Reading between the lines
A critical history of contraception

Gonzalo Herranz

Pilar León-Sanz

José María Pardo

Jokin de Irala

Content

Prologue

Over the last few years, we have been working and discussing on this research project about the history of contraception. As a result of our endeavour, we humbly present to you this book.

We are four Professors of different disciplines working at the University of Navarra. We all have been led, motivated and, above all, taught by Professor Gonzalo Herranz.

The book *Reading between the lines* comprehends a critical history of contraception but it is not a "history" according to the usual meaning of this genre of literature. It is very much original and faithful to historical documentation. During the research, it was inevitable to ask ourselves whether another history of contraception was still necessary. As a matter of fact, there are already many books dealing with this subject: a few of them tell the whole story from antiquity to the present day while others limit themselves to studying the modern era, to what happened in a given country, or to the achievements of the main protagonists in this history.

But what characterizes this book is the inclusion of a well-documented account of little-known, unpublished, and silenced facts with the purpose of shedding more light on some important activities and mentalities of the birth control movement during the 20th century, ignored by the mainstream history of contraception. This is the novelty of the book. Some events happened almost exclusively in the United States which makes sense, since much of the terms with which we denominate contraception originated there. It was in the United States where a strong campaign to promote birth control first appeared and the first contraceptive pill was developed and approved.

The book has a common point with the literature dedicated to the historical study of contraception: it highlights the enormous importance that this reality has had on people, societies and professionals.

We believe that this is an interesting topic for numerous groups of researchers from all over the world and that the book could be a starting point for a new way of researching many new and as well as old issues. Moreover, we also believe that the book applies a new approach to general studies on the History of Medical Ethics. The study of historical realities seeks the analysis of the detailed context and of the origins of the decisions and actions that intervened in the construction of new realities and new models of professional and social ethics. In reading this book, there is a need to read between lines in order to obtain a more complete information of various historical events and processes.

About the book

The first chapter considers the origin of three terms: contraception, prevenception, and birth control, which for decades have referred to the prevention of conception. Given the confusion that has prevailed, it is appropriate to clarify the history of how these words were born. Moreover, it is interesting to delve into partially ignored stories which reveal how different the mentality and the aims of the pioneers of contraception control were.

In continuity with the previous chapter, the second one shows how contraception was in the mind of its authors, and how was it not only something distinct from abortion but by definition, was absolutely incompatible with it.

The topic is pertinent because as it has been in the past decades, the dominant belief in bioethics and medicine is that there is an uninterrupted and intrinsic continuity between contraception and abortion.

At first, contraception was practiced by non-doctors who ran the risk of suffering very harsh penalties because it was an illegal activity. To perform abortions was extremely difficult for doctors. They could advise it in justified cases but it was not easy to put it into practice. Furthermore, it was considered a as an inappropriate practice for those in the medical profession.

The third chapter deals with the changes that occurred in the American medical profession and in contraception particularly in the 1930's. In general, until the second third of the twentieth century, institutional medicine adopted a negative attitude towards contraception. In contrast to the rejection by a great majority of doctors, the use of contraceptive methods spread among the general public especially the well-off. The expansion of contraception use triggered the lucrative production and trade of contraceptive methods (some ineffective and potentially harmful).

As the 1930s advanced, the social and economic importance of contraception required the medical community to consider contraception a fortiori which turned contraception as a conventional but exclusively a medical activity.

The change came with the Resolution of 1937 of the American Medical Association. At its convention held in Atlantic City, the AMA's House of Delegates adopted a new report of the Study Committee on Contraceptive Practices and Related Problems, reversing the same group's earlier rejection of contraception and replacing it with a new spirit of support for birth control.

The chapter analyses the comparison of the 1937 resolution with the previous documents. It induces questions as to what caused the profound change of approach. The 1937 committee's failure to respond to this question provoked widespread speculation regarding the possible existence of undisclosed pressures.

In the fourth chapter, we study the relationship between the stand of the Catholic doctors of the United States which affirmed the report issued in 1937 by the Committee for the Study of Contraceptive Practices, and the causes that led to the approval of those medical practices. We also consider the reactions to the AMA Report of the associations of Catholic doctors and some theologians.

As already indicated in Chapter 3, the committee report of June 8, 1937 signified a radical shift in the AMA's position towards contraception. We must ask ourselves how one could reconcile the strong presence of catholics in the committee whose report contradicts the firm and well-known moral doctrine of the Church of Rome at that time.

We consider Dr. G. Kosmak who, despite his asserted notoriety as a practicing Catholic, never held a position fully consistent with the Church's teaching on contraception. On the contrary, he assumed an increasingly active role in the effort to recognize contraception as a medical correct and morally acceptable activity.

In the case of John Rock who, despite his notoriety as a Catholic was throughout his long career an active promoter of contraception as the responsibility of the doctor. His inconsistency with the doctrine of the Magisterium never caused him problems of conscience.

Evidently, the new attitude of the AMA represented a strong contradiction to doctors and moral theologians who were interested in the ethics of medicine and had embraced the teachings of the encyclical Casti Connubii. But then, the resistance of Catholic doctors against the new situation, strong at the beginning, faded with the passing of time and the changes of the legislation of the states.

The fifth chapter examines the significant role of the Model Penal Code of the American Law Institute (ALI) in the history of contraception. The ALI is a private entity which was founded in 1923 by lawyers, judges, and legal academics to study, clarify, and modernize American law at all levels. One of ALI's most important projects was the drafting of the Model Penal Code (MPC) which has had great influence both in the United States and in other countries.

The text of the code's article on Abortion and Related Offenses (Section 230.3 of the MPC) dealt with the different criminal categories of abortion (unjustified, justifiable, self-induced, fictitious and irregular) and declares unambiguously and for the first time that those contraceptives acting on the developing embryo before the end of implantation are not to be considered by the law as abortifacients (pre-implantational contraceptives, Subsection 7). It was approved at the session of May 24, 1962 after introducing some important amendments. In that same year, the Institute published the Official Final Draft of the MPC. In 1985, they presented to the public the Official Draft with Explanatory Notes which put an end to the project that had begun more than fifty years before. As time passed, the mechanism of action regarding the inhibition of implantation had become common knowledge. Therefore, we must acknowledge that curiously, Subsection 7 was, from 1962, in the end prophetic.

In this timeline we find a decisive terminology change which is reviewed in chapter six. The traditional concepts of contraception coined at the beginning of the twentieth century for the inhibition of fertilization (contraception, prevenception, and birth control) became severely flawed when modern contraceptives (intrauterine devices and oral hormonal preparations) were introduced. It is an exciting story that the meetings of ALI show how the definitions of terms can be mutated in an elegant but harsh manner.

The new definitions were first introduced in the field of medicine by the Terminology Committee of the American College of Obstetricians and Gynecologists (ACOG) through its Terminology Bulletin. They were confirmed years later with the publication of the book, Obstetric-Gynecologic Terminology, published by Hughes under the sponsorship of ACOG. The authoritative nature with which the new terminology was announced and imposed is evidenced by the responses that followers of the new terminology gave to those who challenged the new definitions. They asserted that the criteria they used followed what is defined by the government and the most important medical organizations in the country, and that they represented the official position of national health and medical organizations. But these were health policy reasons and not medical scientific ones.

The seventh chapter tackles the Medical-Biological Aspects of the Papal Commission for the Study of the Problems of the Family, Population, and Birth Rate. Nobody who has taken an interest in the ethical aspects of contraception can ignore the important role they played in the deliberations of this Papal Commission (PC) created by Pope John XXIII and maintained and augmented by Paul VI.

We describe a brief historical summary about the PC. Why was such a Commission formed? The most likely reason was the invitation received by the Holy See from the United Nations to participate in a projected International Conference on Population to be held in New Delhi. This gave rise to the question of which policies could be authorized by the Church to practice birth-control. In this way, with the consent of the Pope, the PC addressed the technical study of birth control methods and their corresponding theological-moral evaluation.

The body of this Chapter mainly focuses on the medical-biological debates of the sessions of the Papal Commission and its conclusions. This will include the way in which the PC, and particularly its medical members, dealt with the biological aspects of contraception, a discussion which would serve as a starting point for the debates and conclusions of the other groups and the entire PC. One of the most urgent issues addressed in the work of the PC was to determine whether the pill acted through an anovulatory effect, or whether it was an abortifacient. Here we can advance that the possible antinidatory effect, the suspicion of its existence especially in the case of intrauterine devices and some hormonal groups although not denied, was not taken into serious consideration and lamentable not mentioned in the final documents of the PC. One must ask, to what could this silence be due? To an involuntary lapse of memory? To a scientific judgment of irrelevance of the data? To a deliberate concealment? In any case, the omission had serious consequences. The Pope did not have significant information to arrive to a considered conclusion of the different types of contraception. The complicity with the new ideas of some of the consultants of the PC makes a very interesting part of our "reading between the lines".

In connection with this last point, in the eighth chapter we consider four protagonists of this history: Edward C. Hughes who was one of the creators of the American Academy of Obstetrics and Gynecology in 1951 and chaired the ACOG in the 1962-1963 period, to become president of its Terminology Committee in 1965;

Raymond T. Holden, member of the Committee on Human Reproduction (1964), whowas the main promoter of the new statement of the AMA on the position of doctors and contraception. The result was considered a milestone that marked the change of the AMA policy with respect to human reproduction and demography;

Thomas Hayes, biophysicist at the University of

California, who introduced the novel concept of the "reproductive act," opposing it to the singular sexual act. Hayes' theory had a significant impact on the final debates and conclusions of the Papal Commission;

And, finally, Sir Alan S. Parkes (1900-1990) who devoted considerable attention to the control of fertility in the human species and was a great promoter of contraception. He actively participated in the population programs of the International Planned Parenthood Federation, the Royal Commission on Population Control and served on the Advisory Committee of the World Health Organization.

The last and ninth chapter is focused on some aspects of the Scientific Research of Contraception. The chapter aims to review some ethical aspects of clinical trials conducted by researchers that developed hormonal contraception. The study takes into consideration the ethical standards of biomedical research of the years 1940-1950. Upon rereading the works published by Pincus, Rock, and their collaborators on their first field trials on the effectiveness and safety of the pill, the reader's attention is powerfully drawn to the attitudes with which women were treated. We study the relegation of women as the subject of experimentation to the status of "human guinea pigs" (or "a cage of ovulating women", in expression of Katharine McCormick). There was a tendency to reduce women to a process of molecularization that has marked for ever the course of contraceptive research

In summary

The summary of the content of the book shows the intention of the authors, declared at the beginning of this foreword, of writing a critical history. That can help to understand its character and the topics it deals with. We also want to highlight the originality and importance of some contributions of the book: to the present day, no one had written a critique about the attitude of the American Law Institute based on written documentation when this institution proposed its first legislation on abortion. The same is true regarding the debates within the American Medical Association that led to a wide professional tolerance of abortion in the USA.

Also, there are no studies that analyzed the double-moral attitude of Catholic doctors who helped introduce contraception as a professional practice and that promoted the idea that Catholic doctors could ethically accept this practice.

No one has so far analyzed the behavior, at least withdrawn and deceptive, of the medical-biological group of the Pontifical Commission constituted by Paul VI which disappointed the Pope's request for an objective and complete evaluation of the mechanism of action of hormonal contraceptives.

READING BETWEEN THE LINES

Throughout the book we have preferred to follow a balanced, reasonable and deliberative style; to argue with data, and objectivity, based on the results obtained from research. It will be up to the reader to decide on the outcomes obtained by the critical reading of the book. We hope that it could provoke the initiation of investigations that would help understand more deeply what had been written between the lines in the existing histories of contraception

Acknowledgments

The authors have not received any financial assistance to carry out this work but wish to thank the support provided by the University of Navarra. The School of Medicine of this university has encouraged our work and allowed us to establish the Study Group on the History of Contraception so that we could freely and independently carry out our research.

We also want to recognize the help given by those who work in the Library of the University of Navarra in the search of the necessary bibliographic material. This book could not have been made without their collaboration.

During the first year of our research, Pedro Gil-Sotres, Professor of Medical History, was part of the group. The authors want to thank Dr. Gil-Sotres for his valuable suggestions and contributions.

Chapter 1. Origins of Modern Contraception: Three Terms for Three Attitudes

In this chapter we will consider the origin of three terms (contraception, prevenception and birth control) with which the prevention of conception was designated for many decades[1].

In 2018, was it interesting to deal with such an old matter? Certainly, it was for several reasons. To begin with, it was necessary to clarify the rather confusing history of how those words were born which allowed us to perceive, once again, how contaminated by false data and gratuitous

---

1 Before going any further, a warning about the use in this book of the term contraception. The recent 23rd edition (2014) of the Dictionary of the Spanish Language of the Royal Spanish Academy admits the term anticoncepción but does not include contracepción. For its part, the Dictionary of Medical Terminology of the Royal Academy of Medicine, in its first edition of 2011, registers contracepción as equivalent to anticoncepción but discourages its use, considering it capable of provoking rejection due to its condition of unnecessary anglicism and of incorrectly formed term. In this book, however, the terms 'contraception' and 'contraceptive' will be used because those are, at least in Spain, the preferred forms by professionals. At the national and regional levels, the associations they form are called societies of contraception and not anticonception. It would, on the other hand, be inappropriate to speak of 'anticonception', when dealing with the origin of the term 'contraception'.

statements the bioethical bibliography was. Furthermore, delving into that history has lead us to understand that these three terms reveal how different in mentality and purposes were the pioneers of conception control. Finally, and perhaps the most relevant reason is that these terms were put into circulation with a main purpose: to point out its total incompatibility with abortion was a basic element of early modern contraception. This last point will be discussed in the next chapter.

1.1.   The origin of the term "contraceptive" (E.B. Foote Jr., 1886)

Apparently, the origin of the word 'contraception' does not seem problematic. Since 1972, the Oxford English Dictionary[2] tells us that the word was used for the first time in 1886 by E. B. Foote, in a publication entitled *The Radical Remedy in Social Science*[3] from which page 89 of the dictionary records the following text: "When it becomes necessary deciding between legal abortion and illegal contraception, they prefer to break the law made by men that condemns the use of contraceptives, to break the natural law that prohibits abortion." But at a close examination, it appears that such attribution is incorrect and ambiguous.

---

[2] Burchfield RW, ed. A Supplement to the Oxford English Dictionary, Vol I·A-G. Oxford: At the Clarendon Press; 1972: 622. The same attribution appears literally in the second edition of the Dictionary (1989), prepared by J.A. Simpson and E.S.C. Weiner (Vol. III: 834).

[3] Foote EB. The Radical Remedy in Social Science or Borning Better Babies Through Regulating Reproduction by Controlling Conception. An Earnest Essay on Pressing Problems. New York: Murray Hill Publishing Company; 1886. To access the virtual version of the book, go to:

https://archive.org/details/02531230R.nlm.nih.gov.

It is incorrect because the fragment quoted in the dictionary does not correspond to that of *The Radical Remedy* in which E.B. Foote used the term contraception. He does it long before, on page 66, at the header of Chapter V: *Why not adopt contraception as a means for the purpose of regulating reproduction and curbing reckless offspring?*[4]. Within those pages the author used the word contraception[5] twenty times.

In addition, the attribution to E.B. Foote is ambiguous, given the peculiar circumstance that E.B. Foote is the name of two authors, the father and the son, who, over many years, shared ideas and editorial undertakings. Hence, it was easy to confuse one with the other since both had the same christian name: Edward. Their complete names, however, were different: the father's name was Edward Bliss Foote and the son's was Edward Bond Foote[6]. To avoid any misunderstanding, Foote Sr and Foote Jr will be used respectively. The one who coined the term contraception was the latter, Foote Jr.

But that is not the opinion of some authorities in the matter. Himes, who is seen as the most complete historian

---

[4] Chapter V. Why not Adopt Contraception as the Means to the End of Regulating Reproduction and Checking Reckless Propagation? *Ibid.*, p. 66.

[5] Actually, the primary neologism introduced by Foote is not contraception, but *contraceptics*. On page 52 of *Radical Remedy*, Foote introduces the new word unequivocally: *"[...] for want of a single appropriate word, I will call them contraceptics –a new coinage literally meaning against-beginning– or something to oppose or prevent conception."*

[6] There is no shortage of information about both Footes, more abundant that referred to Foote Sr (1829-1906) than to the son (1854-1912). Brief biographies or sketches of the Footes can be seen in: Sears HD. The Sex Radicals. Free Love in High Victorian America. Lawrence: The Regent Press of Kansas; 1977: 183-203; Wood JR. The Struggle for Free Speech in the United States; Edward Bliss Foote, Edward Bond Foote, and Anti-Comstock Operations. New York: Routledge; 2008: 11-38. Also Himes (see next note) in pp. 276-281.

of contraception prior to the 1930s, does not allude to the origin of the term in his encyclopedic *Medical History of Contraception* (1936)[7]. What is surprising with the title of his book is the fact that Himes himself published in 1932 an article on the origin of the term contraception[8]. In that article, he states erroneously that Foote Sr was the author of many books on popular medicine[9] and an active pioneer of birth control, who first used the word contraception. He alleges as evidence the erroneous bibliographical reference: the page 1144 of the Plain Home Talk book published in 1881. None of the numerous editions of that title reached a thousand pages. Furthermore, a scrupulous examination of the editions of 1870, 1880, 1892, 1896 and 1899, does not show that Footer Sr used that term[10].

It seems obvious that Himes could not make a

---

[7] Himes NE. Medical History of Contraception. The first edition of the book (1936), with a preface by RL Dickinson, was published by Williams & Wilkins Co, Baltimore. In 1970, the book, with a New Preface by Christopher Tietze, was reprinted by Schocken Books Inc., New York.

[8] Himes NE. Note on the Origin of the Terms Contraception, Birth Control, Neo-Malthusianism, Etc. Med J & Rec 1932; 135: 495-496.

[9] The bibliographic production of Foote Sr was enormously abundant and complex, as were also his commercial initiatives (Gordon L. The Moral Property of Women, A History of Birth Control Politics in America, Urban, Ill: University of Illinois Press, 2007: 112-113). In 1872 he created a publishing company in New York (the Murray Hill Publishing Company) to print and disseminate his numerous titles (more than 60, according to Brodie JF, Contraception and Abortion in 19th Century America, Ithaca: Cornell University Press, 1994: 240). He frequently re-published his popular medicine books: thus, his initial book, *Medical Common Sense* (1858) was later absorbed into *Plain Home Talk* (1870) and this, in its turn, into *Home Cyclopedia of Popular Medical, Social and Sexual Science* (1901). An annotated account of Foote Sr's works appears in: Hoolihan C. An Annotated Catalog of the Edward C. Atwater Collection of American Popular Medicine and Health Reform, Volume III. Rochester NY: University of Rochester Press; 2001: 254-258.

[10] These editions can be viewed at:
https://archive.org/details/63570690R.nlm.nih.gov.

reference to the non-existent page 1144 of the 1881 edition. In reality, he was mentioning page 1144 of a book by Foote Sr, published much later in 1902 which was entitled Home Cyclopedia[11]. It is precisely there, on pages 1143 and 1144, where Foote Sr uses the term contraception. However, he does not to attribute to himself the coining of the word but to to his son, Foote Jr.

It is worth transcribing the revealing and simple story of Foote Sr. to at least rescue it from oblivion because despite its strong testimonial value, it has not been cited by those who have studied the history of contraception. It reads so:

"What is meant by contraceptics? The term being now used on both sides of the Atlantic, I turned to the Standard Dictionary (Funk & Wagnalis, 1895) confidently expecting to find it, but it was not there; then to medical dictionaries with no better success. Asking Dr. E. B. Foote, Jr., where he originally found the term as used in his work entitled "The Radical Remedy in Social Science," he replied that he coined it! The derivation of the word as given by its author, is very simple: merely substituting contra (against) for con in conception. Contraconception would be the full and self-evident form, but too prolix. Contraceptics being a word in actual use at this time, both at home and abroad, a statement of its true origin and definition seems to be quite necessary in this place."

Today, more than a hundred years later, that

---

[11] Foote EB. Home Cyclopedia of Popular Medical, Social, and Sexual Science. New York: Murray Hill Publishing Company; 1902. This book, of 1250 pages, is called by Foote Sr his Complete Work. It consists of a medical section (Parts I and II, of more than 800 pages) an update of his New Book on Health and Disease; and a social section (Parts III and IV, about 400 pages), which is an update of New Plain Home Talk on Love, Marriage and Parentage.

statement remains equally necessary not only because of obscurity and ignorance, but also because of the confusion brought about by the origin of the term 'contraception' by some mistakes of Himes[12] and other authors[13].

1.2. The origin of the term "birth control" (M. Sanger, 191.)

The history of the origin of the expression *birth control* (BC) is very interesting. It is, abundantly documented perhaps in excess which is not surprising, given the

---

[12] For example, Himes states in hiss 1932 article that also Foote Jr had used 'contraception' in 1910, when he wrote: "In all circumstances, contraception is preferable to abortion, and should as far as possible take its place [...]. And when it is found that a married woman can not safely deliver a child, contraception is better than abortion [...]. When, for the poor health of the husband or the wife, or for another reason, it is imprudent, in their opinion, to have a new child, contraception is justified." Foote EB. A Summary of My Views on the Prevention of Conception. Med Pharm Crit Guide 1910; 12: 408: Cit by Himes (note 8, supra: 495). To complete the relation of errors by Himes in his 1932 article, it must be added that he attributes to Foote Jr the authorship of famous pamphlet *Words in Pearl*, by which publication in 1876, Foote Sr was tried and condemned. It has been said, in Himes's apology, that it was not possible for him to obtain any copies of *Words in Pearl* and of *Radical Remedy*.

[13] There are, for example, errors of chronology. It is clear that the word contraception appears in the nineteenth century, specifically in 1886. However, Curran states that it was born in the twentieth century (Curran CE Contraception. In: Clarke PB, Linzey A, eds. Dictionary of Ethics, Theology and Society. Abingdon; Routledge; 1996: 175). Perhaps Curran borrowed the idea from Royle: "The terms 'contraception' and 'birth control' are from the 20th century." Royle E. Radicals, Secularists, and Republicans: Popular Free Thought in Britain, 1866-1915. Manchester: Manchester University Press; 1980: 261. There are also attribution errors originated by the translation of texts. In the English version of Jütte's history of contraception (2003), it is said that "The term 'contraception', now familiar, is not even 100 years old. We found it for the first time in a book by the well-known researcher of sexology, Max Marcuse (1877-1963)." Jütte R. Contraception: a history. Cambridge; Polity Press; 2008: 2. But in this case, the original term is not 'Kontrazeption', very scarcely used in German, but 'Empfängnisverhütung'. Jütte R. Lust ohne Last: Geschichte der Empfängsnisverhütung von der Antike bis zur Gegenwart. München: Verlag C.H. Beck; 2003: 2.

important role it played in the contraceptive movement. Margaret Sanger, the presumed creator of the term, told that story several times. These narratives present variants and even contradictions that immediately arouse interest and critical alertness.

In dealing with the subject, the following order will be followed: first, the transcription of the passages where Sanger relates the creation of the term; then, a clarification as far as possible of the confused circumstances in which the new expression was born; and, finally, some bibliographic data suggesting that the term BC was coined by other individuals.

1.2.1.   Sanger's stories about the origin of BNC

Margaret Sanger included in two of her books separate accounts of how the term BC came about: one is found in My Fight for Birth Control published in 1931; the other, in An Autobiography which appeared in 1938. There is also a third story, marginal in appearance, but extremely prominate in, The Pivot of Civilization which was published in 1922 and has the added value of being the closest in time to the event of 1914 among the three testimonies offered by Sanger.

In *The Pivot*, Sanger tells us:

"Such was the situation in 1914, when I returned to America [...] The amazing growth of this [BC] movement dates from the moment when in my home a small group organized the first Birth Control League. Since then we have been criticized for our choice of the term «Birth Control» to express the idea of modern scientific contraception. [] I have yet to hear any criticism of this term that is not based upon some false and hypocritical sense of modesty, or that does not arise out of a semi-prurient misunderstanding of its aim. On the other hand: nothing better expresses the idea of purposive, responsible, and self-directed guidance of the reproductive powers. [...] Control is guidance, direction, foresight. It implies intelligence, deliberation and responsibility [...]. The term "birth control" has the immense practical advantage of compressing in two short words the response to the mute request of millions of men and women from all countries."[14]

A small group that met at Sanger's house sometime in 1914 gave name to the thriving movement.

Years later, Sanger claims for herself the creation of the new expression. In *My Fight for Birth Control*, her first autobiography, Sanger recalls very vividly that:

"The first thing necessary was to get a name for contraception which would convey to the public the social and personal significance of the idea. A few friends and supporters of the paper gathered together one evening in my apartment to discuss the selection of a distinctive name. We debated in turn Malthusianism, conscious generation, voluntary parenthood, voluntary motherhood, preventception {sic}, the new motherhood, constructive generation, etc. All of these names were cast aside as not meeting the demands. Then we get a little nearer when family control and race control and birth rate control were suggested.

Finally, it came to me out of the blue - Birth Control!

We all knew at once that we had found the perfect name for the cause. There was no further discussion. Our object was attained. The group disbanded to meet no

---

[14] Sanger M. The Pivot of Civilization. New York: Brentano's Publishers; 1922: 11-13.

more."[15]

Finally, in her Autobiography, Sanger seems to have renounced the misappropriation of 1931, and turns back the creation of the term BC to an anonymous contributor. Sanger tells us:

"A new movement was starting, and the baby had to have a name. It did not belong to Socialism nor was it in the labor field, and it had much more to it than just the prevention of conception. As a few companions were sitting with me one evening we debated in turn voluntary parenthood, voluntary motherhood, the new motherhood, constructive generation, and new generation. The terms already in use - Neo-Malthusianism, Family Limitation, and Conscious Generation - seemed stuffy and lacked popular appeal.

The word control was good, but I did not like limitation - that was too limiting. I was not advocating a one-child or two-child system as in France, nor did I wholeheartedly agree with the English Neo-Malthusians whose concern was almost entirely with limitation for economic reasons. My idea of control was bigger and freer. I wanted family in it, yet family control did not sound right. We tried population control, race control, and birth rate control. Then someone suggested, "Drop the rate". Birth control was the answer, we knew we had it. Our work for that day was done and everybody picked up his hat and went home. The baby was named."[16]

It is clear that Sanger considered the expression "BC"

---

[15] Sanger M. My Fight for Birth Control. New York: Farrar & Rinehart Inc.; 1931: 83.

[16] Sanger M. An Autobiography. New York: W.W. Norton & Co; 1938: 107-108.

to be a factor of decisive importance for the expansion of the movement she wanted to promote. She sees in these two brief words the answer "to the silent request of millions of men and women", two words that "have gone around the world as a magical message announcing the arrival of a new dawn."[17]

1.2.2.   The confusing circumstances of the birth of the expression 'Control of births'

Do Sanger's stories reveal the historical reality in which the expression 'B.C.' was born? Did it happen, as she counts in *The Pivot*, on formally creating what would be called BC League? Or, simply, as *My Fight* points out, was it a meeting of friends called to find a new name that could make contraception socially more acceptable? Or, as *My Autobiography* points out, was it about giving a name to the newborn movement?

The variants of the narration of what happened in Sanger's apartment that night, as well as the jubilant or triumphalist expressions with which she concludes her stories, make us suspect that these are strongly idealized memories. It is worth examining in detail some circumstances of this episode, an event that has been magnified some historians of contraception.

It should be noted that the climate in which the meeting was held was certainly not optimistic. Gray has been able to verify that Sanger and her group were those

---

[17] Nor have followers of Sanger been sparing in their praises. From the expression 'BC' it has been said that: "those simple and affirmative words are perhaps the most controversial expression [...] since, in 1859, Darwin introduced natural selection." Katz E, Hajo CM, Engelman PC, eds. The Selected Papers of Margaret Sanger. Vol. 1, The Woman Rebel, 1900-1928. Urbana: University of Illinois Press; 2003: 70.

days under serious difficulties. The Postal Service of the United States had decided to declare illegal the circulation and distribution of the first issues of *The Woman Rebel*[18]. Sanger considered that if she let the journalists know that the pamphlet seizure was an attack on freedom of expression, she would receive massive support from the press. But such support did not occur. On the contrary, the journalists' response, in general quite lukewarm, included some very harsh criticisms: some newspapers came to consider *The Woman Rebel* and its message as something despicable or laughable[19]. It was, in those dramatic circumstances, when Sanger called his group to find a new way to present her message.

There seems to be no doubt that the meeting took place on the apartment Sanger had rented in New York. But what do we know about the date of the event and about when the expression 'BC' was coined?

No one took minutes of the session. Of the stories of Sanger, only the one that appears in *The Pivot* offers a minimum of chronology: the meeting took place in 1914.

---

[18] *The Woman Rebel* was a monthly pamphlet, edited by Sanger, directed mainly to working women, of which seven issues were published between March and September-October 1914. Its marked libertarian and anarchist character, and its ideological aggressiveness in general policy, family and sexuality, caused the seizure by the Postal Office of most of the published numbers.

[19] Gray refers that given the seriousness of the situation, a desperate and depressed Sanger sent to a large number of newspapers an informative note together with a sample of the issues of The Woman Rebel seized by the Post Office. She asked them their view on the unfair and unjust behavior of the police. She hoped that, given the traditional attitude of journalists in favor of press freedom, her action could mobilize new and powerful allies for her cause. The result was just the opposite. Gray describes the negative reactions of some journalists and concludes that the operation of Sanger, "instead of achieving the image of a savior, she was achieving that of a vulgar scold." Gray M. Margaret Sanger: A Biography of the Champion of Birth Control. New York: R. Marek Publ.; 1979: 71-72.

Katz points out that probably it happened in May or June of that same year[20]. In the absence of solid information in Sanger's and others' recollections, it is inevitable to go to the most solid proof of the contemporary bibliography to search when and where the first written mention of 'BC' appears.

Kennedy offers us a first approximation by simply indicating that the term 'BC' is published for the first time in the June 1914 issue of The Woman Rebel[21]. More precise is Engelman's reference[22], stating that, in that issue, 'BC' appears for the first time in an article by Sanger entitled "Suppression", in which reads: "If The Woman Rebel were allowed to publish with impunity elementary and fundamental truths concerning personal liberty and how to obtain it, the birth control movement would become a movement of tremendous power in the emancipation of the working class."[23] Engelman's observation is not entirely accurate: the lines he cites appear in one of the last paragraphs of the article but it was in the first where the author had introduced it for the first time. In fact, the article begins like this: "To suppress is an act of weakness. To suppress an idea is an admission that you are afraid of it, that its life is a threat upon yours. The persistent efforts of the Post office to suppress this paper emphasize its fear of

---

[20] "In May or June they had coined the term BC as an alternative to the more passive expressions commonly used to designate contraception." Katz E, Hajo CM, Engelman PC, eds. Op. Cit. supra, in note 17: 68.

[21] "The *Woman Rebel* discussed and advocated contraception - the June issue for the first time called it 'birth control,' a term devised by Margaret Sanger and some friends." Kennedy DM. Birth Control in America: The Career of Margaret Sanger. New Haven, Co: Yale University Press; 1970: 23.

[22] Engelman PC. A History of the Birth Control Movement in America. Santa Barbara, CA: Praeger; 2011: 23.

[23] Sanger M. Suppression, The Woman Rebel 1914; 1: 25.

the propaganda for birth control."[24] In the absence of future and unlikely, findings, it must be concluded that in the preceding phase is the first written reference of the term 'BC'.

There is no lack, however, in the bibliography on this particular statement wrong ones. For example, Himes, in his aforementioned Note[25], vaguely states that, in his opinion, "the BC term was used for the first time by Margaret Sanger, in April 1914, in an article by The Woman Rebel, a radical publication that then she edited." But a careful reading of that issue does not allow finding such an expression in any of his articles. In his turn, Stillman placed willfully in 1912 the creation of the term[26].

1.3. Origin of the term "prevenception" (W.J. Robinson, 1918)

The third term we have to study is prevenception (and its derivatives prevenceptic and preven-ceptive). For a few years, these new words played a relatively notable role in pro-contraception activism, but they practically fell into oblivion after the death of its creator, William J. Robinson.

Robinson coined prevenception to gather in a single word the classic expression "prevention of conception", which he and many others had been using for a long time as synonymous with contraception. Apparently, there do not seem to be references in the bibliography that accurately indicate the moment in which the new term was born. A

---

[24] Ibid.

[25] Himes, Note on the Origin..., cit supra, note 8.

[26] Stillman JB. Birth Control Movement. In: Ross JA, ed. Encyclopedia of Population, Vol. I. New York: The Free Press; 1982, 58-64, 61.

careful review of Robinson's publications allows to say that 'prevention' comes into light in 1918, because the author did not use that word in his writings before that date, instead, he used indistinctly 'prevention of conception', 'contraception', and ' birth control'[27].

It is in the June 1918 issue of The Medical Critic and Guide[28], one of the magazines that Robinson edited, when the author introduces 'prevenception' for the first time. He did it in an editorial entitled 'Prevenception Against Abortion', in which he enigmatically stated: "Countless times we have shown that there is a radical difference between prevenception and abortion. A difference that is not of degree, but of species."[29]

It is surprising, however, that Robinson in the aforementioned article did not inform his readers that he is introducing a new and original word. Certainly, he did not take long to do so: a month later he affirmed that he, as the editor of the journal, included the new term in a footnote of Goldman's article published in the same magazine[30].

---

[27] Prevenception does not appear in the books Robinson published in 1917: Woman. Her Sex and Love Life. New York: The Critic and Guide Co., 1917; Eugenics, Marriage and Birth Control [Practical Eugenics]. New York: The Critic and Guide Co., 1917; Fewer and Better Babies, or The Limitation of Offspring, 11th and 12th ed. New York: The Critic and Guide Co., 1917.

[28] In the magazine's cover page there is a vivid portrait of the character of the publication: "Critical and Medical Guide. It includes the Dietetic and Hygienic Gazette, and New Medicines of the Doctor. A Magazine of Individuality. No Program outside of Truth, Sincerity and Righteousness. All the readers enjoy equal opportunities before the Editor to express their opinion. All frauds and deceptions will be boldly denounced."

[29] Editorial. Prevenception versus Abortion. Med Critic Guide 1918; 21: 206-207. In the same issue of the magazine, it includes two short editorials (editorialettes) in which it uses 'prevenceptives': Robinson JW (editor). Do we Possess an Absolutely Reliable Prevenceptive? Med Critic Guide 1918; 21: 207; and Reliability of Prevenceptives Tested on Animals, Ibid., 207-208.

[30] Goldman C. Voluntary Checks to Population. Med Critic Guide 1918; 21:

Glossing the term 'contraceptive', Robinson adds that "the Editor has recently introduced, and prefers, the terms "prevenceptive" and "prevenception."[31] Along the second half of 1918, Robinson uses frequently the new terms in editorial articles, letters and notes published in his magazine[32]. Even one of the readers uses both words in a letter to the Editor[33].

Robinson did not feel then the need of defining his neologism because he considered that it was clear to all that it was an obvious contraction of 'prevention of conception', and served as a mere synonym of contraception, a term that deeply displeased him. Neither he explained then the advantages or usefulness of the new expression. He did it only more than 10 years later, when he revealed that he had coined it to eradicate the deceptive word BC[34]. In 1931, in the pages of the Birth Control Review,

---

248-256, at 249.

[31] Ibid., Footnote on page 249.

[32] Vid., for example, Med Critic Guide 1918; 21: 207, 347, 408, 410 and 460.

[33] Gray H. A Few Letters to the Editor. Ibid: 401-402, at 402.

[34] "A word about the term Birth Control. "Birth Control" is misleading. It is a translation of the German *Geburts-Regelung* and is now a permanent addition to our language, which nothing probably will uproot or displace. But it is a bad term, the worst that could have been coined. It is due to that term that prevenception (or prevention of conception) is still so frequently confused in the popular mind with abortion. People know that by abortion they can control the number of births, by abortion they can prevent the birth of a child. Hence when they hear "birth control" they take it as a synonym for abortion. And the term is intrinsically wrong because it is not the birth of offspring that we control, it is the *conception* that we prevent. Prevention of conception, prevenception or conception control, are from every point of view better terms. Prevenception and its adjective prevenceptive have the advantage of being one-word terms, express exactly what we want them to express, and for reasons I explained elsewhere are much preferable to contraception and contraceptive. So, whenever we have the proper occasion, let us use the terms prevenception and prevenceptive. We cannot eliminate the misleading term "Birth Control," from our language, but we can limit its use". Robinson WJ. Practical Prevenception or The Technique of Birth Control.

he repeats again: "BC is a misleading term, [...] the worst of those that could have been coined."[35]

Sanger must have been hurt by Robinson's contempt for her favorite BC expression and she took revenge. In 1931, Sanger, in "My Fight for birth control"[36], referring to the birth of the term "birth control", included prevenception {sic}, in the list of expressions that had to be selected: "Malthusianism, conscious generation, voluntary fatherhood, voluntary motherhood, prevenception, new motherhood, constructive generation, etc. All those names were rejected because they did not meet the requirements." But, when she later tells that same story in her autobiography, prevenception no longer appears; Robinson had been disregarded[37].

Giving the Latest Methods of Prevention of Conception, Discussing their Effect, Favorable or Unfavorable, on the Sex Act; Their Indications and Contraindications, Pointing Out the Reasons for Failures and How to Avoid Them. Hoboken, NJ: American Biological Society; 1929: 6-7.

[35] Robinson WJ. Do Doctors Know About Prevenception? Birth Control Rev 1931; 15: 11.

[36] Sanger, M., My Fight for birth control. New York: Farrar & Rinehart Inc. on Murray Hill; 1931.

[37] Sanger, Autobiography: 108.

Chapter 2. Pioneering Contraception and its Incompatibility with Abortion

This chapter deals with how, in the mind of the pioneers, the prevention of conception is not only different from abortion by nature, but it is, by definition, incompatible with it. For them, there is no possible continuity between contraception and abortion. Biologically and ethically speaking, they were regarded as irreconcilable and antagonistic actions.

Interestingly, the recognition of such a separation is already evident at the moment of its invention and puts into use three terms: contraception, birth control and prevenception. It seems as if the reason that led Foote Jr, Sanger and Robinson to create and spread their new terms was not the desire for greater lexical precision, or the ambition to achieve fame and recognition. The motive that moved them was to make clear the discontinuity between contraception and abortion.

At present, the subject retains a great interest. The prevalent idea in bioethics and medicine has had, for some decades, a seamless continuity between contraception and abortion. They are, as shown by studies on the mechanism of action of both certain types of hormonal contraceptives and intrauterine devices, overlapping entities. Many contraceptives destroy the life of the young embryo. Thus, they are abortive or abortifacient, as it is usually calledThe term 'contragestion' (or contragestation) has been coined to highlight that continuity.

2.1. E.B. Foote Jr.: contraceptives and abortion

As seen today, the legal context in which Foote Jr coined the term 'contraception' appears quite paradoxical: what he wanted to designate as 'contraception' was an infamous and illegal activity and unfit for the profession in almost everywhere, especially in the United States. It was practiced by some marginal doctors or non-doctors who ran the risk of suffering very rigorous penalties. For regular physicians, contraception was severely restricted. They could advise its practice in justified cases but it was not easy for them to provide the means to put it into practice. The paradox was that these same doctors enjoyed a remarkable discretion to perform abortions as long as they offered a therapeutic indication to justify their behavior.

Foote Jr was very deeply convinced of the need to reverse such ambiguous situation which he described as offensive to ethics and to justice[38]. In 1886, perceiving that his death was near (intuition that resulted erroneous)[39], he

---

[38] He did it mainly because he was an agnostic and a freethinker, strongly anti-Catholic. He abandoned the practice of medicine (though not his father's business) to promote libertarian causes such as the repealing of Comstock laws. He was extremely generous and provided personal and financial support to the Free Speech League.

[39] Harman tells the circumstances in which Foote Jr wrote Radical Remedy: "He felt that he had a few months to live and that this book was the most

wanted to collect in a small book his message in favor of controlling conception and condemning abortion[40]. He himself felt morally obliged to disseminate information in the society about what, in his opinion, was the radical remedy for the ills affecting individuals, families and society. Unlike other promoters of conception control, he considered essential that this information be based on the data of science. Only on this condition, contraception could become the main procedure to eradicate the serious social and moral wound of abortion.

For Foote Jr, the scientific basis of contraception was non-negotiable. It is not without significance that, when he spoke for the first time on contraceptives, he did so after lamenting the ignorance that in Malthus's time reigned over the physiology of conception[41] while he could benefit from the progress of physiological science. In 1886, Foote Jr pointed out his strong conviction that thanks to new knowledge in the physiology of reproduction, the problem of the control of conception could be faced with a new light. Recent science made it possible to distinguish "between the mere prevention of conception and the forcible

---

important legacy he could leave, so he dedicated the remaining energy to that task. He was surprised to continue living, but he was still convinced that his 'Radical Remedy' was the most important thing he or anyone else could have done." Harman L., A Letter. In: Schroeder T, ed., Edward Bond Foote. Biographical Notes and Appreciatives. New York: Free Speech League: 1913: 62-65, in 64.

[40] Foote EB. The Radical Remedy, in Social Science or Borning Better Babies Through Regulating Reproduction by Controlling Conception. An Earnest Essay on Pressing Problems. New York: Murray Hill Publishing Company; 1886.

[41] Foote Jr points out that for the control of population, Malthus limited himself to recommend celibacy, late marriage and marital continence, while condemning all other remedies as improper procedures or indecent acts, among them abortion. Foote Jr considers that Malthus, cleric and philosopher, was guided more by his theological convictions and not by the facts of science. Understandably, in 1826, when Malthus wrote, "there was far less facts in science to appeal to than at present." Foote, Radical Remedy, p. 51.

interference with the product of conception which constitutes abortion. There is an important distinction and difference in which persons who lack instruction in the physiology of reproduction are bound to ignore."[42]

After briefly describing the process of fertilization in which the microscopic gametes fuse together, Foote Jr concludes: "the joining of two such minute elements effects impregnation or conception, and the result is the beginning of a new organism in what is called the product of conception. Any interference with the natural growth and development of this germ of life at any stage of its uterine life causes its abortion, and is therefore destructive of a living entity [...]. Thus, we make clear the distinction between contraceptics, which prevent conception, and abortives, which interfere with the actual living product of conception."[43]

It is clear for Foote Jr that there is a decisive biological and moral frontier between abortion and conception control which he wants to underline with the new term 'contraception'. On the one side of that border are the contraceptive methods which prevent the reunion of the gametes, an action from which no harm is derived for the nascent life. On the other, the abortive procedures, condemnable at the light of sexual physiology and moral considerations.

Foote Jr feels impelled to cry out against the illogical legislative situation of his time: "[...] if the laws were obeyed, the practical result would be a great number of abortions where contraception might served instead; but the fact is that physicians and laymen take liberties with the

---

[42] Ibíd.

[43] Ibíd., 52.

law, and where it becomes a necessity to decide between lawful abortion and unlawful contraception, they prefer to break the man-made against contraceptics rather than the natural law against abortion."[44]

Foote Jr never abandoned his conviction about the insurmountable moral and biological distance that separates contraception and abortion. In 1910, two years before his death, in an article summarizing his views on contraception, he states: "In all circumstances, contraception is preferable to abortion, and should take its place as far as possible [...]. When it is discovered that a married woman can not bear a child safely, contraception is better than abortion."[45]

2.2. M. Sanger: birth control is incompatible with abortion

As indicated in the previous chapter, Sanger and/or someone of her collaborators coined the term BC in 1914. In stories written years later which Sanger left us on the subject, we can find no references as to how the author considered the possible relationship between BC and abortion. We lack a document that, like *Radical Remedy* of Foote Jr, deals specifically with the matter, and, therefore, must study the problem through documents published more or less after putting in circulation the term BC. It is a difficult task because for some years, Sanger's position on the matter changes apparently for more pragmatic and political reasons than for substantive or ethical reasons until

---

[44] Ibíd., 88-89.

[45] Foote EB. A Summary of My Views on the Prevention of Conception. Med Pharm Crit Guide 1910; 13: 408 (Cit. en Himes NE. Medical History..., p. 281.)

she later arrives at a consolidated position.

The same year, 1914, Sanger distributed a pamphletentitled *Family Limitation*, brief but intentionally subversive. It basically contained information about the contraceptive methods then practiced. Despite the fact that the printing and distribution of the pamphlet were carried out clandestinely and caused several problems with the police and the judges, the pamphlet had to be reissued several times within a few years[46]. Sanger introduced some notable text variants in successive editions[47].

In the first edition, a tolerant attitude toward abortion is insinuated as interruption of pregnancy is seen as an inevitable and final expedient when contraception has failed. Sanger says to her readers that only then "the only remedy is abortion. When one has been convinced that an abortion is necessary, do not indulge in medicines of any kind. [...] Never allow a pregnancy to run over a month. [...] It is for each woman to decide this for herself, but act at once, whichever way you decide" (p. 5).

That broad tolerance for abortion has been almost abandoned three years later. In the sixth edition (1917), we find, along with some minimal references to the physiology of human reproduction (fertilization, nidation), the

---

[46] Sanger M. Family Limitation. In none of its editions does this 16-page booklet carry an indication of the place or year of its printing. Data are available, however, which assure that the first edition was printed in New York, in 1914. It reached its eighteenth, and perhaps last, edition, in 1922.

[47] Jensen has studied, from the political point of view, the evolution of Sanger's ideas in the successive editions of the pamphlet, especially the transition of rhetorics: from the initial leftist the later liberal. Jensen JM. The Evolution of Margaret Sanger's "Family Limitation" Pamphlet, 1914-1921. Signs 1981; 6: 548-567. McCann reproaches Jensen for not paying attention to the sexual rhetoric. McCann CM, Birth Control Politics in the United Status, 1916-1945. Ithaca, NY: Cornell University Press; 1999: 36.

following warnings: "... By taking the above precautions you will prevent the ovum from making its nest in the lining of the womb [...] and a week has elapsed with no signs of menstrual flow, then it is safe to assume conception has taken place. Any attempt to interfere with the development of the fertilized ovum is called an abortion. No one can doubt that there are times when an abortion is be justifiable but they will become *unnecessary when care is taken to prevent or avoid conception*. This is the *only* cure for abortions."[48]

It was in 1918 that Sanger took a firm stance on the problem and directly confronted the issue in an article whose title was *"Birth Control or Abortion?"*. After verifying her view that the limitation of the family is inevitable, she wonders how it would be practiced: whether with the normal and scientific methods of BC, or with an abnormal and often dangerous surgical operation. For Sanger, the solution is to prevent fertilization, to prevent the encounter of sperm and ovum through BC procedures. "But if preventive means are not used and the sperm meets the ovum and development thus begins, any attempt at removing it or stopping its further growth is called abortion. [...] While there are cases where even the law recognizes an abortion as justifiable if recommended by a physician, I assert that the hundreds of thousands of abortions performed in America each year is a disgrace to civilization. There is the case in a nutshell. Family limitation will always be practiced as it is now being practiced – either by Birth Control or by abortion. We know that. The one means health and happiness – a stronger, better race. The other means disease, suffering, death."[49]

---

[48] Sanger M. Family Limitation. Revised, Sixth ed.; 1917, pp. 4 and 5. Italics in the original.

In the previous quote, it is clear that for Sanger, BC and abortion belong to different biological and ethical areas. In the following years, Sanger riveted the same ideas and persisted in giving them scientific foundation. But her basic idea does not change. So, for example, in the chapter *Contraceptives or Abortion?* of a book she published in 1920, we find repeated, literally, many fragments of the article quoted above[50]. Sanger did not stop insisting on the radical, exclusive difference that separates the BC procedures and the practice of abortion. She had no patience for the fact that the public frequently hold them both equivalent and considered abortion as a further method of BC.

In 1931, following the promulgation of the encyclical Casti connubii by Pope Pius XI, Sanger again affirmed her position against abortion[51]. "Although abortion may be resorted to in order to save the life of the mother, the practice of it merely for limitation of offspring is dangerous and vicious. I bring up the subject here only because some ill-informed persons have the notion that when we speak of birth control, we include abortion as a method. We certainly do not. Abortion destroys the already fertilized ovum or the embryo; contraception, as I have carefully explained, prevents the fertilizing of the ovum by keeping the male cells away. Thus, it prevents the beginning of life."

---

[49] Sanger M. Birth Control or Abortion? Birth Contra Rev 1918; 2: 3-4.

[50] Sanger M. Woman and the New Race (With a Preface by Havelock Ellis). New York: Brentano's; 1920: 118-129.

[51] In addition to a brief commentary (Sanger M. Comments on the Pope Encyclical, Birth Control Rev 1931; 15: 40-41), Sanger left an unpublished article (Sanger M. Birth Control Advances, A Reply to the Pope), from which the above quotation is taken. Accessible in:

http://www.nyu.edu/projects/sanger/webedition/app/documents/show.php?sangerDoc=236637.xml.

To confirm Sanger's rejection of abortion as a procedure to limit the offspring it might be interesting to remember the information, she had given to the women who attended her first clinic since 1917: "To each group we explained simply what contraception was; that abortion was the wrong way —no matter how early it was performed it was taking life; that contraception was the better way, the safer way— it took a little time, a little trouble, but was well worth while in the long run, because life had not begun."[52]

2.3. W.J. Robinson: prevenception and uncertainty before abortion

Robinson's position on prevenception and abortion is complex since two contradictory attitudes seem to coexist in him. On one hand, he tenaciously manifested from 1918 his personal and practical conviction that prevenception was the priority and almost universal solution to the problems that human reproduction could pose to the point that the diligent practice of prevenception would end up making abortion unnecessary. On the other hand, and paradoxically, Robinson admitted the need for certain abortions because while recognizing that abortion always presented itself as an evil, he accepted that sometimes, it represented a lesser evil compared to the catastrophic consequences that could result from not practicing it, consequences that were not only biological but also social, economic and eugenic. This led him throughout his life, especially at the end of it, to promote the repeal of the laws against abortion.

What is interesitng above all is that, in spite of his

---

[52] Sanger M. An Autobiography. New Cork: W.W. Norton Publ.; 1938: 217.

moral ambiguity, Robinson coined the term 'prevenception' for rejection and not only for prevention of abortion. Indeed, it seems that Robinson's basic intention in putting his neologism into circulation was to establish the maximum possible distance between contraception and abortion. In the editorial in which he used the new word for the first time, Robinson says: "Times without number we have shown that there is a radical difference between prevenception and abortion. A difference not in degree but in kind. We have shown that a great many advocates of prevenceptive measures are sincerely opposed to abortion in any form."[53]

A few months later, he returns to the subject in another editorial in which he criticizes with great harshness the cynical attitude of those doctors who do not perceive any moral difference between prevenception and abortion, so, in practice, they opt for the latter. Robinson writes that they recognize abortion as the destruction of a life, while prevention simply means preventing the sperm from coming into contact with the egg. But they conclude that the end result, being identical in both cases, is preventing children from coming to this world; the crime was the same."[54]

In 1920, he exposes those same views with even more vigor. Responding to a letter from a doctor who maintained that from different perspectives (sociological, eugenic, ethical), there are no differences between prevenception and abortion[55], Robinson, who had earned a just reputation

---

[53] Robinson WJ. Prevenception versus Abortion. Med Critic Guide1918; 21: 206-207, 206.

[54] Robinson WJ. Editorials. A Doctor on Prevenception and Abortion. Critic & Guide 1918; 21: 410.

[55] Dekker H. Prevenceptive and Abortion - Are They on the Same Ethical

for radical extremism, wrote: "I confess that I am not radical enough to consider abortion on the same ethical plane as prevention of conception. As we have tried to make clear so many times, one of the reasons for our persistent advocacy of prevenception is to do away with the justification for or the necessity of abortion. Even if abortion were as harmless and safe a procedure as our contributor claims it to be, it would still be ethically objectionable. [...] They are two essentially different acts. In prevenception we prevent the spermatozoa from coming in contact with the ovum. We do this by either mechanical, chemical or physiological means. There is no destruction of any kind. And, ethically prevenception is exactly similar to abstinence. Prevenception is neither less nor more than abstaining from the act. But abortion is a different matter. There we destroy something already created".[56]

And to confirm that conviction on abortion, Robinson alleges that he never practiced an abortion. He affirms, however, that his behavior was not based on moral considerations, but on mere psychological feelings. As early as 1912, he had said: "... strange as this statement may seem, I have never personally performed an abortion." And he adds that he abstained not because of moral superiority, but out of sheer cowardice[57], or "and partly by a feeling of disgust which I could not overcome."[58] Thirty years later, in what could be called his ethical testament on prevenception

---

Plane. Med Critic & Guide 1920; 23: 213-214.

[56] Robinson WJ. Comment by the Editor. Critic and Guide 1920; 23: 215.

[57] Robinson WJ. Sexual Problems of To-Day. New York: Critic and Guide 1912: 155. The same text is preserved and unmodified through the multiple editions of this book: the 12th edition was published in 1923.

[58] Robinson WJ. The Ethics of Abortion. New York Medical Journal 1914; 100: 897.

and abortion, he repeats the same opinions: "There is no reason why this question could not be discussed [the repeal of the laws against abortion] calmly, judicially, without bias and without fear. And I can do this the more readily, because, strange as this statement may sound to you, I personally have never produced an abortion. Yes, it is twenty years since I received my M.D. degree, and during that time I have not committed one single abortion. I know that this sounds strange, but it is so. But, pray, do not for a moment imagine that it was on moral ground that I refused the hundred of pleading, weeping, heart-broken, distracted women, married or unmarried, who begged and entreated to be freed of the fruit of their womb. No, I repeat, it was not moral superiority; it was cowardice principally."[59]

Gordon has questioned the sincerity of Robinson's personal refusal to perform abortions[60]. She simply raises the suspicion that Robinson, in printed and privately distributed reports, admitted that he had 'wiped wombs'[61]. The same suspicion is also expressed by Derr, MacNair and Naranjo-Huebl[62].

It must be concluded that Robinson's attitude of duplicity in the face of abortion (the refusal to practice it

---

[59] Robinson WJ. The Law Against Abortion. Its Perniciousness Demonstrated and Its Repeal Demanded. New York: The Eugenics Publishing Company, Inc.; 1934: 120-121.

[60] Gordon L. Woman's Body, Woman's Right. Birth Control in America, 2nd ed. Penguin Books: 1990: 170.

[61] Robinson WJ. Dr. Robinson and Saint Peter. How Dr. Robinson Entered the Heavenly Gates and Became St. Peter's Assistant. New York: Eugenics Publishing Co.; 1931: 24-25.

[62] Derr MK, MacNair R, Naranjo-Huebl L. Reproductive Wrongs Unto Death: Eugenic Strictures (Late Nineteenth-Early Twentieth Centuries and Beyond). In: Derr MK, MacNair R, Naranjo-Huebl L, eds. ProLife Feminism. Yesterday and Today. 2nd ed. Bloomington, IN: Xlibris; 2005: 107-113.

and demanding its legalization) opens a gap in the conviction of the pioneers of abortion, who maintained the incompatibility of abortion and prevention of fertilization. In Foote Jr, that conviction was absolute and based exclusively on ethical reasons. The firm opposition of Sanger to abortion came, rather than from moral convictions, from social and political conveniences, for it was clear that for the society of that time to accept contraception required to interpose a great distance between contraception and abortion. In Robinson, such incompatibility is fractured because he did not renounce to tolerate the practice of legal abortion for therapeutic and socioeconomic indications.

Chapter 3. The Medical Profession and Contraception: From Rejection to Acceptance

3.1. The institutional contempt for contraception

Although there are significant differences from one country to another, it can be said that in general and until well into the twentieth century, institutional medicine (both national corporations and associations of specialists) adopted a negative or openly condemning attitude towards contraception.

At that time, the idea that the practice of contraception was not proper medicine prevailed among physicians. It had no scientific basis because the methods and materials that where used had not been validated experimentally. Hence, nobody knew to what extent they were effective. And, what was worse is that all were aware that they were sometimes capable of inducing considerable damage. It was also firmly held that with the exception of the rare cases in which a new pregnancy was seriously contraindicated from a clinical point of view, the prevention of conception was not a legitimate medical activity; doctors did not consider themselves capable of evaluating economic or of social convenience reasons invoked by the vast majority of women who came to them seeking contraceptive advice.

In addition, at that time and in most countries, contraception was not accepted by legislation and public morality. In fact, there were very few physicians who participated in social movements in favor of conception control. The great majority understood that this matter was more of groups and individuals dedicated to promoting women's rights and radical feminism. However, there were some doctors who became active supporters of contraception and decided to fight for its approval by the professional institutions for various reasons such as the prevision of a demographic catastrophe, the eugenic utopia, the high infant mortality or simply the precarious life of some poor and prolific families.

In contrast to the institutional rejection by doctors, the practice of the contraceptive methods then available was extended among the general public especially in the affluent class. Apart from its important effects on the social ethos, conception control favored the production of contraceptive agents, an "industry" that over the years managed to move many millions of dollars. It became inevitable that the lack of legal regulation, misleading advertising and the absence of control of the quality of the products offered in the market ended up facilitating the diffusion of ineffective or potentially harmful methods and products.

In the late 1930s, the social importance of contraception and its economic relevance forced organized medicine to get involved in the matter and pay attention to it. Striking changes of attitudes in the profession followed and the lack of interest mixed with the contempt of earlier times mutated little by little into recognition and approval. This is a history worth considering with due detail and to carry out such pending task, we will analyze what happened in the United States at that time.

3.2. The complex history of rejection: from 1912 to 1936

With regard to contraception, the first third of the twentieth century was a quiet time for medical institutions. None of them were ever seriously worried about the possibility of changing their official position rejecting contraception. The activism in favor of the control of conception, however, gave its first steps at that time. Although it lacked enough power to force major changes in the attitude of the medical profession, it did not stop implementing strategies to favor them. The most significant of these strategies consisted in capturing the collaboration of leading figures in medicine with a twofold purpose: on one hand, to promote the progressive acceptance of contraception within medical organizations; and on the other hand, to make doctors the main propagators of birth control.

The 1912 presidential speech that Abraham Jacobi pronounced in the annual session of the American Medical Association – is usually chosen as the first episode of this story. In that speech, Jacobi spoke about the decline of infant mortality and made a tangential reference to contraception although he did not name it as such nor did he say a word about the techniques or policies of conception control[63]. Despite this, the promoters of the contraceptive movement have elevated Jacobi's address to the status of a historical milestone that inaugurated the desired alliance between the birth-control movement and institutional medicine. It is an obvious exaggeration used as a persuasive propaganda tool[64]. Over the years, however, the meaning attributed to Jacobi's discourse became common among historians of contraception but unfortunately, none of them tried to evaluate its real impact on institutional medicine[65].

Furthermore, it is unjustified to state that Jacobi's

---

[63] At one point, Jacobi alluded to the scarcity of resources available to reduce infant mortality from what he intuitively deduced "that is why it has become an indispensable suggestion that only a certain number of babies should be born into the world. As long as not infrequently even the well-to-do limit the number of their offspring, the advice to the poor —or those to whom the raising of a large family is worse than merely difficult— to limit the number of children, even the healthy ones, is perhaps more than merely excusable. I often learn that an American family has had ten children but only three or four survived. Before the dead ones succumbed, they were a source of expense, poverty and morbidity to the few survivors. For the interest of the latter and the health of the community at large, they had better not have been born." That's all Jacobi said in his address about offspring control. Jacobi A. The Best Means of Combating Infant Mortality. JAMA 1912; 58: 1735-1744.

[64] The idea was imagined and spread by W.J. Robinson. Robinson, admirer, friend and, later, literary executor of Jacobi, urged him to refer in his speech to the control of births. Years later, in a retrospective, Robinson stated that "after Dr Jacobi, the Nestor of American Medicine, the founder of Pediatrics in the United States, and President of the American Medical Association (the highest honor a physician can receive) came out openly for Birth Control. Some other physicians who at first did not want to hear anything about it joined the movement and it then progressed with accelerated momentum." Robinson W.J. Twenty-Five Years of Progress. Birth Contr Rev 1927; 11: 323.

[65] Thus, for example, the generic desire expressed by Jacobi in his speech that fewer and better children be born is willfully changed by V. Robinson (son of W.J Robinson) into a social action program: "in his presidential speech [Jacobi] advocated the need to disseminate among the public the best methods to control unwanted and undesirable fertilization." Robinson V. Pioneers of Birth Control in England and America. New York: Voluntary Parenthood League; 1919: 72. But Jacobi did not say a word of contraceptive methods.

speech provoked much controversy and division about contraception among doctors[66]. Certainly, other aspects of Jacobi's address —for example, what Jacobi said on the role of midwives in obstetric care or on the dispute of childbirth in the hospital or at home, or on infant feeding— received both wide criticism and applause. But it is not justified to affirm that Jacobi's intervention broke the dominant contraceptive consensus or divided the doctors[67]. The brief and oblique allusions of Jacobi to offspring limitation passed practically without any comment68. JAMA did not publish a single letter to the editor about the speech. And Jacobi himself, in a farewell article published a year later wherein he comments on his presidential speech, makes no allusion to the question of fewer and healthier children[69]. V. Robinson points out that Jacobi's prestige made him relatively immune to the attacks of his colleagues and that some critical opinions were expressed only until three years later[70].

---

[66] For example, Gordon, whose observations on Jacobi contain frequent errors, adds one more when she affirms that this shocking speech "was more a product than a cause, more a culmination than a beginning, of the revival of medical birth control activism". Gordon L. The Moral Property of Women. A History of Birth Control Politics in America. Urbana: University of Illinois Press; 2002: 115. As it will be seen below, the immediate impact of Jacobi's speech was minimal.

[67] Pearson M. Millennial Dreams and Moral Dilemmas. Seventh-day Adventism and Contemporary Ethics. Cambridge: Cambridge University Press; 1990: 57.

[68] Reed notes that Jacobi's colleagues ignored Jacobi's proposal that they should assume a leading on the implementation of birth control (Reed J. The Birth Control Movement, Princeton, New Jersey: Princeton Legacy Library; 2014: 46). For her part, Chesler says that when Jacobi raised, in his speech to the AMA, for the first time the problem of contraception, there was no appreciable clamor (Chesler E. Woman of Valor: Margaret Sanger and the Birth Control Movement in America. New York; Simon & Schuster: 147).

[69] Jacobi A. A Final Word to the Fellows and Members of the American Medical Association. JAMA 1913; 61: 633-635.

The resistance of institutional medicine to contraception was steadfast in 1924. That year, the experience of 1912 was repeated in a certain way. The then President of the A.M.A., William Pusey, mentioned in his presidential address the social problems of medicine including birth restriction. He acknowledged that in those years, medicine had no satisfactory program for birth control. He opted for theorizing the demographic and eugenic potential of contraception and ignored its possible medical indications or its role in the health of the individual patients[71]. An editorial article published months later in the Association's journal pointed out that, given the total lack of research carried out "in a scientific and ethical spirit and approaching the subject without bias, there is a wide divergence of opinion and a vast amount of argumentation."[72] This situation of apathy invited doctors and their associations not to be involved in birth control policies due to the lack of satisfactory methods and programs to carry them out.

The resistance of the profession to the alleged social and economic indications of contraception for which doctors declared themselves incompetent was outspoken in

---

[70] Robinson V. Pioneers of Birth Control: 73.

[71] In his speech, Pusey expressed himself as a fervent follower of social Darwinism: "It is clear that our civilization is committed to a sort of socialism to the effect that the economically fit and competent will take care of the weak and inefficient. It is an unconscious endeavour to set aside the law of natural selection and counteract nature's cruel but salutary process of eliminating the unfit." Pusey W.A. Some of the Social Problems of Medicine. JAMA 1924; 82: 1905-1908. A year later, Pusey advocated in favor of sterilization of the deficient and birth control to prevent dysgenic reproduction. He insisted that, if poor people did not reproduce themselves, poverty and high taxes for social welfare could be eliminated. Pusey W.A. Medicine's Responsibilities in the Birth Control Movement. Birth Contr Rev 1925; 9: 134-136, 156-158.

[72] Editorial. The Prevention of Conception JAMA 1924; 83: 2020-2021.

those years. They thought that the collective interest of professional institutions should be limited to discussing whether there were pathological situations in which the control of conception could be medically necessary, that is, in which well-defined clinical situations might it be acceptable to recommend a more or less prolonged delay of a new pregnancy[73]. The attitude of the medical institutions in other countries was practically the same: contraception for non-medical indications was seen as something alien to the medical profession.

3.2.1. The first fissures in the block

It was precisely in the mid-1920s when, as a result of certain social forces, some cracks began to appear in the solid block of the institutional rejection of contraception although radical changes would not occur until the next decade.

Perhaps the more important stimulus came from the most radical segment of feminism. Within it, two positions had emerged on how to promote contraception. They disagreed about the convenience of seeking the collaboration of doctors and their organizations. On one hand, Margaret Sanger, with her American League of Birth Control, considered that the alliance with doctors was essential to introduce contraception into society. She even proposed a bill that she called the "law of doctors only " to put the exclusive application of techniques for birth control in their hands. On the other hand, Mary Dennet, with her

---

[73] "Medical leaders in contraception soon realized the resistance of the profession to "social" indications and confined their discussion to the necessity of birth control in well-defined pathologic circumstances -tuberculosis, heart and kidney disease, and pelvic abnormality." Kennedy D.M. Birth Control in America: The Career of Margaret Sanger. New Haven: Yale University Press; 1970: 180.

League of Voluntary Paternity, struggled to keep the contraceptive movement far from medicine because she considered that giving doctors the leadership in this field was tantamount to betraying the essence of the movement[74].

The history of the rapprochement between contraceptive activism and institutional medicine and consequently, of the fracture of institutional unity, was long and complex. At first, the 'secular' activists adopted the aggressive and confrontational attitude of the first feminism in which the rebellion against the prevailing social order (and especially against the doctors who helped preserve it) was linked to a campaign to publicize the contraceptive methods among women of the working class. The propaganda instrument was a clandestine and short-lived pamphlet entitled 'The Woman Rebel'[75].

After various vicissitudes, that first rebellious and anti-medical attitude changed into its antithetical position. From 1918, the League's policy focused on attracting doctors to the 'cause' and thus on being able to socially legitimize the movement of birth control. Sanger understood that without the cooperation of the medical profession it was practically impossible to win the social battle in favor of contraception[76].

---

[74] The history of the Sanger-Dennett struggle can be seen in the chapter on Birth Control and the Law, by Kennedy D. op. cit., pp. 218-223; and also in Engelman P. A History of the Birth Control Movement in America. Santa Barbara: Praeger, ABC-CLIO, LLC; 2011: 113-126. Sanger, for her part, took care to collect in the Birth Control Review some news informing about the proposals and suggestions that some doctors presented to their associations in favor of recognizing contraception as an activity of organized medicine: Sanger M. The Doctors and Birth Control. Birth Contr Rev 1923; 7: 144-145.

[75] Relatively few, although interesting, are the articles and notes on contraception that appear in The Woman Rebel, whose seven issues appeared between March and September-October 1914. They can be viewed at: http://wyatt.elasticbeanstalk.com/mep/MS/ docs / MS.lb.html.

The change of objectives and accent was recorded when its anarchist pamphlet "The Woman Rebel" was replaced by the publication entitled "Birth Control Review", with a more formal and academic content[77].

Despite Sanger's and the birth control activists' attempts to recruit doctors for their cause, the medical community remained refractory to the contraceptive movement. For many years the Birth Control Review collected, commented on and amplified any news or simple rumor about the lukewarm cooperation of some doctors or their associations with the movement of fertility control. Following an editorial line of optimism in the inevitable social triumph of contraception, the Review paid special attention to the actions and attitudes of local medical associations or the AMA itself, celebrating some trivial events as major advances[78].

---

[76] "From 1918 on, Sanger had concentrated on gaining support from the medical profession. Her commitment to the target of a nationwide chain of clinics under medical auspices led to her most ambitious campaign. In 1919, she set up the National Committee for Federal Legislation for Birth Control in Washington, D.C. Its objective was to legalize the use of the mails and other interstate carriers for contraceptive materials and information so that doctors could prescribe freely for their patients." Lader L. Margaret Sanger: Militant, Pragmatist, Visionary. http://www.ontheissuesmagazine.com/1990spring/Spr90_Lader.php.

[77] The full text of the journal, published between February 1917 and January 1940, is available at: https://lifedynamics.com/library/#birth-control-review.

[78] Sanger, who acted as Editor of the Birth Control Review until 1929, was concerned with tireless perseverance to publish in the magazine editorials, notes and news that informed of the initiatives and suggestions that some doctors proposed to their colleagues, requesting that contraception be recognized as an acceptable activity for a correct professional practice. For many years, the magazine functioned as a sounding board that exaggerated the importance of this information to the point of falsifying them at times. For example, in an editorial published in 1923, the reader is led to suppose that the statement of the President of the Medical Society of the State of New York is gratuitous when she assured that the majority of the members of the Society were against contraception, since she did not cite the source of that data. When it was clarified that such data was

By contrast, the Review did not spare any occasion to bitterly criticize the resistance that physicians and their organizations opposed to the theory and practice of birth control which they still considered a matter inappropriate for the medical profession. It is easily understandable, therefore, that Birth Control Review gave much prominence to the actions and writings of a few doctors in favor of contraception. Some of them, like William Robinson and Robert Dickinson, played an important role in both academic medicine and the long debate searching for the acceptance of birth control by the profession and society. It should not be forgotten that an element that facilitated such medical acceptance was the attitude, that was shared by all, of a complete rejection of non-therapeutic abortion.

3.2.2. The AMA responds to pro-contraceptive pressure

Only from the mid-1920s onwards did members or associations of physicians address petitions to the House of Delegates, urging it to take an active role in favor (and, occasionally, against) the legal and professional regulation of contraception begin to be presented and debated in the annual sessions of the AMA[79]. In fact, as of 1925, the consideration of these petitions was never absent from the agenda of the annual meetings. Along the first years, they

---

based on the answers to a questionnaire sent to the medical societies of the counties, the editorial reply of Sanger was very expressive: "the medical profession -with a large number of honorable exceptions- has not been able, until now, to realize the immense amount of disease, suffering and death that afflicts women and children in our great country for lack of adequate and scientific education on contraception." Editor. Doctors and Birth Control. Birth Contr Rev 1923; 7: 144-145.

[79] The reluctance that the AMA had shown until the mid-1920s to include contraception in its debates comes from old. In 1902, the House of Delegates decided by vote "to indefinitely postpone resolutions that recommend [...] means that prevent or shorten gestation". Blasingame F.J.L, ed. AMA Digest of Official Actions, Vol. I: 1846-1958. Chicago: American Medical Association; 1959: 69.

focused on requesting AMA to mediate in favor of enacting legislation recognizing the right of doctors to offer information on birth control in their offices, clinics or dispensaries to women in whom contraception was medically indicated[80]. Later, the requests sought the creation of a committee to rule on the quality and efficacy of contraceptives then in use. It was precisely because of the committee's influence that contraception ceased to be seen as an empirical and unprofessional practice to become a recommendable medical activity.

It is worth detailing the historical course of the positions of the AMA over a little more than a decade to understand the ethical-professional background of such a radical and, to some extent, unexpected change. In a first stage, the leaders of the AMA used the powerful resources that the regulations put in their hands (reasoned decisions, administrative silence, opportunistic delays, transfer to consulting bodies) to repel the initiatives presented. Finally, AMA directors transferred the responsibility to the Committee for the Study of Contraception and limited themselves to follow the Committee's opinion; the AMA then changed from rejection to acceptance.

The first formal petition occurred in 1925 when the Section of Obstetrics, Gynecology and Abdominal Surgery of

---

[80] Fishbein points out that in 1922, "at the meeting of the Board of Trustees previous to the St. Louis session, there came a resolution from the Council on Health and Public Instruction which was to create much concern in ensuing years. It dealt with the prevention of conception and proposed that the American Medical Association take action to secure modification of federal laws which interfered with the right of the physician to give advice by mail on this subject. The Board of Trustees decided at this time that the question was one on which it could not take action." Fishbein M. The History of the American Medical Association, 1847 to 1947. With the Biographies of the Presidents of the Association by Walter L. Bierring, and with Histories of the Publications, Councils, Bureaus and Other Official Bodies. Philadelphia; W.B. Saunders Co; 1947: 328.

the AMA itself submitted a resolution to the House of Delegates recommending "the alteration of existing laws, whenever necessary, so that doctors could legally inform about contraception of their patients in the ordinary course of their practice."[81] The trustees declined such undertaking. Two years later, the Section of Obstetrics sent the petition again to the Board of Trustees[82]. The next year, the Board offered the following answer: "In view of the great lack of unanimity of opinion with respect to the matter that deals with the resolution, this Board of Trustees returns the issue with all respect to the House of Delegates."[83]

Previously, in 1926, the Board of Trustees had already expressed its intention of remaining silent on the issue, when it left aside a petition of the National Catholic Social Welfare Conference requesting the AMA to intervene in the proposed change of the federal criminal code so that the regulations on contraception would not be relaxed[84]. The Board decided to abstain from the matter and not to issue an opinion, referring to "the absence of data based on adequate scientific research."[85]

---

[81] There is no mention of this proposal in the Minutes of the 76th Annual Session of the AMA, in Atlantic City, May 25-29, 1925, as they appear published in the JAMA (JAMA 1925; 84: 1635-1667). The same happens with the Proceedings, House of Delegates, or with the Digest of Official Actions, of the AMA Archives (http://ama.nmtvault.com/custom/About.jsp). The only precise reference to the mentioned initiative is found in the documentary Appendix, pp. 431-432, of Dickinson R.L. Control of Conception, Present and Future. Bull NY Acad Med 1929; 5: 413-434.

[82] Resolution on Contraception. Minutes, House of Delegates. Seventy-Eighth Annual Session of the American Medical Association, Held at Washington, D.C., May 16-20, 1927: 60.

[83] Resolution on Contraception. Minutes, House of Delegates, Seventy-ninth Annual Session, Held at Minneapolis, Minn., June 11-15, 1928: 27.

[84] Communication from National Catholic Welfare Conference. Minutes, House of Delegates, Seventy-Seventh Annual Session, Held at Dallas, Texas, April 19-23, 1926: 39.

With time, the requests became more frequent; its content and arguments offered slight variations as did the answers and the reasons given by the directors of the AMA. In the 1932 session in New Orleans, an innovation was introduced which years later would be decisive: the motion asked for the creation, within the AMA, of a Committee to study birth control. The expected negative response of the influential Reference Committee argued that being a very controversial issue, it was not advisable at that time to present it to the debate of the profession[86]. The motion was reiterated in Milwaukee in the session of 1933 where once again the creation of a Committee was requested. The committee would be in charge of the study of birth control in all its aspects, paying special attention to the methods, the medical indications for their use, and the ways of instructing the public and physicians on the subject. The motion included a significant caution which was never abandoned in the future – the creation of the Committee was not to be interpreted at all as an endorsement of contraception by the AMA[87]. At first, the Reference Committee on Hygiene and Public Health decided to recommend the resolution and send it to the House of Delegates but after a debate, the Committee opted to submit the proposal to a vote of the Chamber as a result of which the Resolution was left on the table[88].

---

[85] Supplementary Report of Board of Trustees. Ibíd., 44.

[86] Resolutions on the Appointment of a Committee to Study Birth Control. Minutes, House of Delegates. Eighty-third Annual Session, Held at New Orleans, La., May 3-13, 1932: 45.

[87] Resolutions on Creation of the Committee for the Study of Birth Control. Minutes, House of Delegates. Eighty-fourth Annual Session, Held at Milwaukee, Wis., June 12-15, 1933: 50-51.

[88] Ibíd., 88.

In 1934, the position of the institutional rejection of the AMA to the control of births was maintained although some signs of ambiguity were perceptible then. At the Session held in June in Cleveland, a new resolution was presented to create a Committee on Contraceptive Methods which would study the therapeutic value and effectiveness of contraceptive agents in use at that time or that manufacturers could put on the market in order to make it easier for doctors to give an informed response to the general public. Although it was again stated that the creation of the Committee did not imply any endorsement by the AMA of birth control[89], it was accepted that the results of these studies could be published in JAMA, the official organ of the Association[90]. The Reference Committee on Hygiene and Public Health that preferred to assume a neutral position this time returned the resolution to the House of Delegates without making any recommendation on it. At the same time, they requested the opinion of the Chamber on the matter. The Chamber once again left it on the table[91]. For its part, the Birth Control Review, in sharp contrast to the criticisms expressed in previous years, praised the action of the AMA which, at last, recognized even for bizarre and deviant reasons that birth control was a medical problem. It also predicted that the official medical sanction of contraception would soon arrive[92].

---

[89] Resolutions on Contraceptive Methods. Minutes, House of Delegates. Eighty-fifth Annual Session, Held at Cleveland, Ohio, June 11-15, 1934: 42.

[90] Resolution on Contraceptive Devices and Methods. Ibíd., 53.

[91] Resolution Referred Back to the House by the Reference Committee on Hygiene and Public Health. Ibíd., 59.

[92] Editorials. Birth Contr Rev 1934; 2: 1-2.

3.2.3.   The transition from 1935 to 1936

At the 1935 session in Atlantic City, the decision to create a committee to study contraception was finally taken. By doing so, the Board of Trustees gave an answer to the intense pressure that both outside and within, the Association had been created in favor of the medical acceptance of contraception. The requests to the AMA continued to increase[93] and in order to evaluate them, it was decided to set up a Special Reference Committee which concluded that none of the received requests could be approved in its current tenor as a resolution proposal. That led the Special Committee to replace the requests with a draft of its own.

The first thing that Special Committee said was that any resolution taken on the matter could not be interpreted as a statement or action for or against the control of births. It added some other considerations to this clause: that the use of contraceptives, so generalized but outside the law, had been stimulated by non-medical groups and especially by commercial interests[94]; that the effects which contraceptive products could have had on the health of the population were unknown and required that they be studied in an exact and extensive manner; that there was a lot of confusion in interpreting federal and state regulations

---

[93] In the 1935 session, the following requests were taken into consideration: those of the Medical Societies of several States (New York, Arkansas, Maine and New Mexico), the District of Columbia; some Counties (Berks, Gage, Portag), and a number of scientific societies. See: Resolutions on Contraception. Minutes, House of Delegates, 86th Annual Session, Atlantic City, June 10-14, 1935: 34.

[94] Reed notes that it was the concern about the great magnitude of the contraceptive business what led the AMA to create in 1935 its Committee on Contraception. Reed J. Doctors, birth control, and social values, 1830-1970. In: Vogel M.J, Rosenberg C.E, eds. The Therapeutic Revolution: Essays in the Social History of American Medicine. University of Pennsylvania Press; 1979: 109-133: 122.

on the subject. The Committee concluded with a recommendation to the Board of Trustees to create a competent committee to study these problems so that a report could be offered to the next session of the AMA although it was provisional[95]. The Board of Trustees approved this proposal on June 11 and created the Study Committee on Contraceptive Practices and Related Problems, to which they entrusted the thorough investigation of the problem of birth control[96].

3.2.4.   The Resolution of 1936

At the 1936 session in Kansas City, the Committee for the Study of Contraceptive Practices and Related Problems presented through the Reference Committee for the Executive Session the report commissioned by the Board of Trustees[97]. It was a document that required to be known in detail in view of the corresponding resolution of 1937 so as to perceive the remarkable differences existing between both documents. The 1936 report generally disapproved of contraception, relying more on data and professional opinions than on ethical arguments. It was composed of a short introduction, a long reference to the problem of overpopulation in the Western world, and four groups of considerations: eugenic, economic, moral and medical. It

---

[95] Report of the Special Reference Committee. Ibíd., 45.

[96] In the Report presented by the Committee at the following session (Kansas City, 1936), it was stated that it "had been appointed by the Board of Trustees of the AMA in accordance with the resolutions approved on June 11, 1935 by the House of Delegates." Report of Committee to Study Contraceptive Practices and Related Problems. Minutes, House of Delegates. Eighty-Seventh Annual Session, Held at Kansas City, Mo., May 11-15, 1936: 53.

[97] Report of Committee to Study Contraceptive Practices and Related Problems. Minutes, House of Delegates. Eighty-Seventh Annual Session, Held at Kansas City, Mo., May 11-15, 1936: 53-55.

concluded with several recommendations.

After recognizing the extent of the problem and the role played by organized propaganda in favor of contraception, the report alluded to the little attention that medicine had given to the issue and to the widespread ignorance on the subject which equally reigned among doctors and the public. The committee declared that after having reviewed a large amount of bibliography, its purpose was to offer an examination of the the current ideas concerning the general use of contraceptives as well as on the acceptable medical indications.

The report was quite shocking. It presented a reductive, purely physiological view of man by declaring that the human animal had always wanted to avoid conception as a natural consequence of coitus. Its reflections on the problem of overpopulation sounded as having a slightly racist accent, since they were limited to the western world and specifically to the demography of the white populations, to whom they provided the greatest social dignity. Three quarters of the text devoted to the demographic problem included long bibliographic quotations: the first one dealing with the convenience of reducing the birth rate of all social strata and not only of the upper class in order to avoid the risk of a "racial suicide of the educated part of our population"; the second referred to the decrease in the birth rate in the whole world and not only in Europe, to conclude that "the general belief that the decline in fertility is limited to the nations of Western civilization is false".

In the committee's view, apart from the case of a few rare hereditary diseases, the limited knowledge of human genetics did not offer a firm basis to justify the limitation of conception for eugenic reasons. The committee did not participate in the optimism of those who thought that a greater dissemination of contraceptive information would tend to establish a better social and economic equilibrium in society. In addition, the only social sector that did not grow as a result of contraceptive propaganda were the upper classes of society.

The committee had not found a reliable evidence that the dissemination of contraceptive information had improved the economic condition of low-income groups nor was the committee aware of any type of contraception that was reasonably adequate and effective for a large portion of the population.

The moral considerations of the committee were very poor and almost disappointing. They were limited to report that coitus was accepted as a normal marital function but that there were differences of opinion about methods to prevent conception. Finally, it pointed out that there were no moral objections concerning the selection by married couples of the supposedly infertile period of the cycle for intercourse.

In its medical considerations, the committee recognized that voluntary limitation of conception may be necessary to safeguard the health of some women. It included a list of diseases in which a pregnancy is not desirable (active tuberculosis, nephritis, heart disease, certain psychopathic conditions, etc.), although it recognized that the ability of women to bear a pregnancy without affecting their health is so variable that no general rules can be offered. The marriage of individuals with mental or physical abnormalities that contraindicate reproduction was discouraged.

The committee reviewed the contraceptive methods and devices available then. It pointed out that some were more or less innocuous and relatively effective if used intelligently but it considered that all mechanical devices introduced into the neck or body of the uterus were potentially dangerous. In several scientific publications the effectiveness of the different available techniques were evaluated but aside from continence, none were 100% safe.

The committee finally referred to some professional medical aspects: it did not find evidence of legal limitations interfering with the freedom of the doctor to advise his patients to use contraception; in its opinion, contraceptive offices should not be established outside of doctor's control; and the doctors who, for non-medical reasons, considered it improper to inform or advise their patients about contraception, even if the pregnancy is contraindicated, should not be criticized; but these doctors should not dissuade their patients from obtaining contraceptive advice. Lastly, the committee raised the need for physicians and medical students to acquire sufficient knowledge on the control of conception.

The final recommendations of the resolution were three: the first one requested that, given the incompleteness of the report, a committee be appointed to continue this study and report back to the House; the second recommendation requested that a group should be constituted with the responsibility of developing criteria for the evaluation of contraceptive materials; the third one proposed a repudiation of the propaganda directed to the public by non-medical organisms which, unfortunately, some doctors had been part. The Committee reproached these bodies for creating an entirely false sense of values with respect to the important role of pregnancy and parenting.

The Reference Committee for the Executive Session

only approved the first and third recommendations but not the second one because it estimated that there was not enough knowledge about the matter and that the disavowal of certain contraceptive products could, by inference, mean the approval of others. The House of Delegates, not without having promoted a vote of appreciation to the Study Committee on Contraception for the work done, adopted the Report and its first and third recommendations as proposed by the Reference Committee.

The Dallas Resolution received harsh criticism from the American Birth Control League, which called the document contradictory, replete with prejudices, confusions and evasiveness, and reproached it for omitting the role of birth control in reducing both criminal abortion and the resulting maternal deaths[98].

3.3.   The resolution of 1937

It is considered, in general, that the approval of the Report of the Study Committee on Contraceptive Practices and Related Problems by the House of Delegates during the AMA Session held in Atlantic City in 1937 was more than a great novelty, a true historic landmark[99]. It overturned the long and accepted tradition of dislike or rejection of contraception that the Association had maintained for decades in order to establish in its place a new attitude of acceptance and active support for birth control. Nothing shows this change of position better than the radical

---

[98] Editorial. Organized Medicine Dodges the Issue. Birth Control Rev 1936; 3 (10) (n.s.): 1-3.

[99] Report of the Reference Committee on Executive Session. 2. Report of Committee to Study Contraceptive Practices and Related Problems. American Medical Association. Proceedings of the House of Delegates. Eighty-Eighth Annual Session, Held at Atlantic City, N.J., June 7-11, 1937: 65-67.

contrast between the reports of 1936 and 1937 which were both prepared by the Committee for the Study of Contraceptive Practices.

What innovations does the 1937 document offer? It is practically a new writing in its entirety which differs in style, content and conclusions with its namesake of 1936. The latter had paid attention to the demographic, eugenic, economic, moral and medical aspects of contraception; the 1937 document exclusively reduced its considerations to the strictly professional medical area of the private relationship between doctors and patients, whatever the socioeconomic group to which patients belonged. It established that the correct places to advise and inform on contraception (dispensaries, clinics and doctor's offices) had to have a legal license and be under medical control. As the only agreement with its 1936 Report, it pointed out that the medical indications of contraception there included remained valid but considered, however, that the limitation of births was a matter to be determined case by case, taking into account the circumstances according to the judgment of parents and doctors. It affirmed that the doctor was free to give information to his/her patients concerning contraception – information that would be provided only when in his/her judgment the medical necessity of the case demanded it. Medical necessity was the only legal justification for contraception. Consequently, the control of the conception had to be under medical supervision.

The Report stated that ignorance about contraception not only occurred among the general public but also affected many doctors. It established accordingly that medical students had to be thoroughly educated on fertility, sterility and also on the therapeutic application of contraceptive methods. Lastly, it insisted that the AMA had to investigate contraceptive products and techniques.

The report concluded with three recommendations: 1. That the AMA did what was necessary to make clear to physicians their legal rights regarding the use of contraceptives; 2. That the AMA undertook the investigation of the materials, devices and methods recommended or used for the prevention of conception in order to evaluate their properties, their physiological, chemical and biological effects, and published the results to inform the profession; 3. That the Council of Medical Education and Hospitals of the AMA be asked to promote the teaching and learning of the various factors pertaining to fertility and sterility, including their positive and negative aspects.

The Report was presented to the Chamber of Delegates by the Executive Reference Committee which, in addition to endorsing it with its authority, considered it appropriate to correct the style of the first recommendation and sought the expert opinion of the Pharmacy, Chemistry and Physical Therapy Councils on the second recommendation as well as the view of the Committee of Medical Education and Hospitals on the third recommendation. The Executive Committee requested to not dissolve the Contraception Study Committee, but that it remained available to provide the information and assistance requested. After giving course to these requests, the report was entirely approved.

Logically, the decision of the AMA was acknowledged by individuals and groups in favor of birth control as a great victory that had required long years of struggle[100]. The

---

[100] "The history of human progress as well as the history of medicine will record a decisive victory on June 8th, 1937, when the American Medical Association gave its first official recognition to birth control as a legitimate part of medical practice." Editorial. American Medicine Accepts Birth Control. Birth Contr

resolution also reached a resounding and immediate echo in the media. Using the chronicles of their own correspondents and the notes published by the news agencies (Associated Press and Reuters)[101], the newspapers, magazines and radio station presented it to the public as one of the great triumphs of a modern and progressive society.

Some also reported that the resolution had received unanimous approval from the House of Delegates[102]but that did not correspond to what happened in Atlantic City. On one hand, the minutes of the AMA Session made no mention of that unanimous vote[103]. It appears questionable

---

Rev 1937; 4 (n.s.) (6): 1-2; Sanger M. Hail and Farewell. Nat Birth Contr News 1937 June: 3-5, available at:

http://sangerpapers.org/sanger/app/documents/show.php?sangerDoc=301 422.xml.

101 In an editorial article, we read: "A veritable deluge of representatives of the press and of the various illustrated magazines descended on Atlantic City several days before the session and worked busily throughout." It then points out, apart from the five reporters who had won that year the Pulitzer Prize for journalism, correspondents of the important newspapers of New York and Philadelphia, Detroit, Washington and Chicago, as well as from the magazines Time, Newsweek and Life were present in the session. Editorial. The Atlantic City Session. JAMA 1937; 108: 2124-2125.

[102] Almost all the newspapers that gave notice of the Atlantic City resolution refer to that unanimity. The Tribunetribune of Altoona, Pennsylvania went ahead to publish it the same day, June 8: "Birth control was recognized as proper medical practice by the American Medical Association today, when an unanimous vote of its House of Delegates, governing body of the American medicine, ended completely a 25-year long opposition to contraceptives." Birth Control Approved by Medical Assn. Altoona Tribune, June 8, 1937, p. 1.

[103] American Medical Association, Proceedings of the House of Delegates. Eighty-Eighth Annual Session, Held at Atlantic City, NJ, June 7-11, 1937. But curiously, in an editorial of the official journal of the AMA, it is stated that such unanimity was given: "The Contraception Committee presented a simple, dignified report of its deliberations, which was unanimously adopted by the House of Delegates." Editorial: The Atlantic City Session. J Am Med Ass 1937; 108: 2124-2125.

that the 170 members of the House of Delegates representing more than 105,000 AMA associates at the time had been unanimous on such a divisive issue[104]. It seems unlikely that the matter was discussed in the plenary sessions because these were not the place to prepare, through deliberation and voting, decisions and documents that represented the genuinely democratic view of the associates[105]. The usual practice implemented since the beginning of the AMA was much simpler: the Board of Trustees presented to the House of Delegates the final texts of the decisions to be adopted and previously prepared by the Executive Committees with the input of the thematic committees. It was assumed that the final documents did not need to be debated[106]. Such action nowadays would be

---

104 The data are in the Report of the Secretary of the Association to the House of Delegates. American Medical Association, Proceedings of the House of Delegates. Eighty-Eighth Annual Session, Held at Atlantic City, N.J., June 7-11, 1937: 6.

105 In the first two thirds of the twentieth century, given the organizational structure of the AMA, the contrast of opinions was limited to the lower levels of the association, that is, to the medical societies of the counties and, to a lesser extent, to those of the states. The system of indirect representation followed at the national level theoretically placed the decisions in the hands of the House of Delegates, although, in reality, the decisions were taken by the Board of Trustees, which granted the House the simple task of endorsing them. The schedule of the annual sessions of the AMA was always overloaded and there was no time for debates. It was possible to send in advance opinions and suggestions when the documentation on the matters to be discussed was sent to the delegates with some anticipation. The House was, therefore, not an instance where opinions that differed from the monolithic view of the ruling group could be presented. Similarly, the official magazine of the Association, JAMA, followed the editorial practice of not publishing, or very rarely, diverging opinions. See Hyde D.R, Wolff P, Gross A, Hoffman E.L. The American Medical Association: Power, Purpose, and Politics in Organized Medicine. Yale Law J 1954; 63: 937-1022, especially 942-47; and Freidson E. Profession of Medicine. A Study of the Sociology of Applied Knowledge. Chicago: The University of Chicago Press; 1970: 27-28.

106 Not without a point of complacency and some paternalism, an editorial article, published in the JAMA two years before, affirmed: "The House of Delegates functioned efficiently and completed its business with such celerity that

considered as strongly paternalistic. The idea that the 1937 Resolution was unanimously approved was, in all probability, introduced by an Associated Press news agency, which was reproduced by innumerable publications[107].

---

many observers commented on the apparent quiet of the proceedings. This was no doubt due to the fact that the reference committees were so well selected and so assiduous in the performance of their duties that most of the difficulties were ironed out in the committees. Many listened for hours to those representing various points of view and the reports which they brought in took cognizance of these expressions and were therefore adopted without opposition from the floor." And the editorial concluded: "It is desirable that all those who are interested in the policies of the American Medical Association make a thorough study of these reports and familiarize themselves with the problems concerned. Only to the extent to which all the membership of the association is familiar with these activities and supports them can the association function efficiently." Editorial. Policies Adopted by the House of Delegates. JAMA 1935; 104: 2351.

[107] Although most newspapers limited themselves to offering an edited transcript of the Associated Press office, some others (for example, the Daily Times, of Burlington, NC., The Monroe News-Star, of Monroe, Louisiana, or the Telegraph, of Nashua, NH) opted to reproduce more or less widely the article by Howard W. Blakeslee, scientific editor of Associated Press and one of the winners of the Pulitzer Prize who were invited to the Atlantic City session. In it, Blakeslee attributed a transcendental dimension to the Resolution of Atlantic City: "According to some of the leaders of the thought of the AMA, the decision on control of the births adopted by the Association goes much more beyond the contraception. It is the recognition of change in the biological way of thinking based on the knowledge of the human body, mind and spirit." Birth Control Policy Change for Reaching. The Telegraph, Nashua, N.H., June 9, 1937, p. 7.

3.4.   What happened to the 1937 resolution?

Contrary to what was proclaimed by birth control activists, the Atlantic City resolution was not in itself an unlimited approval of contraception, a blank check that the AMA had placed at the discretion of its members. It was rather a cautious and provisional document which, in order to become an effective norm, required, as indicated by its three final recommendations, that the AMA itself accomplished certain assignments and made certain clarifications.

It is interesting to inquire about what the Board of Trustees of the AMA did as an executive body to comply with these recommendations. Judging from what is recorded in the minutes of the House of Delegates and in the pages of its official organ, the Journal of the American Medical Association, in the years that followed 1937, the Association worked very little on contraception. Interestingly, the most salient aspect of this scarce activity was the return in 1938 to the old position of neutrality: the AMA as an institution once again refrained from backing or opposing the control of the population[108].

Specifically, what did the AMA do to comply with the first Recommendation: to do what is necessary to make it clear to the doctors about their legal rights in relation to the use of contraceptives? Apparently, this task was limited to finding that four states had included in their legislation the exclusive authorization to doctors and pharmacists to

---

[108] "In 1935 and again in 1938, the House of Delegates adopted a 'neutral' stance on this matter, stating that the AMA neither endorsed nor opposed the control of the population." Report of the Reference Committee on Miscellaneous Business. Supplementary Report G. American Medical Association. Proceedings of the House of Delegates, 18th Clinical Convention. Miami Beach, Florida. Nov. 30-Dec 2, 1964: 94.

"control the sale and distribution of devices, medicines and medicinal preparations considered of some use for the prevention of conception and venereal diseases". The Reference Committee of the Executive Session thought that the enactment of those laws was a step forward to the right direction[109]. But it did nothing to clarify the rights of physicians. Those rights could not be taken for granted both by virtue of the diversity of the legal regulations among the states and as well as in the discordant interpretation of the sentence of the famous case *United States vs. One Package*. In effect, the Journal had published in April of 1937, two months before the Atlantic City Resolution, an editorial article stating that this sentence was not, as the promoters of birth control intended, "a bill of rights of the profession", making contraception legal but an authorization granted to doctors in several states to import contraceptive materials from abroad, if they wish so[110].

With respect to the second Recommendation –to promote research on materials, devices and contraceptive methods in order to determine their properties and physiological, chemical and biological effects, and to publish the corresponding results–, the activity of the AMA was very poor. The Council of Pharmacy and Chemistry, on one hand, and the Physical Therapeutics Committee on the other, organized a "Council of Counsels on Contraceptives"

---

[109] Report of the Reference Committee on Executive Session. Proceedings of the House of Delegates, AMA. Eighty-Ninth Annual Session, Held at San Francisco, Calif., June 13-17, 1938: 73.

[110] Editorial. Contraceptive Advice, Devices and Preparations still Contraband. JAMA 1937; 108: 1179-1180. A critical response to that Editorial, presenting the views of the Legal Advisory Committee of the National Committee for Federal Legislation on Birth Control, was published in: Ballard F.A et al. Contraceptive Advice, Devices and Preparations. JAMA 1937; 108: 1819-1820. The final answer by the AMA is found in: Woodward W.C. Contraceptive Advice, Devices and Preparations. JAMA 1937; 108: 1820.

and appointed their corresponding members who chose to follow a conservative general policy and act more as a body of compilation of data than as an advisory body[111]. Its first and only report concerning the use of roentgen rays in contraception[112] was published in the section of the Pharmacy and Chemistry Council of the Journal in November 1938. That report caused some disappointment because of the poor technical quality of its content and by dealing almost exclusively with the use of roentgen radiation in abortion and not, as would have been proper, in contraception[113].

The life of the Council of Councils was brief. As early as 1942, the Council of Pharmacy and Chemistry autonomously declared that in the future it would evaluate contraceptives on the same basis as therapeutic agents using a set of criteria prepared by the Advisory Committee[114]. But the number of contraceptive materials evaluated was minimal; the Secretary of the Pharmacy Council affirmed that the devices studied were two[115]. For some time, the Council seemed satisfied with publishing works by authors external to it. In 1939, it published a review article by Stein[116] and another by Dickinson[117] in 1943. This line of passivity

---

[111] Councils' Committee on Contraceptives. Proceedings of the House of Delegates. Ninetieth Annual Session, Held at St. Louis, Mo, May 15-19, 1939: 18.

[112] Report on the Use of Roentgen Rays for Contraception. JAMA 1938; 111: 1767. Although the report is not signed, Reed points out that it was the work of a Committee on Contraceptives, under the presidency of Gamble, in 1939. Reed J. The Birth Control Movement and American Society. From Private Vice to Public Virtue. Princeton, NJ: Princeton University Press; 1984: 245.

[113] Frank RT. Report on the Use of Roentgen Rays for Contraception. JAMA 1939; 112: 169-170.

[114] Smith A.E. Council on Pharmacy and Chemistry. JAMA 1943; 123: 1043.

[115] Ibíd.

[116] Stein I. Contraceptive Methods. JAMA 1939; 112: 1311-1314.

was confirmed in 1938 by the report that, at the request of the Study Committee on Contraceptive Practices, presented through the Reference Committee of the Executive Session to the Board of Trustees. The report was adopted despite the fact that it contradicted the resolution taken in the previous year in Atlantic City[118].

Only in 1944 a chapter on contraceptives (creams, diaphragms, syringe applicators, occlusive rings) that were considered an innovation and whose need was long felt appeared in the annual series "New and Nonofficial Remedies"[119].

The third recommendation –the promotion in medical schools of an instruction on fertility and sterility in its positive and negative aspects– was not taken care of by the Board of Medical Education and Hospitals. It remained ignored for a quarter of a century until 1964, when the matter was reactivated by the Committee of Human Reproductionwhich was established the previous year. This new committee, which had been commissioned by the Board of Trustees to review the previous statements of the AMA on contraceptive practices, affirmed in its report that

---

[117] Dickinson R.L. Conception Control. JAMA 1943; 123: 1043-1047.

[118] "It is not the function of the American Medical Association to tell physicians what therapeutic advice they shall offer patients. However, it has been its policy to investigate various procedures, devices and drugs, and to publish the results of such studies in its official publications for the information of the profession. The instructions to the Council on Pharmacy and Chemistry and the Council on Physical Therapy to investigate further the materials, devices and procedures used for the purpose of contraception do not indicate any change in the usual policy of the Association, nor do they constitute an endorsement by the Association of contraceptive practices." Report of the Reference Committee on Executive Session. Proceedings of the House of Delegates, AMA. Eighty-Ninth Annual Session, Held at San Francisco, Calif., June 13-17, 1938: 73.

[119] Book Notices. New and Nonofficial Remedies, 1944. Chicago: American Medical Association; 1944. JAMA 1944; 125: 1000.

"the last established policy statement relative to contraceptive practices had been made by the Association in 1938", so that nothing practical had been done to comply with the third Recommendation[120].

As already mentioned above, the Atlantic City Resolution of 1937 was not completed with the responses of the committees to the petitions done by the House, nor was it formally ratified after the partial retraction adopted in the AMA Session of 1938 held in San Francisco. This did not prevent it, despite its shortcomings and inaccuracies, to orient, over many years, the application by American doctors of contraceptive practices, among which, since the late 1950s, the use of progestin steroids, including IUDs.

3.5.   Motives behind the 1937 Resolution

A critical consideration of the 1937 Resolution, considering what had happened before and after that year, can not avoid the question on which could be the reasons behind the change, or better the rupture, that that resolution brought about in the AMA's contraceptive policy.

In fact, the Resolution of 1937 ignored and partly contradicted the considerations contained in the 1936 Report. The disagreement between both reports is even more shocking if one takes into account that more than half of the members were present in both committees[121]. The

---

[120] "The Committee is of the opinion that educational programs on this subject have never been included in the curricula of medical schools." Report of Reference Committee on Miscellaneous Business. Supplementary Report G American Medical Association. Proceedings of the House of Delegates, 18th Clinical Convention. Miami Beach, Florida. Nov. 30-Dec 2, 1964: 95.

[121] The 1937 Committee consisted of the same five members of the 1936 Committee (Drs. Davis, Kosmak, Bloss, Rock, and Woodward) to whom the Board had added four new ones (Coventry, O'Shea, Cooke, and Plass). In contrast, the

only point in common with both reports is that they affirmed the existence of the medical indications of contraception. Evidently, the 1937 Committee considered it irrelevant to criticize the reasons given by the 1936 Committee for denying its support for contraception. But curiously, the 1937 Committee opted to remain silent on the reasons that could justify its diametrical change of position. Between the lines, two reasons that could have influenced the favorable decision to contraception can be inferred. The first one is the existence of medical indications to advise contraception; but as indicated, it did not require a new Resolution, since such indications had been included in the 1936 Report to which the Resolution refers. The second one notes that "the voluntary and intelligent postponement of pregnancies for the health and general welfare of mothers and children may be desirable". But this suggestion appeared implicit in the Report of the previous year[122].

The silence kept by the 1937 Committee on the reasons that induced it to change so radically its previous position provoked the speculations of some observers. Benjamin, for example, attributed a preponderant role in the change to the pressure exercised by the movement in favor of contraception especially the National Medical

---

composition of the 1938 Committee was almost entirely new, with the exception of Bloss (Booth, Hayden, Wright, Lee, Bunce, Fenton, Bloss, Cullen and Sensenich). It is not strange, therefore, that he adopted a cold stance with regard to the 1937 Resolution.

[122] In the Medical Considerations that appeared in the 1936 Report of the Study Committee on Contraception, one can read these two: "It must be recognized that the capacity of women to bear children without impairment to health is an individual matter and varies to such a degree that no general rules can be offered here". And "The Committee has been unable to find evidence that existing laws, federal or state, have interfered with any medical advice which a physician has felt called on to furnish his patients." Report of Reference Committee on Executive Session. JAMA 1936; 106: 1911.

Committee for State and Federal Legislation on Birth Control, on the AMA and its Committee[123]. Reed, who recalls that in the report, no mention was made of the criticisms to AMA's policy by non-medical organizations and by a considerable number of doctors[124], pointed out that, shortly after the 1936 AMA Session in Kansas City, Dickinson maintained a three-day meeting with three members of the Committee (Davis, Plass and Kosmak). According to Reed, Dickinson refuted point by point the contents of the 1936 Report and managed to change the position of the Committee, as would be seen the following year in Atlantic City[125]. Kennedy presumed that the Committee's new attitude may have been influenced by several causes: the then recent judicial decision of the *U.S vs. One Package* case, the change of composition of the Committee, or the dangers of the free commercialization of contraceptives[126].

There seemed to be no solid reasons for such assumptions. On one hand, the committee of 1937 which did not omit to cite the aforementioned judicial sentence in its Report gave it a merely confirming value of the freedom enjoyed by doctors in almost all States to advice their patients on contraception in the case that their medical needs required it. On the other hand, it did not seem that the addition of four new members to the Committee was the cause of the new attitude since, although we ignore the intensity and content of the internal debates of the

---

[123] Benjamin H.C. Lobbying for Birth Control. Publ Opin Q 1938; 2: 48-60, at 57.

[124] Reed J. The Birth Control Movement and American Society. From Private Vice to Public Virtue. Princeton: Princeton University Press; 1984: 190.

[125] Ibíd., 187.

[126] Kennedy D.M. Birth Control in America. The Career of Margaret Sanger. New Haven: Yale University Press; 1970: 215.

Committee in the preparation of its Report, it did not seem likely that a radical confrontation could occur between the newly incorporated members who were a minority and those who had drafted the 1936 Resolution. Finally, the magnitude of the contraceptive industry and trade was already very considerably striking at that time and had been growing from year to year[127]. But the fact that it was in the hands of non-medical groups and, that it represented a danger for the health of the population was not a new idea, since, according to Reed, in 1935 it had been the main reason for creating the Committee[128]. The AMA itself recognized this in an editorial article published by the JAMA[129] in 1938.

3.6. Criticism from medical ethics

It is time to ask about the ethical considerations that underlined the AMA Reports on contraception.

Practically none. It is only in the 1936 report that a very short section devoted to "moral considerations" appeared[130].

---

[127] "In 1937, Americans spent $ 38 million on condoms and more than $ 200 million on 'feminine hygiene'." Reed J. The Birth Control Movement: 239. A detailed explanation of the volume of the contraceptive industry can be seen in: Tone A. Contraceptive Consumers: Gender and the Political Economy of Birth Control in the 1930s. J Soc Hist 1996; 29: 485-506.

[128] According to Reed, "AMA continued to ignore the problem until 1935, when the business of 'feminine hygiene' boomed, based on unscrupulous advertising, and flourished in the absence of medically recognized regulations that discriminated against such methods and products, forced the formation of a committee to investigate the situation." Reed J. The Birth Control Movement: 186-187.

[129] Editorial. The Business of Birth Control. JAMA 1938; 110: 513.

[130] These considerations literally say: "Coitus is accepted as a normal marital function, but differences in opinion arise as to methods of preventing conception. Apparently, there is no moral objection to selection of the assumed nonfertile portion of the month for coitus by the married couples." Proceedings Kansas City

In the subsequent reports no allusion was made to the ethical aspects of contraception. Such fact is particularly surprising in the 1937 Report which offered no ethical justification for the radical change it introduced. It appears as if the authors of the Report were sure that the expected unanimous adoption of the document by the Chamber of Delegates would dispense them from dealing with the ethical aspects of their proposal.

In summary, for the directive bodies of the AMA, contraception was not an ethical issue. Therefore, the ethical debate on contraception was pointless.

Session. JAMA 1936; 106: 1911.

Chapter 4. Catholic Doctors and the Professional Approval of Contraception

There are at least two important points to consider regarding the attitude that American Catholic doctors upheld towards the 1937 AMA's institutional resolution on contraception after adopting the report drafted by the Committee for the Study of Contraceptive Practices. The first point refers to the participation in the drafting of the aforementioned Report of some Catholic doctors who were members of the committee. The second point deals with the reactions expressed by the associations of Catholic doctors in the aftermath of the adoption of the Report.

When dealing with both aspects, it must be taken into account that seven years earlier, Pope Pius XI had published the encyclical *Casti connubii* in which, as it is well-known, the Pontiff had confirmed with great energy the Church's traditional condemnation of artificial contraception[131], a

---

[131] In paragraph 56 of this encyclical letter, dated the last day of 1930, the Pontiff reiterated in very firm terms the moral condemnation of contraception: "[The Catholic Church] ... through our mouth proclaims anew: any use whatsoever of matrimony exercised in such a way that the act is deliberately frustrated in its natural power to generate life is an offense against the law of God and of nature,

doctrine which had remote precedents in the teaching of the Magisterium[132] and enjoyed the general adhesion of the Catholic faithful[133]. But as is shown below, such position was not embraced by the members of the AMA Committee whose status as Catholics was publicly known.

4.1. Catholic doctors in the AMA Committee of 1936

In 1936, when the Chamber of Delegates of the AMA published the resolution of the committee for the Study of Contraceptive Practices in which the institutional refusal to control births was maintained, no one, neither in the media of public opinion nor within the organization, alluded to the presence of Catholics among the members of the committee. This had been constituted by virtue of a decision adopted in the Atlantic City session of 1935, and, as established in the by-laws, its five members were chosen by the Board of Directors. The members appointed to the committee were: Carl Henry Davis, who would act as president, George W. Kosmak, James R. Bloss, John Rock and William C. Woodward. Two of them, John Rock and George Kosmak, who were among the most prominent

---

and those who indulge in such are branded with the guilt of a grave sin."
http://w2.vatican.va/content/pius-xi/en/encyclicals/documents/hf_p-xi_enc_19301231_casti-connubii.pdf.

[132] Noonan JT. Contraception: A History of Its Treatment by the Catholic Theologians and Canonists. Enlarged Edition. Cambridge, Mass: Belknap Press; 1986. Particularly interesting is the Decision of the Congregation of the Holy Office of May 21, 1851 (page 403).

[133] That contraception was incompatible with Catholic morality was then a profound and undoubted conviction for the Catholic faithful and their pastors. According to McGreevy, "Catholics in the 1930s included contraception, forced sterilization, euthanasia and abortion in the same category of abhorrent actions." McGreevy JT. Catholicism and American Freedom: A History. New York: W.W. Norton; 2003: 223.

gynecologists of the moment, were well-known Catholics[134]. Therefore, there could be reasons to suspect that the open rejection of contraception issued by the Committee in 1936 depended on the religious convictions of Catholics present in it, since two of its five members were well-known Catholics and two others had studied at Catholic universities and taught, or had taught, in some of them[135]. But nobody drew attention to that circumstance.

It is possible to assume that such a numerically disproportionate presence of Catholic physicians in the Committee was merely the result of chance, but it is equally possible to suspect that it was due to a deliberate purpose of the AMA Board of Trustees which considered that the presence of Catholics in the 1936 Committee could have played an important role both in guaranteeing the maintenance of the traditional institutional condemnation of the contraception, as well as in testifying that the AMA had no anti-Catholic prejudices[136].

---

[134] Already in the 1930s, the fact that Rock was a Catholic was of general knowledge. In the literature on contraception, his name often appears linked to the epithet "devout Catholic". Although less frequently, George Kosmak is characterized as a "practicing Catholic". See, for example, Reed J. Doctors, birth control, and social values, 1830-1970. In: Vogel MJ, Rosenberg CE, eds. The Therapeutic Revolution: Essays in the Social History of American Medicine, University of Pennsylvania Press, 1979: 109-133, in 121; or Engs RC. The Progressive Era's Health Reform Movement: A Historical Dictionary, Wesport, CT: Greenwood Publ. 80, or simply from "Catholic gynecologist": Gray M. Margaret Sanger. A Biography of the Champion of Birth Control. New York: Richard Marek Publishers, 1979: 286.

[135] Carl Henry Davis, chairman of the Committee, although not Catholic, was Professor of Gynecology and Women's Diseases and Director of the Department of Obstetrics and Gynecology at the School of Medicine at Marquette University, Milwaukee, a Catholic university. William C. Woodward had studied medicine at Georgetown University, also a Catholic university, and taught medical law at its School of Medicine.

[136] It should not be forgotten that in the AMA, the appointment of members of the Committeescommittees was a function granted to the Executive Committee

4.2. Catholic doctors in the AMA Committee of 1937

When the committee presented its interim report in 1936, they asked the House of Delegates an extension to finish its assignment. The Board of Directors not only accepted the petition but also, in anticipation of the increased work that the committee should do, they decided to expand the number of its members to nine, adding to the five already in office another four: William A. Coventry, Richard J. O'Shea, Willard R. Cooke and Everett D. Plass[137].

As indicated in the preceding chapter, the Committee Report of 1937, once adopted as a resolution by the House of Delegates, signified a radical shift in the AMA's position towards contraception which, from rejected as unfit for medicine, came to be included among the acts proper to it. And, it happened again that nobody, neither in the media of public opinion nor in the internal sphere of the AMA, drew attention to the presence of Catholics in the Committee.

This silence makes incites to seek an answer to the question on how to reconcile the strong presence of Catholics in the committee with the contents and conclusions of a report which were clear contradictions with the firm and well-known moral doctrine of the Church of Rome. Did the Catholic members of the Committee justify their dissident conduct? In the Proceedings of the corresponding sessions of the AMA (Kansas City, 1936; Atlantic City, 1937), no indication is found on the subject[138].

---

of the Board of Trustees which enjoyed full freedom to elect them. The Board was not required to make public the reasons for those appointments.

[137] Richard O'Shea, one of the new members, was a Catholic.

[138] That is natural since there was a norm in the AMA to keep secret the deliberations of its annual Sessions. The Sessions' Proceedings' contain -besides

Are there in the literature data that could illuminate the problem? Some can be found: a few and indirect information related Kosmak, many referred to Rock.

George Kosmak, despite his asserted notoriety as a practicing Catholic, never held a position fully consistent with the Church's teaching on contraception. Certainly, he firmly opposed the movements in favor of contraception directed by non-physicians and equally disapproved the contraception for hedonic or socio-economic purposes. But already in his first publications, he affirmed with great energy that physicians enjoyed the power to recommend contraception when they considered it necessary according to rigid medical criteria[139]. Subsequently, influenced by Dickinson and his own participation in the National Maternal Health Committee which he entered to find a responsible alternative to the professionally suspicious activities of the Birth Control League led by Sanger[140], he assumed an increasingly active role in the effort to recognize contraception as a medical activity. He did so from his influential positions as president of the Medical Society of the State of New York, editor of the American

---

the President's address, other greetings, and some news on social events- the written texts of the documents presented to, and of the resolutions taken by the House of Delegates and the Board of Trustees but not the transcription or summary of the debates on the matters considered. Neither there is in the accessible AMA's archives any documentation from the preparatory sessions of the committees.

[139] "... we may assume that there can be no question or difference of opinion regarding the necessity for contraceptive measures in certain cases. The tuberculous, the cardiac, the nephritic are only among the more common general illnesses that demand abstention from childbearing, and there are local or obstetrical situations that must likewise be considered." Kosmak GW. The Broader Aspects of the Birth Control Propaganda as it Should Interest the Physician. Am J Obstet Gynecol 1923; 6: 276-285, in 281.

[140] Engs RC. The Progressive Era's Health Reform Movement: A Historical Dictionary. Wesport, CT: Greenwood Publ. Group; 2003: 80.

Journal of Obstetrics and Gynecology, and, above all, as a member of the House of Delegates of the AMA and its Committee for the Study of Contraception. He firmly supported the Resolutions of 1936 and 1937made by the House.

Kosmak never declared himself a Catholic in his articles. On the contrary, his distancing from Catholic doctrine is well evident in numerous writings he published in defense of the medical and social indications of contraception: "The indications [of contraception], both medical and social, using the latter term in its wider implications, have been established in a more satisfactory manner; adequate scientific research of means and methods has served to demonstrate the ineffectiveness of earlier procedures, and the thought has gained ground that the physician should exercise his prerogatives in employing contraceptive methods as a part of his legitimate practice."[141] In addition, he was disenchanted by the limitations of the rhythm method: "How can such a method of self-control be imposed on the large group of people who are most in need of a method of child spacing or contraception that is free from failures?"[142] However, he did not conceal his fears about the long-term effects of contraception not only on population growth but also on "the decision of men and women not to accept their procreative responsibilities."[143]

John Rock played a very important role in the adoption of contraception by the AMA. Curiously, none of the two

---

[141] Kosmak GW. Contraceptive Practices. Am J Obstet Gynecol 1940; 40: 652-654.

[142] Kosmak GW. The Responsibility of the Medical Profession in the movement for 'Birth Control'. JAMA 1939; 113: 1553-1559, 1556.

[143] Kosmak GW. Contraceptive Practices. Am J Obstet Gynecol 1940; 40: 652-654.

biographies so far published by Rock mention its participation in the Committee for the Study of the Contraception[144]. In a footnote to his book *The Time Has Come*, Rock affirms that he was a member of that committee and lists the recommendations of the Report which, he says, was adopted unanimously. However, he does not explain why he and the whole committee decided to abandon their previous opinion and assented to the AMA's attitude toward contraception[145].

It is worth noting that Rock, despite his notoriety as a Catholic, was throughout his long career an active promoter of contraception as a professional responsibility of the doctor. His discrepancy with the doctrine of the Magisterium never caused him problems of conscience. His biographer, McLaughlin, without indicating source or date attributes to him some very significant words: "very early in my life I separated biology from theology and I never confused them again."[146]. Indeed, in 1931, shortly after the publication the encyclical *Casti connubii*, Rock, along with other distinguished doctors of Massachusetts, signed a letter requesting the legalization of contraception in that State[147]. The following year, in one of his annual reviews on

---

[144] These two biographies are: McLaughlin L. The Pill, John Rock, and the Church. The Biography of a Revolution. Boston: Little, Brown and Co.; 1982; and Marsh M, Ronner W. The Fertility Doctor: John Rock and the Reproductive Revolution. Baltimore: Johns Hopkins University Press; 2008.

[145] Rock J. The Time Has Come. A Catholic Doctor's Proposals to End the Battle over Birth Control. New York: Alfred A. Knopf; 1963, 79, Note 3.

[146] McLaughlin, op. cit., p. 27. Asbell mentions the testimony of Katharine McCormick who explained that Rock was a "reformed Catholic" and whose position is that "religion has nothing to do with medicine and how to practice it, and that, if the Church did not interfere in his affairs, he would not interfere with hers." Asbell B. The Pill: A Biography of the Drug That Changed the World. New York: Random House; 1995: 130.

[147] Ames O. Massachusetts Doctors Take the Initiative. Birth Contr Rev 1932;

advances in obstetrics, he referred to contraception as the most correct recommendation a doctor can offer in cases in which a new pregnancy could ruin the woman's body or her mental health, or could even put her life in danger. In an allusion barely disguised to the encyclical, Rock warned that the doctor cannot put aside his duty to prescribe very effective contraceptive methods: "blindly to prescribe continence or refuse to treat according to sound medical principles [...] may bespeak in the physician merely a deviation of allegiance to another profession than that which concerns us here –medicine."[148].

Years later, in 1949, Rock and Lock published a book devoted to a detailed description of the contraceptive procedures then in use. Because of Fr. Carroll of the Catholic University of America, the volume included a chapter on the view of the Catholic morality about those procedures[149].

In conclusion, it seems appropriate to affirm that Kosmak's and Rock's ideas and behavior on contraceptive practices has nothing to do with their being regarded as "practicing Catholic" and "devout Catholic".

4.3. Reaction of Catholics (doctors, moralistic theologians and pastors) to the resolution of the AMA of 1937

It has already been pointed out that the decision of the

---

15 (2): 51-52.

[148] Rock J. Progress in Obstetrics. N Eng J Med 1932; 206: 77-87, 77-78.

[149] Rock J, Loth DG. Voluntary Parenthood New York: Random House; 1949. Loth was at the time Director of Public Information of the American Federation of Planned Parenthood. The book did not receive much praise. Vid., Tietze C. Voluntary Parenthood. Quart Rev Biol 1950; 25: 12.

AMA of June 8, 1937 clashed heads with the doctrine of the Catholic Church on contraception and with the widespread conviction among the Catholic faithful that contraception was contrary to the morality of the Church.

The new attitude of the AMA was in turn a strong setback for doctors and moral theologians interested in the ethics of medicine who had agreed to the teachings of the encyclical. Knowing how these doctors and theologians reacted to the new situation created in the AMA is a matter of no little interest since it is scarcely known and has therefore been little investigated. The issue is also complex since it involves not only looking at the general and professional press for the opinions expressed but also analyzing the professional and moral arguments that served as support for the critics of the AMA resolution on contraceptive practices.

Unfortunately, one of the parties in litigation preferred to remain silent. The AMA followed a rigid restrictive policy regarding the information issued by its governing bodies. On one hand, the sessions of the House of Delegates were held behind closed doors so that only the final communiqués were made public but the content of the debates in the event that they had taken place, was not made public. On the other, the editors of JAMA, following a policy consolidated over the years, did not publish articles, comments or letters to the editor expressing disagreement with the decisions of the governing bodies of the institution. In fact, there was no room in its pages for a reasonable discussion of the decisions taken in the annual sessions including ethical issues. It is therefore necessary to limit these considerations to what is published by the Catholic party (doctors, moral theologians and pastors).

It seems certain that the Resolution of June 1937

came, in a certain way, to break a period of relative tranquility between the AMA and its Catholic membership. Before 1937, there were no reciprocal misunderstandings. With the encouragement of their pastors and the technical assistance of the National Catholic Welfare Conference (NCWC), Catholics were above all interested in social justice and many Catholic doctors were busy in extending medical care to all social strata in the often dramatic circumstances of the great depression.

Concerning contraception, Catholic doctors wanted for some time now to clarify the confused and indeterminate legal regulation inherited from before. In 1926, the NCWC itself had submitted a motion to the AMA session in Dallas, Texas requesting that the House of Delegates incite the United States Congress to legislate on contraceptive practices and birth control. The initiative did not prosper. The House, persisting in its position of non-intervention in such a delicate matter, preferred to abandon the initiative of the Catholics and, without further explanation, returned their proposal to the Board of Trustees, which decided to archive it. That behavior generated in the Catholics a point of distrust in the internal democratic management of the AMA. They made this clear in 1932 when the NCWC informed that it had sent a proposal to the House of Delegates of the AMA meeting in the session of New Orleans requesting again the creation of a Committee to investigate the procedures of birth control. The petition was denied unanimously in a secret session. The NCWC regretted that what had been discussed in that session had not been made public[150].

---

[150] NCWC Inquiry into Birth Control Rejected by Medical Assn. The Guardian/Arkansas Cath 1932; May 28: 7.

Two days after the approval of the 1937 Resolution by the AMA, the News Catholic Service spread the news, dated June 10, that the Federation of Catholic Medical Guilds meeting in Atlantic City had issued a declaration condemning in impassioned language the aforementioned resolution. The Guilds affirmed that Catholic doctors did not want to align themselves with colleagues who subscribed a pagan philosophy and who tried to turn the medical profession into the gravediggers of the nation or, by means of abortion and euthanasia, in its executioners. They added that "the practice of artificial contraception for any reason is the perversion of the moral order of things, productive of mutual distrust on the part of the spouses using it, and its use even for medical reasons is a potential, if not, and actual weapon for the undermining of the virtues upon which Christian civilization is based." And concluded: "There is no human necessity which can confer on the doctor the right to take life or to prevent it [...]. Whatever legal rights may exist with regard [to artificial contraception] now or may be granted in the future, the Federation asserts that legal rights are not necessarily moral rights and are not infrequently in direct opposition to God's rights."[151]

Curiously, the text of the same news item refers that 75 delegates who attended the meeting of the aforementioned Federation of Catholic Medical Guilds had also been "delegates to the AMA national convention". It would be interesting to know if some of them took part in the AMA's House of Delegates meeting in which the 1937 Resolution was voted. If such was the case, it is difficult to find an explanation to the unanimous approval of the Resolution unless they abstained from voting or voted

---

[151] Catholic Physicians Denounce Medical Assn. for Birth Control Recognition. The Guardian, June 19, 1937: 4.

against conscience.

To the rejection of the doctors joined the simultaneous condemnation of Catholic moralists. Thus, Fr. Cox, SJ, professor of Ethics at Fordham University, besides disapproving the decision of the AMA as "a still further advance of the popular and pagan ideology with regard to life at its source and all its phases which has brought about a world situation reconcilable neither with reason nor common sense", planned the creation of a "legion of decency" to oppose both the producers of contraceptives and the physicians who approve of their use[152].

The reaction of the executive committee of the Catholic Hospital Association was not long in coming. In its resolution of June 18, 1937, it requested the AMA to clarify the confused situation created by the discrepancies between the report and the press headlines about the resolution and the recommendations of the House of Delegates. The Catholic Hospital Association recognized that the AMA had changed its attitude to contraception but found that the resolution was imprecise on many points so it asked the AMA to define precisely what its attitude was. In addition, the Catholic Hospital Association refused to accept that the resolution was an authentic expression of the opinion of all the members of the House of Delegates[153]. As expected, given the policy of the AMA, the request of the Catholic Hospital Association remained unanswered.

Logically, the condemnations by the members of the episcopate arrived in time, as shows the immediate and

---

[152] Legion of Decency Proposed Against Firms and Doctors Dealing In Contraceptives. The Guardian, June 19, 1937, p. 4.

[153] Schwitalla AM. The American Medical Association and Contraception. Hosp Progr 1937; 18: 219-224.

well-considered statement of Mons. Rummel, Archbishop of New Orleans. The prelate lamented the change of attitude of the AMA because it affected a very serious and vital issue that could profoundly affect the religious, moral and social life of the nation. He said: "It is unfortunate that a group of men who enjoy such great prestige should make themselves liable to the breakdown of one of the most important pillars of society, namely, a righteous, God-fearing use of the sacred privilege of marriage and a morally sound development of the american home and family."[154]

The echo of the Catholic response went far: The Sunday Times of Perth in Western Australia, after harshly commenting on the decision of the AMA "to take charge of 342 contraception offices and the millions of dollars of the contraceptive trade", alluded to the "violent reaction of the Catholic clergy and the declaration of the Federation of Catholic Medical Guilds." It wondered what would be the behavior of the new President of the AMA, the Catholic Dr. Abell, with respect to the new Resolution. This last, curiously, was approved in the interval between the election of Abell and his inauguration[155]. Finally, the correspondent in New York of the South African Medical Journal gave a detailed description of the actions of the AMA, the Federation of Catholic Doctors and the American League for Birth Control or National Medical Council on Birth Control[156].

---

[154] Prelate Flays Medical Assn. in Statement. Blow Dealt at America Home, Prelate Says. The Guardian, 1937; June 19: 4.

[155] Doctors Approve Birth Control. Violent Catholic Protest. Sunday Times, Perth, WA. Sunday August 1, 1937: 1.

[156] From Our New York Correspondent. American Letter: Contraception Approved, and Combated. South Afr Med J 1937, Aug. 14.

Chapter 5. How the Lawyers Lead the First Attack on the Human Embryo

5.1.   The Model Penal Code of the American Institute of Law and its Article on Abortion and Related Offenses

A fact barely noticeable when it occurred but that had extraordinary importance due to its legal and social effects, was the presentation by the American Law Institute (ALI)[157] regarding the article on Abortion and Related Offenses which was to be included in the Model Penal Code (MPC), an ambitious project which the Institute was working up[158].

---

[157] The American Law Institute (ALI) is a private entity founded in 1923 and formed by jurists (judges, university professors, lawyers) of high academic and professional level which devotes its attention to study and propose improvements of the North American legal normative and procedures, with the purpose of improving their contents and mode of application. It exerts extraordinary influence and its publications are highly appreciated. It is not risky to say that the ALI, in virtue of the high quality and scope of its productions, has become a parallel legislative power. For general information about the ALI, see: https://www.ali.org/about-ali/. For the history of the ALI, see: Frank JP. The American Law Institute 1923-1998. Hofstra Law Rev 1998; 26: 615-639.

The text of the article was made known in the tentative draft debated at the session of the Institute held on May 8, 1959. Under the then designed as section 207.11, the different criminal categories of abortion (unjustified, justifiable, self-induced, fictitious, irregular) were dealt within the first six subsections of the article; in the final Subsection 7, an allusion was made to the non-abortive nature of pre-implantation contraceptives[159]. The aforementioned article which in the final text appears numbered as section 230.3 was definitively approved at the session of May 24, 1962, after introducing some important amendments[160]. On that same year, the Institute published the official final draft of the articulated text of the MPC. It was only after 23 years later in 1985 that the official final draft with explanatory notes was published; its articulated text was enriched with the authoritative Revised Comments. In this way, the project which began over fifty years before was culminated[161]. At present (2018), a new version of the MPC is being elaborated by the ALI.

---

[158] The project of ALI to draft an MPC was born in 1931 with the intent of remedying the chaotic state of codified criminal law in the United States. The endeavor was interrupted before the Second World War but resumed in 1951, thanks to the financial support of the Rockefeller Foundation (Wechsler H. The Challenge of a Model Penal Code, Harvard Law Rev 1952; 65: 1097-1133). Throughout the late 1950s, successive drafts of different parts of the code were debated, edited and published. The final draft was published in 1962. On the successive stages of preparation of the MPC drafts, see: Beyer HS. Model Penal Code Selected Bibliography. Buff Crim Law Rev 2000; 4: 627-639.

[159] American Law Institute. Model Penal Code. Tentative Draft No. 9. May 8, 1959. Philadelphia, PA: The Executive Office, ALI; 1959: 144-146.

[160] The main differences between Section 207.11 of the 1959 draft and Section 239.3 as drafted in 1963 include some new indications of justifiable abortion, the requirement for legality of a physicians' certificate, and lastly, a redefinition of fictitious abortion.

[161] American Law Institute. Model Penal Code. Official Draft and Explanatory Notes. Philadelphia, PA: The American Law Institute; 1985.

In the 1960s, the MPC was received by most of the jurists as a very significant advance and worth of all praise. Such a favorable welcoming, however, was not universal; some reviewers highlighted a number of remarkable shortcomings in the MPC's legal technique and more importantly, some European authors denounced the questionable philosophy underlying the whole project[162].

Despite those criticisms, section 230.3 had an almost immediate and a resounding effect on abortion legislation. It was adopted almost literally by the Criminal Code of several American States. In addition, it inspired the legislation of abortion in other countries and with the passing of years it exerted more or less directly a strong influence on the practice and legal regulation of contraception and abortion in the world.

5.2. Subsection 7

The impact of section 230.3 on Abortion and Related Offenses was felt not only in the legislative field. It also rose great interest in the academic field. Countless comments have been published in books and journals dealing with its achievements and shortcomings. What is truly striking, however, is that one of its paragraphs, Subsection 7, hardly aroused the attention of experts despite the novelty of its content and the seriousness of its ethical and anthropological implications. In fact, instead of being the object of a deserved critical debate, the Subsection 7 was practically ignored as if it had fallen in the blind spot of the retina of lawyers.

---

[162] Fletcher GP. Dogmas of the Model Penal Code. 2 Buff. Crim. L. Rev. 3 1998-1999.

Its text says: *"§ 230.3 (7) Section Inapplicable to Prevention of Pregnancy.* Nothing in this section shall be deemed applicable to the prescription, administration or distribution of drugs or other substances for avoiding pregnancy, whether by preventing implantation of a fertilized ovum or by any other method that operates before, at or immediately after fertilization."

Subsection 7 prescribed, on one hand, that the other paragraphs (1 to 6) of the section 230.3 were not applicable to contraceptive methods. In other words, contraception had nothing to do with abortion. On the other hand, however, it established that medicines and other substances used to prevent pregnancy were to be considered simple contraceptives despite the fact that that they operate after fertilization. In the late 1950s, such statement implied an unprecedented novelty. Indeed, Subsection 7 introduced for the first time in society the notion that the induced loss of young human embryos which until then was considered a very early form of abortion could no longer be considered or penalized as an abortion with the condition that such an embryonic loss or destruction was mediated through a mechanism that operated between fertilization and implantation. In this way, the concept of contraception was considerably broadened by adding to its own field of action (prefecundational, that is, acting to prevent conception or fertilization) an alien and improper territory (the post-fecundational, which interferes with the development of the embryo between fertilization and implantation).

5.2.1.   Subsection 7, approved without debate

The novelty and seriousness of the text of Subsection deserved a serious and well-reasoned debate. Regretfully, that debate did not take place. In contrast with the

meticulous discussion of the drafts of the preceding Subsections, no exchange of views was allowed on Subsection 7. One circumstance contributed effectively to this silence: by decision of the ALI governing bodies, the Subsection 7 was excluded from debate. In effect, the council of the Institute and its advisory committee had considered the matter in advance and concluded that contraception should not enter into the subject matter of a Penal Code since, in its opinion, it would be preferable to regulate it by means of administrative regulations devised to control the advertising and distribution of those products[163].
 An immediate consequence of the council's decision was to eliminate contraception from the agenda of the MPC preparation meetings despite the desire of some participants to discuss the issue[164]. Subsection 7 thus acquired for some members of the institute the status of a "taboo" subject; for others, given the undisputed academic authority of the ALI Council, the ethical irrelevance of the pre-implanted embryo was established as "legal truth".

Exclusion from the debate ensured the extraordinary stability of the text: the wording of Subsection 7 remained unchanged throughout the complex succession of drafts,

---

[163] The explanation offered was based on several reasons, among which were the persistence in some of the states of abusive ("that goes beyond the permissible limits of the intervention of criminal law in matters on which moral citizens may be in reasonable and responsible disagreement) or obsolete legislation (Comstock laws); the non-application in other states of norms that sought to limit the sale and use of contraceptives to the prevention of diseases; and the fact that many states lacked criminal rules on the matter. These explanations are repeated with little change in: ALI. Model Penal Code Commentaries, Part II Sec 368, 1980: 440.

[164] ALI. MPC. Tentative Draft No. 9. Submitted by the Council to the Members for Discussion at the Thirty-sixth Annual Meeting, May 20, 21, 22 and 23, 1959. Philadelphia: The Executive Office, The American Law Institute; May 8, 1959: 161-162.

which modified, as noted above, almost all the other paragraphs of the Section. The aforementioned fixedness of the text is maintained from March 25, 1959 when the Subsection was first introduced in the preliminary draft[165] until May 24, 1962 when the definitive Proposed Official Draft was approved[166].

Perhaps the exclusion of debate inside the ALI contributed to the silence of legal literature on Subsection 7. The number of comments on that subsection was in strong contrast with the abundant publications dealing with the other paragraphs of Article 230.3 which logically attracted the attention of jurists. But Subsection 7 was put aside; practically no author showed the slightest interest in its juridical implications. In several articles, the text of the whole section is reproduced[167] but only a few authors referred in passing to some partial aspect of Subsection 7 but none considered it deserving of a detailed analysis. Thus, for example, Meloy only inquires into the meaning of the term "drugs or other substances" to conclude that the MPC establishes a difference between chemical substances

---

[165] The original draft was presented to the ALI meeting on March 25, 1959. by the principal rapporteur, Herbert Wechsler. It was accompanied by a Memorandum addressed to the ALI Council in which it was recalled that the Council had approved the Rapporteur'srapporteur's recommendation that participants abstain of presenting new legal proposals on contraception. Preliminary Draftpreliminary draft of Articlesarticles 207 & 208, March 25, 1959.

[166] American Law Institute. Model Penal Code Proposed Official Draft (May 4, 1962). Philadelphia, PA: The American Law Institute; 1962.

[167] For example: Barnard Jr. TH. An Analysis and Criticism of the Model Penal Code Provisions on the Law of Abortion. Cas W Res L Rev 1967; 18: 540-564; Polityka T. From Poe to Roe: A Bickelian View of the Abortion Decision – Its Timing and Principle. Neb. L. Rev. 1974; 53: 31-57, in 44-45; Linton PB. Planned Parenthood v. Casey: The Flight from Reason in the Supreme Court. St. Louis U. Pub. L. Rev. 1993; 13: 15-137, in 25-26; Merz JF, Jackson CA, Klerman JA. A Review of Abortion Policy: Legality, Medicaid Funding and Parental Involvement, 1967-1994. Women's Rts. L. Rep.1995; 17: 1-61, in 4.

and mechanical devices[168]. Albright, Byrne and Crooks accuse the subsection of vagueness, ambiguity, lack of medical basis, and offering a biased moral vision but do not present the reasons in which they support their opinion[169]. Mietus and Mietus criticize some errors contained in the ALI commentary on § 207.11 such as the statement that only the fourth month of gestation the fetus is firmly implanted in the uterus when it has not yet developed many of the characteristic and recognizable features of humanity or that the difference between the embryo as "being initiated" and the fully formed fetus justifies the ethical and juridical position that distinguishes between lives that can be discarded and lives worthy of being saved[170]. Kutner criticizes the ALI for its simplistic behavior to avoid the ethical problem of pre-implantation control of fertility when it appeals to the strategy to assert without giving reasons that the prohibition of abortion is not applicable to the pre-implantation phase[171]. Grisez notes that Subsection 7 is a clear invitation both to develop pharmacological abortifacients such as the morning after pill and to legitimize through an explicit exemption the probable abortifacient techniques of birth control such as the IUD[172]. Marshall and Donovan point out with regard to Subsection 7 that the "wording used posited two beginnings for the

---

[168] Meloy S. Pre-implantation Fertility Control and the Abortion Laws. 41 Chi.-Kent L. Rev. 183-206, 1964, en 203-205.

[169] "Prevention of conception is expressly exempted from the section." Albright JP, Byrne PB, Crooks NP. Church-State Religious Institutions and Values: A Legal Survey 1960-1962, Notre Dame L Rev 1962; 37: 649-719, in 703.

[170] Mietus AC, Mietus NJ. Criminal Abortion: "A Failure of Law" or a Challenge to Society? Am Bar Ass J 1965; 51: 924-928, in 925.

[171] Kutner L. Due Process of Abortion. Minn LR 1968; 53: 1-28.

[172] Grisez G. Abortion. The Myths, the Realities, and the Arguments. New York: Corpus Books; 1970: 238.

same pregnancy, i.e., fertilization and implantation. This double beginning of pregnancy apparently posed no problem for these solons."[173]

5.3. Looking for possible reasons for the decision of ALI

The importance of Subsection 7 itself and, in particular, the magnitude of the consequences that later should derive from it, invite us to inquire about the reasons persuading the ALI members to belittle the ethical value of the re-implanted embryo. We cannot forget that in the mid-twentieth century, fertilization was held as the basic biological event of sexual reproduction – a process where not only an individual was generated but also the parental inheritance was transmitted and the genetic sex of the new human being was established. In those years, to negate the ethical significance of fertilization was a very bold and unheard-of assertion. Therefore, we must ask what were the arguments of the ALI for considering in their MPC the idea that the human embryo in its early days of development was a dispensable legal non-entity which the criminal system could ignore.

All that the ALI offers on that question appears in its comments to Article 207, and more specifically in the explanations on Subsection 7 that deals with the relationship of abortion with contraception. There it reads: "Subsection (7) draws the line between abortion and contraception so as to avoid applying the article to the techniques that prevent pregnancy even when they act shortly after fertilization. Recent research on contraception

---

[173] Marshall R, Donovan C. Blessed are the Barren. The Social Policy of Planned Parenthood. San Francisco: Ignatius Press; 1991: 247.

shows that certain methods of birth control by oral ingestion of medicines prevent the fertilized oocyte from being installed in the wall of the uterus, a necessary precondition for fetal development."[174] Unfortunately, the ALI experts did not give any bibliographic indications on where and by whom those recent investigations were published[175]. We must remember that in the late 1950s, the knowledge on the abortifacient effect of oral contraceptives was more a matter of conjecture than of scientifically demonstrated facts. The leaders of ALI had apparently the presentiment that in the end, an abortifacient effect of contraceptives could not be excluded. Consequently, they included in the prevention of implantation of a fertilized as one modality of contraception. It was an arbitrary but a prudent and astute decision.

In 1959, Subsection 7 could not be supported by clinical trial data that objectively demonstrated the mechanisms of action of the new contraceptives in women. At that moment, there were only suspicions and suggestions. For example, at the V Conference of Planned Parenthood (Tokyo, 1955), Pincus reported that data from his trials on women suggested that progesterone could act on implantation[176]. And although the results of

---

[174] American Law Institute. Model Penal Code. Tentative Draft No. 9, May 8, 1959. Philadelphia: American Law Institute, Executive Office; 1959: 161.

[175] The ALI jurists should be thanked, however, for their frank recognition that the oral ingestion of certain pharmacological agents prevents the implantation of the embryo in the endometrium, an issue that in the following years many researchers and bioethicists denied or concealed jealously.

[176] "There is a suggestion in our data that in women exogenous oral progesterone may act as an antifertility agent for reasons other that its ovulation-inhibiting action. The frequent occurrence of atypical endometrial and already-mentioned indication of suppressive action on endogenous progestin suggest possible effects on ovum and sperm transport and implantation." Pincus G. Some Effects of Progesterone and Related Compounds Upon Reproductive and Early

experimental tests on animals are not to be directly extrapolated to the human species, Pincus and colleagues published in the same year that most of the eggs taken after intercourse from the fallopian tubes of rabbits treated with progesterone appeared fertilized, but no offspring was born from any of the treated animals did any offspring was born[177]. In a related paper on the research done in women and as well as in other publications in those years, they say nothing about such an abortifacient effect[178]. Only in 1959 in the discussion following the presentation of an article by these authors at the Symposium on Steroids for Fertility Control of the American Society of Pharmacology and Experimental Therapeutics (Atlantic City, April 14, 1959)[179] when Greenblatt observed that "the success of this enterprise depends perhaps more on induced endometrial changes that may be hostile to implantation"[180], Pincus replied that Greenblatt's suggestion was interesting but that it should wait to be fully tested[181].

It should also be remembered that in 1960, one year later, the 'pill' was approved by the FDA for contraceptive usebut on a statistically questionable basis. The FDA itself

---

Development in Mammals. Acta Endocr 1956. Suppl. 28: 18-36, 3 in 34.

[177] Pincus G, Chang MC, Hafez ESE, Zarrow MX, Merrill A. Effects of Certain 19-Nor Steroids on Reproductive Processes in Animals. Science 1956; 124: 890-891.

[178] Rock J, Pincus G, Garcia CR. Effects of Certain 19 Nor Steroids on the Normal Human Menstrual Cycle. Science 1956; 124: 891-893.

[179] Pincus G, Rock J, Chang MC, Garcia CR. Effects of Certain 19-Nor Steroids on Reproductive Processes and Fertility. Fed Proc 1959; 18: 1051-1055. This work was presented at the Symposium on Steroids for the Control of Fertility of the American Society of Pharmacology and Experimental Therapeutics, Atlantic City, April 14, 1959.

[180] Greenblatt RB. Discussion. Fed Proc 1959; 18: 1055-1056.

[181] Pincus G. Reply to Discussion, Fed Proc 1959; 18: 1056.

had authorized it in 1957 for certain gynecological indications after evaluating its efficacy and safety but without having precise knowledge of its mechanism of action. Around 1960, the idea prevailed, especially divulged by Pincus and Rock, that the mechanism of action of oral contraceptives was anovulatorybut the effects of these agents on the early embryonic development or on the process of implantation were unknown. A little later, Garcia stated that "the prevention of implantation offers more than ordinary interest because it implies the possibility of post-coital control. However, even if there are many laboratory strategies, these have not been applied nor have been proven to be inapplicable to human beings."[182]

As regards to the methodological difficulties, one must add the extended disinterest to explore in detail the mechanism of action of the new contraceptives. Such a lack of concern soon took root among the advocates of contraception, individual researchers, social agents or pharma industry people alike. It alleviated economic concerns from manufacturers and at the same time released physicians and biologists from the burden of clarifying whether and to what extent these agents acted through an antinidatory mechanism, a "thorny" study, since the confirmation of an early abortifacient effect of contraceptives could suppose the loss of an important sector of the market in those years.

The ethical background of this neglect is revealed by contrast, by what happened in China, a country where the limitation of births was imposed by law and where the population submitted submissively to the prescriptions of

---

[182] Garcia CR. Clinical Studies on Human Fertility Control. In: Greep RO, ed. Human Fertility and Population Problems. Cambridge, Mass: Schenkman Publ Co. 1963: 43-63, at 44.

doctors. These two factors favored the investigation of the mechanisms of action of contraceptives including those acting after fertilization[183].

In any case, the inhibition of implantation was a well-known and accepted issue in the development of contraceptive methods. Thus, Bishop affirms in 1960, "There is, in fact, evidence that some of these gestagens do not inhibit ovulation and perhaps the ideal oral contraceptive will be one that prevents implantation or produces a cervical barrier without inhibiting ovulation."[184]

With the passage of time, the mechanism of action by inhibition of implantation has become common knowledge. In 1973, Morris and van Wagenen created the terms "interceptive" and "interception" to designate respectively the agents and the process of preventing implantation[185]. And in 1999, some of the world's largest contraception agencies (UNDP / UNFPA; WHO; World Bank) together with the Rockefeller Foundation launched an initiative to study the molecular biology of implantation and the effects on

---

[183] See, for example: Fried J, Ryan KJ, Tsuchitani PJ, eds. Oral Contraceptives and Steroid Chemistry in the People's Republic of China. A Trip Report of the American Steroid Chemistry and Biochemistry Delegation. CSCPRC Report No. 5. Washington, D.C.: National Academy of Sciences; 1977. There it is reported that "after an active agent is found, more extensive physiologic studies will be carried out to determine its mechanism of action, for example, whether it inhibits ovulation, prevents implantation, or has other effects" (p. 46). And more specifically: "Chinese investigators conclude that while anordrin may have had an effect in inhibiting ovulation, this was inconsistent [...]. The primary mechanism of action is assumed to be anti-implantation" (p. 56). "It could be demonstrated that the primary effect [of quinegenastrol] was in the genital tract rather than the egg itself, a desynchronization between the zygote and the uterus resulting in an anti-implantation effect" (p. 59).

[184] Bishop PMF. Oral Contraceptives, Practitioner 1960; 85: 158-162, in 161.

[185] Morris JM, van Wagenen G. Interception: The use of postovulatory estrogens to prevent implantation. Am J Obstet Gynecol 1973; 115: 101-106.

fertility of the manipulation of the factors involved in its mechanism[186].

In the end, it must be recognized that Subsection 7 of the MPC, although at the time of its writing it was misleading because of its unsubstantiated claims, was ultimately prophetic. It was not based on scientific evidence but on the desire to introduce contraception as something required by the society of the moment and thus give legal sanction to the change of attitude of the public towards sexuality. The history of the Subsection 7 corroborates the views of an anonymous editorialist of the British Medical Journal in 1974 who wrote, "The dust is settling a little after these earlier controversies and the articles written in the fifties and sixties often showed more of their writers' attitudes to sexual mores than of interpretation of the available evidence although these attitudes were rarely overtly expressed."[187]

---

[186] Griffin PD. Pushing the Frontiers of Science. The WHO/Rockefeller Foundation Initiative on Implantation. Int J Gynecol Obstetr 1999; 67: S111-S116.

[187] Editorial. Stopping the Pill. BMJ 1974; 2: 517-518.

Chapter 6. Changing the Words to Change the Minds

As it was shown in Chapter 2, what the pioneers and the general public had in mind was that modern contraception was understood as prevention of conception. This view was massively dominant until the mid twentieth century. At that time, contraceptive methods intended exclusively to prevent the union of the gametes. Everyone recognized that in order to qualify an instrument as a contraceptive, it was necessary that it had acted before fertilization. By their very nature, contraceptives had nothing to do with the destruction of human zygotes or embryos. Social morality and professional ethics of the time hold firmly that the life of the newly conceived was intangible.

This view of contraception as an exclusive impediment to fertilization began to burst when the suspicion arose after the introduction of some of its new forms (intrauterine devices and oral hormone preparations) that part of their efficacy could be due to a post-fertilization effect, specifically an anti-implantation one, with the consequent loss of very early embryos. The promoters of contraception, from the ideological and industrial point of view, immediately realized that if such a suspicion was confirmed, it could have been very serious could have lead to undesired consequences for their population policy or their businesses, particularly in those countries or cultures where for social or religious reasons, a deep respect was professed to the human embryo from its conception.

Once convinced of the reality of the abortive effect (more intense in the case of the IUDs than in the case of hormonal contraceptives), the promoters had to design actions to favor the social acceptance of the new contraceptives. They realized that perhaps the most effective measures to be taken were two: on one side, to discourage research and publications on the mechanism of action of these contraceptives; on the other, to trivialize the problem by changing the terminology, proposing, and later imposing new meanings for the terms 'conception' and 'gestation' (and, consequently, "abortion").

It is this latter strategy that interests us now. According to the new terminology, the term "conception" would no longer be synonymous with "fertilization" but ought to be defined as "the implantation of the fertilized egg". Therefore, "gestation" would mean in the future "the state of the woman from conception, understood now as the finished implantation, until the expulsion of the products of that conception". According to the new definitions, the first two weeks of development do not belong to gestation; they were provisionally located in a biologically and ethically indeterminate limbo which was initially and inappropriately named as the stage of the "fertilized egg"[188], a stage that disappeared afterwards from the new nomenclature[189].

---

188 American College of Obstetricians and Gynecologists (ACOG). Terminology Bulletin no. 1: Terms used in reference to the fetus. Insert circulated with the September 1965 issue of the journal Obstetrics and Gynecology, the official organ of the ACOG.

Very few times in the history of medicine, the new molding of a pair of words has had such an enormous relevance. It makes an amazing story because of its audacity and its profound ethical and social effects. It has been naturally related by different authors from very different perspectives[190]. However, it is worthwhile to revise and complete it with previously unpublished details.

6.1. A fleeting antecedent of the new terminology: Velpeau and Meigs

6.1.1. The Velpeau's intuition

Apparently, no author until now has alluded to the interesting fact that two obstetricians, one French, Alfred Velpeau, and the other an American, Charles Meigs, anticipated the changes that were to be introduced more than a century later, in the meaning of the basic terms "conception" and "gestation" as used in the science of reproduction and in the study of early human development.

It was Alfred Velpeau who, in 1829 and against the general opinion, proposed that fecundation and conception ought to be considered as two different phenomena. Velpeau based his considerations exclusively in data from the comparative biology of his time, completely alien to whatsoever ethical consequences his view could imply. In his Elemental Treatise on the Art of Midwifery[191], he tells us

---

[189] Hughes EC, ed. Obstetric-gynecologic Terminology, with Section on Neonatology and Glossary of Congenital Anomalies. Philadelphia: F.A. Davis; 1972.

[190] We owe above all to Grisez the systematic investigation of the change of terminology. Members of many pro-life organizations have used extensively Grisez's findings. Grisez G. Abortion, The Myths, the Realities, and the Arguments. New York: Corpus Books; 1970, especially the section "Abortion in the Initial Stages of Pregnancy", pp. 106-116.

that in the reproduction of mammals, there are several successive phases, namely: generation, fertilization, conception and gestation. In his view, these are phases well differentiated each in itself so that the terms which designate them could not be taken as synonyms. For Velpeau, *reproduction* designates the whole function; *generation* should be reserved exclusively for the simple creation of gametes (what we now call gametogenesis); *fertilization* would simply express the action that brings together the two gametes in which one of them would vivify the other (Velpeau frequently uses vivification as a synonym of fertilization); *conception*, which etymologically means to retain, can only designate the action that causes the fertilized gametes to be retained in the sexual organs; *gestation* designates the later development of the gametes vivified and conceived inside the animal. Finally, at the end of pregnancy occurs the *expulsion* or *delivery*.

What did Velpeau understand by conception as a phase well-differentiated from the fertilization that precedes it and the gestation that proceeds it? He does not say it clearly. On one hand, as it has just been pointed out, he understands by conception the retention of the fertilized germ in the genital tract. On the other hand, the author tells us that "conception comprehends what takes place between the instance of vivification and the moment when the fertilized gamete begins to develop whether it attaches itself for this purpose to some point of the generative passages or be expelled in order to undergo the process of incubation exteriorly."[192] Apparently Velpeau gave

---

[191] Velpeau AALM. Traité Élémentaire de l'Art des Accouchements, ou Principes de Tokologie et d'Embryologie. Tome Premier. Paris: J.B. Baillière; 1829: 131-132.

[192] Velpeau A. An Elementary Treatise on Midwifery: or Principles of

conception a double meaning. On one side, it represented what we now call implantation. On the other, it could correspond to a transitory stoppage of development (as it happens in the diapause that in some species precedes implantation or in the case of delayed external incubation).

Appealing to his knowledge of comparative reproductive biology, Velpeau gives the example of the reproduction of ophidians and birds in which there is conception but not gestation[193]. That affirmation is questionable because among the ophidians, there are viviparous snakes in which all the embryonic development is internal; and oviparous snakes, which lay their eggs when the embryos are at a more or less advanced stage of their development[194]. Years later, Velpeau prudently recognized the speculative and provisional nature of his ideas. He explained: "But since this is an abstract point, in a sense, of the great function before us, any other detail on the subject would be completely useless."[195] In summary, the great French doctor launches an ingenious and interesting suggestion which, nevertheless, needs the support of more

---

Tokology and Embryology. Transl. by Ch. D. Meigs. Philadelphia; John Grigg; 1931: 101.

[193] Ibíd., 143-144. In 1829 not much was known about the embryology of reptiles so Velpeau's example had no firm foundation. Today it must be taken as a mistake. In fact, in the birds the processes of segmentation and blastulation begin already during the transit of the fertilized egg along the oviduct: a slow process in the chicken (Patten BM. Early Embryology of the Chick, Philadelphia: Blakiston Co, 1920); more rapid in the pigeon, where the formation of the primitive line begins two hours after incubation, so gastrulation is very advanced at the time of laying (Patterson JT. On Gastrulation and the Origin of the Primitive Streak in the Pigeon's Egg: Preliminary Notice, Biol Bull 1907; 13: 251-271).

[194] White ME. Oogenesis and Early Embryogenesis. In: Aldridge RD, Sever DM, eds. Reproductive Biology and Phylogeny of Snakes. Boca Raton, FL: A.K. Peters / CRC Press; 2011: 101-102.

[195] Velpeau AALM. Traité Complet. Tome I, 2ème éd. Paris: J.B. Baillière; 1835: 152.

refined scientific data.

6.1.2. Meigs: a firmer and more radical vision

Velpeau's ideas were introduced into the Anglo-Saxon medical world by Charles Meigs. He did not simply translate to English the books of his admired Parisian doctor but refined many of his ideas and concretely Velpeaux's theory on the stages of reproduction. Meigs included his new and better articulated vision of the nature of fertilization and the conception in all the five editions of his prestigious manual[196]. He did not rely in the same way as Velpeau did in a comparative biological perspective but in what we call today the preimplantation loss of embryos. He does this by arguing with great vigor that fertilization is not conception, pointing to the fact that a woman can have a fertilized egg in her organs without having conceived since the fertilized egg "may be washed away in a torrent of blood, or carried off amidst a quantity of mucus. In such case, the woman has been fecundated but she has failed to conceive."[197]

As in 1849 the process of implantation of the human embryo in the endometrium was insufficiently known, it was not possible to distinguish between the initial implantation phase, adhesion / fixation of the embryo to the endometrium, and the posterior stage of endometrial invasion by the trophoblast. We can suppose, however, that what Meigs referred to as "conception" could correspond to the entire process of implantation even though Meigs does

---

[196] The first edition (Meigs CD. Obstetrics: The Science and the Art. Philadelphia: Lea and Blanchard) appeared in 1849; the fifth was published two years before Meigs' death (Meigs CD. Obstetrics: The Science and the Art. Philadelphia: Henry C. Lea; 1867).

[197] Meigs CD. Obstetrics: The Science ...; 1849: 157. "Conception is the affixation ... ", says the 5th ed, 1867, in p. 182.

not mention in his book the trophoblastic invasion or the development of primary villi. He merely states that "conception is the fixation ("affixation", says the 5th edition instead of "fixation" as in the previous four) of a fertilized egg on to a living surface of the mother; it is the formation of an adhesion to, or a union with, the uterus, the trunk, etc., of the mother."[198]

What is relevant to us about Meigs' ideas (conception is not fertilization; the fixation of the embryo to the mother's genital tract) lies in the fact that the future redefinition of conception as implantation was anticipated a century before, a matter which we will be dealing with later on. But before this, we must consider how the scientific community received the view of Meigs.

6.1.3. The echoes of Meigs' concept

An extensive review of the obstetrics books of the second half of the nineteenth century reveals that the proposal of Meigs (conception is the fixation of the embryo) did not win the adherence of his colleagues. The authors who quoted it were only few and even less those who approved it. On the contrary, an overwhelming majority of authors adhered to the traditional thesis that fertilization, impregnation and conception are synonymous and mark the beginning of gestation.

The concept of Meigs is apparently mentioned for the first time in 1855 in a "New American Edition" of the book by the English professor Francis Ramsbotham[199] which

---

[198] Ibíd.

[199] Ramsbotham FH. The Principles and Practice of Obstetric Medicine and Surgery, in Reference to the Process of Parturition: A new American Edition, revised by the Author, with Notes and Additions by W.V. Keating. Philadelphia: Blanchard and Lea; 1855.

numerous editions and reprints were published in London and Philadelphia. That 1855 edition informs that not only was it revised by Ramsbotham but it was also completed with notes and additions by William Keating[200], a gynecologist who was part of the circle of Meigs and who became later his successor in the chair of Obstetrics and Gynecology in the Jefferson Medical College of Philadelphia. The Ramsbotham/Keating explanation of the terminology deserves to be transcribed: "Conception, on the other hand, is the fixation, upon some living surface of the mother, of a fecundated ovum; for, as had been well remarked by Prof. Meigs, a female may have a fecundated ovum without having conceived; her ovaries are acting well; the cell-germs are extruded, and are vivified by the sperm-cells during the act of copulation; and yet, owing to a morbid condition of the lining membrane of the uterus, by means of which it fails to form the memhrana decidua, the fecundated ovum is not caught and retained in the uterus or perhaps has been carried away in a gush of menstrual blood and lost in a quantity of mucus. Such a woman may be fecundated without conceiving."[201]

Years later, although without attributing its authorship of Meigs, the argument reappears in a somewhat picturesque account of T. Gaillard Thomas, probably the most eminent obstetrics professor of his time[202]. Thomas stresses the difference between fertilization and conception: "A still more marked influence [than that of ovulation], however, is excited by the meeting of the zoosperm and ovule in some part of the uterine tract. [...]

---

[200] Ibíd., (v).

[201] Ibíd., 82-83.

[202] Mohr JC. Abortion in America. The Origins and Evolution of National Policy, 1800-1900. New York: Oxford University Press; 1978: 239.

Impregnation and conception, as it should be understood, are two entirely different things. Ova may become impregnated twelve times a year and yet conception may not result. Conception is the fixation of the impregnated ovum and instantaneously on its occurrence a communication is set up through the nervous system while the whole economy of the woman begins to change."[203]

Meigs' argument was slightly modified by Hodge when he considered conception as the first stage of the gestation process. This author state: "Physiologists have well established that in the mammalia, this generative function comprehends three distinct series of phenomena: first, germination; second, fecundation; third, gestation [...], gestation or pregnancy, which means the retention and carrying of the product of fecundation to the full term of fetal life, when the new being is prepared for another mode of existence."[204]

These are the very few references contained in the obstetric literature of the nineteenth century on equations "conception equal to fixation (implantation)" and "conception not equal to fertilization" postulated by Meigs. In contrast, that same bibliography appears massively dominated by the traditional view of conception, which, on one hand, establishes the equivalence and synonymy of the terms conception, fertilization and impregnation; and on the other, recognizes conception as the initial moment of gestation. Thus, it does not seem well grounded the opinion

---

[203] Thomas TG. Abortion and Its Treatment, from the Standpoint of Practical Experience: A Special Course of Lectures Delivered at the College of Physicians and Surgeons, New York, Session of 1889-1890. New York: D. Appleton and Co.; 1890: 4-5.

[204] Hodge HL. The Principles and Practice of Obstetrics. Philadelphia: Blanchard and Lea; 1864: 48.

recently expressed by Chung et al., affirming that there has been a long history of ambiguity in the language that has been used to describe the beginning of pregnancy and invoke as proof the explanation given by Meigs[205].

In summary: as we have just seen, to situate the beginning of gestation at implantation and not at fertilization is not a recent invention. It is also long standing the idea of making a distinction between fertilization and conception: two phenomena that had been considered equivalent until Velpeau and Meigs gave conception the new meaning of implantation. The theory of Velpeau and Meigs was short-lived. But after being forgotten for decades, it surprisingly resurfaced in the mid-twentieth century when the promoters of contraception proposed, or rather imposed the equation conception equals implantation.

In order to understand how the meanings of conception and gestation, which was forgotten for so long, were reintroduced in the modern language of medicine, it is necessary to briefly review the role played by the "physiological control of fertility" in the understanding of modern human reproduction.

6.2. Adaptation to change: the 'physiological control of fertilization'

In the acceptance by many scientists of some antinidatory agents as if they were mere contraceptives, what was known as "physiological control of fertility" played a decisive role. It was a new approach to the

---

[205] Chung GS, Lawrence RE, Rasinski KA, et al. Obstetrician-gynecologists' beliefs about when pregnancy begins. Am J Obstet Gynecol 2012; 206: 132.e1-7.

problem of searching for contraceptive procedures which were scientifically based. The trend for physiological control of fertility arose as a rejection of the inefficient products and gadgets contrived by empiricists.

This new approach started from the study of the physiology of reproduction in the human species with the purpose of identifying its most vulnerable points particularly those related to the production and transport of gametes, the different phases of the fertilization process, and also the receptivity of the endometrium. Only with that knowledge it would be possible to design a strategic plan and select the most promising procedures in efficacy and safety to achieve the maximum control capacity at the minimum cost of undesirable biological effects. In contrast to the precedent contraceptive procedures which were intuitive, cumbersome, inelegant and potentially harmful, the techniques derived from physiological control promised to be effective, discreet, innocuous and scientifically based.

The possibility of interfering with the development of the zygote in the stage from fertilization to the implantation of the blastocyst was already included in the first discussions on the physiological control of fertility. At a meeting of the National Maternal Health Committee held in 1933, the possibility of using "hormones preventing nesting of ovum" was included in a "Future Research Program on Birth Control"[206].

In the early 1950s, several articles were published on

---

[206] National Committee on Maternal Health. Program for Future Research on Birth Control. Memorandum on March 23, 1933, conference between Drs. Frank, Hartman, Dickinson, Bryant. *Center for the History of Medicine, Countway Library, Harvard University.*

http://collections.countway.harvard.edu/onview/file_upload/0002360_dre f.jpg.

the theoretical possibilities of interfering with implantation. In 1952, Pirie lectured the members of the Eugenic Society on the biochemistry of conception control. He concluded that the implantation of the zygote offered good perspectives of inhibition and good probabilities of specificity and acceptance. Without referring to the ethical aspects of his conclusions, he dictated that the initial stages of implantation (adhesion and fixation of the blastocyst's trophectoderm to the endometrium) prior to the beginning of the formation of the placenta belonged to the conception process and thus fell within the proper field of contraception. Pirie, an author of the modern times, was the first to include the nidation of the embryo into the stage of conception[207]. But at that time, such an idea was strange or unacceptable since it was "officially" asserted that gestation begins with fertilization and that the control of fertility was synonymous with the prevention of fertilization[208].

But the inhibitory effect of implantation could not remain for a long time as a relatively remote theoretical possibility. Some researchers began to consider it as an objective easy to reach and very useful. It was at the International Planned Parenthood Conference in 1955 in Tokyo when Pincus himself spoke about this effect: "There is a suggestion in our data that in women exogenous oral progesterone may act as an antifertility agent for reasons

---

[207] Pirie NW. The Biochemistry of Conception Control. Eugen Rev 1952; 44: 129-140, in 134.

[208] In 1953, at a conference on pregnancy loss, emphasis was placed on the massive loss of embryos before implantation which were considered as failed pregnancies. "With some qualms and after extensive discussion, the term gestational loss was used to indicate the total post-conception reproductive deficit." Engle ET, ed. Pregnancy Wastage, Proceedings of the Conference Sponsored by the Committee on Human Reproduction, National Research Council, on behalf of the National Committee on Maternal Health, Inc. Springfield, IL. CC Thomas; 1953: 141.

other that its ovulation-inhibiting action. The frequent occurrence of atypical endometrial and already-mentioned indication of suppressive action on endogenous progestin suggest possible effects on ovum and sperm transport and implantation."[209]   Hence,   in   1955,   embryonic preimplantation development and implantation were already enrolled in research projects that sought reliable procedures to interfere with them[210]. The researchers were aware that methods targeting these biological targets ran the risk of not receiving broad social acceptance[211].

Although some authors expressed certain ethical objections about post-fertilization contraception[212], it was gradually ceasing to be problematic among many scientists in the following years[213]. The need to say not a word before the general public on the abortifacient effect of the new contraceptives, resulted in the coinage of a new term.

---

[209] Pincus G. Some Effects of Progesterone and Related Compounds upon Reproduction and Early Development in Mammals. Papers on Biological Research Presented at the Fifth International Planned Parenthood Conference Held at Tokyo, Japan, from October 24th to 29th, 1955. Acta Endocrinologica 1956, Suppl. XXVIII: 18-36, in 34.

[210] Nelson WO. Survey of Studies Relating to Vulnerable Points in the Reproductive Processes. Papers on Biological Research Presented at the Fifth International Planned Parenthood Conference Held at Tokyo, Japan, from October 24th to 29th, 1955. Acta Endocrinologica 1956, Suppl. XXVIII: 7-17, in 8.

[211] Ibíd., 15.

[212] For example, Stone stated in a very popular publication: "the method raises an important ethical question unlike the other contraceptive methods, it destroys a life already begun". Stone A. The Control of Fertility. Sci Am 1954; 190 (4): 31-33. Even harder were the criticisms of moralists: Gibbons WJ, Burch TK. Physiologic Control of Fertility: Process and Morality. Am Eccl Rev 1958; 138: 246-277.

[213] See, for example: Parkes AS. Quest for an Ideal Contraceptive. Proc Soc Stud Fertil 1953; 5: 20-26; Nelson, WO. Survey of Studies Relating to Vulnerable Points in the Reproductive Processes. Fifth International Conference of Planned Parenthood, Tokyo, 1955. Acta Endocr 1956; Suppl XXVIII: 7.

6.3.   A new terminology for post-fertilization contraception is born

As is said above, the main objective (ethical, not biological) of the new terminology was to induce in the public the belief that the methods of fertility control that acted inhibiting either the development of the zygote in its first days or the implantation of the blastocyst were to be considered ordinary contraceptives. For many people then and now, the terminological amend was not able to change their certainty that it was wholly incorrect and unacceptable to classify abortifacient agents as contraceptives. To obviate this difficulty, the promoters of the new terminology proposed and methodically imposed a very simple idea: to declare the stage of embryonic development that goes from fertilization to the end of implantation as ethically neutral. In other words, the first fourteen days of the developing human embryo were to be considered as ethically irrelevant.

To that effect, a few and new definitions were sufficient. The new definitions were introduced in the field of medicine by the Committee on Terminology of the American College of Obstetricians and Gynecologists (ACOG) through a circular entitled *"Terminology Bulletin"*[214]. That provisional leaflet catalyzed the publication years later of the book *"Obstetric-Gynecologic Terminology"*[215] edited by Hughes under the sponsorship of the ACOG. In both

---

[214] Committee on Terminology, American College of Obstetricians and Gynecologists. Terms Used in Reference to the Fetus. Terminol Bull, No. 1, Insert in Obstet Gynecol, 1965; 26 (3).

[215] Committee on Terminology. American College of Obstetricians and Gynecologists. Hughes EC, ed. Obstetric-Gynecologic Terminology with Section on Neonatology and Glossary of Congenital Anomalies. Philadelphia: FA. Davis Company 1972.

publications, the conception is not defined as the fertilization of the oocyte by the sperm but as the implantation of the fertilized egg in the uterus (*Bulletin*) or the implantation of the blastocyst (*Terminology*). In addition, pregnancy, in the *Bulletin*, is defined, as "the state from conception to the expulsion of the products of such conception" while in *Terminology* it is defined as "the state of the woman after conception and until the termination of pregnancy"[216]. When defining "abortion", no publication makes reference to the minimum developmental age required of the product of fertilization in order to be considered an abortion. The only condition required is that the gestational age be less than 20 weeks of development, an age which obviously includes the product of fertilization in the days of its pre-implantation development[217]. A conclusion is unavoidable: the definitions of the terms related to early development were elaborated carelessly by the Committee of Terminology.

As was noted in the previous chapter, however, it was not in the ACOG publications where the new system of ideas was introduced for the first time. In 1959, the American Law Institute (ALI) manifested in a clear and explicit way the ethical irrelevance of the antinidation effect and, consequently, the embryo in its preimplantation days.

---

[216] Some explanations on the origin and meaning of the new terminology introduced by the ACOG Committee are discussed in detail in Chapter 8, in the section dedicated to Edward C. Hughes and the Obstetric-gynecologic Terminology.

[217] The Bulletin states that the product expelled must weigh less than 500 g and its gestational age less than 20 weeks. In Terminology, preference is given to weight over the calculated age when the abortus weights less than 500 g; in the event that this information is ignored, the duration of the pregnancy will be used which must be less than 20 completed weeks (139 days) calculated from the first day of the last normal menstrual period. Significantly, the Bulletin discourages the use of the terms "early abortion" or "late abortion".

In its influential Model Penal Code, contraceptives are defined as drugs or substances that in order to avoid pregnancy, act before, during or immediately after fertilization or in some way prevent the implantation of the fertilized egg[218]. The jurists founded their opinion on the idea that "contraception research indicates that some methods of birth control through the oral ingestion of medicines prevent the fertilized egg from being established in the wall of the uterus, a necessary precondition for fetal development"[219]. For the ALI, it was a sufficient reason to annul the ethical value of the pre-implanted embryo, its willful decision to declare as contraceptives the procedures acting after fertilization, a paradigmatic example of how the change of words implies a change of reality.

The new meaning of the terms "conception", "gestation" and "abortion" never got general approval among physicians. However, it became an "official" terminology in many academic and health care institutions. The history of the lexical mutation has been told with great precision and detail by Grisez[220], so it is not necessary here to recapitulate that history which, on the other hand, has been profusely divulged by the followers of the pro-life movement.

The following section is devoted to present a feature of the terminological mutation that has not received the attention it deserves: the dogmatic and almost despotic way according to which the equation "conception equals

---

[218] American Law Institute. Model Penal Code. Tentative Draft No. 9, May 8, 1959. Philadelphia, PA. The Executive Office, The American Law Institute; 1959: 144.

[219] Ibíd., 161.

[220] Grisez G. Abortion, The Myths, The Realities, and The Arguments. New York: Corpus Books; 1970, pp. 106-116.

implantation" was adopted and disseminated by the world's most important and influential health and medical institutions.

6.4. The terminological change is imposed by authoritarian fiat

The terminological change introduced by the ACOG was not promoted by new discoveries which invited a change of the terminology for scientific reasons until peacefully shared. Truly, anovulatory pills did not demand any terminological change since in theory, their mechanism of action was exclusively prefecundative[221]. The rationale behind the decision of the ACOG's Terminology Committee to introduce its new and revolutionary definitions have never been revealed. The justification which the bulletin offers us about the new definition could be qualified with fairness as a pathetic alibi. In fact, the committee explains that "this definition has been selected deliberately because union of sperm and ovum cannot be detected clinically unless implantation occurs."[222] From a logical point of view, such an explanation in itself is an invalid conclusion. In

---

[221] A convincing proof of this assertion is offered by John Rock himself, one of the creators of the contraceptive pill. He advocated the use of high doses of hormones to ensure the pill's anovulatory mechanism of action since he knew that reducing the hormone contents of the drug implied an unavoidable risk of embryo loss. When Chang and Pincus proposed him to try a morning-after pill, Rock's cold response made it clear that he had no desire to continue down that path: "I feel that it [such a pill] is an abortifacient", he told them. This episode is related in Asbell B. The Pill. A Biography of the Drug that Changed the World. New York: Random House; 1995: 348. Asbell had probably taken it from Lader L. Three Men Who Made a Revolution. New York Times Mag, April 10, 1966: 8-9, 55-56, 63, 66, at 55.

[222] ACOG. Terminology Bulletin No. 1: 1. As it is easy to suppose, this Bulletin's inappropriate justification was not included by Hughes in his book on *Terminology*.

1970, Ramsey refuted convincingly the idea of conception as implantation: "The basis for the theoretical assertion that life begins with implantation is the merely practical consideration that the "union of sperm and ovum cannot be detected clinically unless implantation occurs." If this is the case, one may correctly draw the conclusion that a scientist's clinical knowledge that life has started begins with implantation. We could say that *pregnancy* begins with implantation, if saying this is not a redundancy. However, to declare categorically that new life begins with implantation is to make oneself ignorant of the [first] six or seven days. This proposal can only be set down as self-serving. As a layman, I can only express surprise if it is a statement of scientific fact that fertilized ova before implantation have not been 'clinically detected'."[223]

And yet, despite its obvious deficiencies (lack of scientific justification, conflict of moral interests and absence of logic), the new definition of conception triumphed throughout the world, andit did in a spectacular way. Its lack of intrinsic rationality was more than compensated for by the strong and authoritarian support provided by many important world and national medical and health institutions. Many of them threw the weight of their authority in spreading and imposing the new terminology as the only correct language. The new definitions, initially targeted on the ACOG's membership, were promptly adopted by the International Federation of Gynecology and Obstetrics (FIGO) and following in its footsteps by practically all the national associations of obstetricians and gynecologists. Within a few years, they

---

[223] Ramsey P. Reference Points in Deciding about Abortion. En: Noonan jr JT, ed. The Morality of Abortion. Legal and Historical Perspectives. Cambridge, Mass. Harvard University Press; 1970: 60-100, in 65.

were embraced by the World Medical Association and many national medical associations, among them are: the American Medical Association (AMA) and the American Medical Women's Association (AMWA); by the World Health Organization (WHO/OMS), the Food and Drug Administration (FDA), the National Institutes of Health (NIH) and many other governmental agencies in the United States and abroad.

The generalization of the new terminology did not come by way of the critical evaluation of its objectivity and usefulness but by the fiat of the managers of professional organizations or the officers of government's agencies. Hughes' *Terminology* acted in many cases as a catalyst of the lexical change thanks to its supposed authoritativeness. Over the years, the *Terminology* became itself its own source of legitimate lexical expertise[224]. In exceptional cases, some organizations alleged a democratic process of consultation with their membership to legitimate the new semantics. The results of those surveys were never audited or published but declared as massively in accordance with the new definitions. Such is the case, for example, of the Department of Health, Education and Welfare (DHEW, now the Department of Health and Human Services, DHHS) of the United States[225].

---

[224] This is the case of the WHO / WHO. In 2003, he states that "A WHO Technical Report considered that gestation begins when the implantation is already completed, and that implantation is the process that begins with the adhesion of the denuded blastocyst of the pellucida to the uterine wall (days 5- 6 post-fertilization). Cook R, Dickens BM, Fathalla MF. Reproductive Health and Human Rights: Integrating Medicine, Ethics, and Law. Oxford University Press; 2003: 291. The Technical Report referred to is: Mechanism of Action, Safety and Efficacy of Intrauterine Devices: Report of a WHO Scientific Group. Technical Report Series 753. Geneva: WHO; 1987: 12.

[225] The history of this case began on November 16, 1973 when the Director of the NIH, Robert S. Stone, published in the Federal Register (38 FR 31738-31747)

The authoritarian nature with which the new terminology was disseminated and indoctrinated appears clearly in the answers that the adherents of the new terminology give to those who challenge the new language. They usually argue that they simply follow what is defined by the government and the most important medical organizations in the country. In their view, the new terminology represents the official position of national health and medical organizations. Truly, they are on the side of health policy and not of medical science.

---

a draft for public consultation on the special procedures required for the protection of vulnerable subjects in biomedical research. The fetus was already defined in that draft as "the product of conception from the time of implantation until the time of delivery" (p. 31739). On August 23, 1974, the Register informed that many (about 450) critical comments to the proposed definitions had been received, demanding that pregnancy should be defined as initiated in the fertilization of the egg. But, while the Department has no argument with the conceptual definition as proposed above, it sees no way of basing regulations on the concept. Rather, in order to provide an administrable policy, the definition must be based on existing medical technology which permits confirmation of pregnancy (39FR30647 and ff, in 30651). Evidently, DHEW officials preferred administrative efficiency and set aside valid conceptual objections.

Chapter 7. Biology and Medicine in the Papal Commission for the Study of the Problems of the Population, Family and Birth

No one who is interested in the ethical aspects of contraception can ignore the important role played in them by the Pontifical Commission for the Study of the Problems of Population, Family and Birth (PC)[226]. In the public opinion, the PC is usually considered a group of highly competent experts with firm convictions, who, at the end of their work, became tragically divided into two fractions: a large majority, which recommended to change the traditional doctrine of the Catholic Church on the intrinsically disordered nature of contraception; and a small minority, favorable to the maintenance of the perennial teaching on the subject. As is well known, Paul VI did not accept the proposal of the majority, and reaffirmed in his encyclical Humanae vitae the traditional view. Since then, the PC is

---

[226] In the Encyclical *Humanae Vitae*, Paul VI named the Commission "the Commission for the Study of the Problems of the Population, the Family and the Birth". That could be taken by its official name. In practice, it is usually abbreviated to Papal Birth Commission or simply Papal Commission.

usually presented in the great majority of publications as a victim of the conservatism of the Roman Curia[227].

When more than fifty years have passed since the creation of the PC and, despite the fact that most of the documentation that it produced is still under secrecy, it is convenient to review some topics of interest, which in this chapter will be circumscribed to the medical-biological aspects. Virtually nothing has been published on the subject. The present study benefits, on one hand, from the insertion on the Internet by Germain Grisez of a small part of the documentation of the PC[228]; and, on the other, from the access to another set of documents bequeathed by John Marshall, member of the PC from the first moment, to the Library of the University of Notre Dame[229]. It is a material of enormous interest that, although incomplete, allows for an exploratory and provisional study, pending the access to the full archive of the PC, including the documentation delivered by its Secretary to Pope Paul VI[230].

---

[227] The bibliography on the PC is very abundant and has contributed to create certain views that logically dominate public opinion on the subject. In general, they do not save praise for the opinion of the majority and strongly reprove the imperviousness to innovation of the minority. That is the version offered by the two works that, in more detail, have dealt with the history of the PC: Kaiser RB. The Encyclical that Never Was. The Story of the Commission on Population, Family and Birth, 1964-66. Revised edition. London: Sheed & Ward; 1987 (The original edition, published in 1985, was: The Politics of Sex and Religion: A Case History in the Development of Doctrine, 1962-1984, Kansas City, Mo, Leaven Press, 1985); and McClory R. Turning Point. The Inside Story of the Papal Birth Control Commission. New York: Crossroad; 1995.

[228] Accessible at: http://twotlj.org/BCCommission.html.

[229] Gently lent to one of us (GH) by Mons. Pegoraro, Vice Chancellor of the Pontifical Academy for Life.

[230] This documentation available today is composedpartly of answers to questionnaires, summaries of debates, reports of sessions and documents provided by the commissioners. From its reading, one can infer the decisive role played by his General Secretary, Henry de Riedmatten, in the activity of the COP.

7.1. A brief historical synthesis of the Papal Commission

There are different versions on the origin of the PC. McClory notes that it was Cardinal Leo Suenens who urged Pope John XXIII to create a small commission to study in detail the problem of birth control[231]. Harvey affirms that it was Archbishop Sheehan of Baltimore who, with the support of Cardinal Cicognani, pressured John XXIII to establish a PC; and that Sheehan, once appointed a member of the Commission, got the necessary donations to start it[232]. Kaiser, on the other hand, tells a story, not proven, according to which the PC was suggested to John XXIII by his Secretary, Loris Capovilla, so that it could studyaside from the demographic aspects, those related with the doctrinal and pastoral problems of fertility in the marriage. In addition, he recommended to the Pope that in order to organize this Commission, he should ask Suenens for help, given the long experience of the Belgian prelate in the matter[233]. Shannon offered the most probable version of the genesis of the PC. He refers that when the Holy See

---

He not only became the intellectual conductor of the Commission thanks to the timing and programming of the plenary and group sessions, but at the same time, it acted as spokesman for the Commission before the Pope and as a transmitter of the indications of the Supreme Authority to the Commission. In addition, he personally wrote numerous reports and summaries of the sessions, prepared questionnaires and work agendas, and enjoyed considerable autonomy in his activity. On many occasions, and to avoid delays in the progress of the work programmed, the documents drafted by de Riedmatten were not reviewed by the Executive Committee, nor by the members designated *ex officio* for that function.

[231] McClory R. Turning Point ... p. 40.

[232] Harvey JC. André Hellegers and Carroll House: Architect and Blueprint for the Kennedy Institute of Ethics. KIEJ 2004; 14: 199-206, in 204. However, Sheehan was appointed to participate in the V session, in 1966, so it does not seem likely that it would help the start-up of the small CP of 1963.

[233] Kaiser RB. The Encyclical ... p. 66.

received an invitation from the United Nations to an International Conference on Population, the documentation came to the Swiss Dominican, Rev. Henri de Riedmatten of the Vatican representation to the international organizations in Geneva, who suggested the creation of a group that would respond to the United Nations questionnaires[234].

John XXIII created that group on April 27, 1963. The majority of the persons appointed to the PC that year were active participants in the seminaries organized by Cardinal Suenens in Louvain. Pope John died before the Commission could meet for its first session but Paul VI welcomed the PC and confirmed its membership. All the activity of the PC took place during Paul VI's pontificate.

At the first session of the PC (Louvain, October 12-13, 1963), its six members[235] tried to fulfill the request received: a report to be sent to the programmed United Nations Population Conference in New Delhi, a conference that apparently never met. This first session of the PC was not communicated to the public. The report ratified the current moral doctrine of the Church although it left open the issue on which methods of birth control could be approved by the Holy See. Just in that question was contained the germ of what came after[236].

---

[234] Shannon WH. The Lively Debate. Response to Humanae Vitae. New York: Sheed & Ward; 1970, p. 76.

[235] It is not easy to make a complete and accurate nominal list of the members of the PC. Several lists have been published. Henry de Riedmatten includes in the Final Report of the PC a list of the members who participated in the final session. On the other hand, McClory (Turning Point ..., pp. 188-190), Kaiser (The Encyclical ... pp-297-299) and Shannon (The Lively Debate .. pp. 210-212) offer their lists, which show small differences between them. The most reliable is that of de Riedmatten, which adds to the list of members, that of observers, guests and consultants.

Before the second session (Rome, April 3-5, 1964), the PC was enlarged with two demographers and five theologians. Its agenda included two points. First, how the Church should respond to the United Nations and governments on the demographic question; the other, how should the morality of birth control be approached[237]. Again, the PC confirmed the traditional doctrine but left for later the study of contraceptive methods which would have to be treated as a priority in the next session.

The third session (Rome, June 13-14, 1964), just a month and a half after the second, was summoned urgently to answer some concrete questions: the primary purpose of marriage (relationship between responsibility of marriage), and an evaluation of the means by which couples could put into practice responsible fatherhood (the rhythm and the pill). The PC, now composed of fifteen members (two theologians had been added to it), decided by majority opinion to confirm the traditional doctrine on the first two points and manifested its opposition to use of the pill for birth regulation although it considered that a definitive pronouncement of the Pope on the matter would be premature. In that session, only two members of the PC were doctors.

Before the fourth session (Rome, 25-28 March 1965) the PC underwent a radical change in number and qualification of its members; their number grew to fifty-eight and they were very diverse intellectually and sociologically. Their task was to offer the Pope recommendations for immediate action regarding the uses

---

[236] Kaiser RB. According to this source, the PC discussed the morality of the contraceptive use of the pill but upon recognizing the need of more information, the final decision was postponed. The Encyclical ... p. 68s.

[237] Ibíd., 73.

of the pill, assuming that there had been doctrinal advances on that matter. It began with a plenary meeting where Noonan spoke on the history of changes in the canonical discipline on issues that seemed doctrinally consolidated. The purpose of Noonan's intervention was to open a way for a change of attitude towards contraception. The members were divided into three sections: Theologians; Doctors and Psychologists; and Demographers, Sociologists and Economists. Although there was much exchange of ideas and a perceptible improvement of the PC as a coordinated working team, four days were not enough to respond to a so wide problem and to reach conclusions. Once again, it was necessary to continue studying the issues.

The fifth and last session (Rome, April 18 to June 15, 1966) was very long and complex. By decision of the Supreme Authority, the hitherto members of the Commission were renamed "experts". The PC proper was then reconstituted to a group of sixteen members (fourteen of them - seven Cardinals and seven Bishops - were new to the PC, while two Bishops came from the previous Commission), with the task of reviewing and delivering the final recommendations of the experts to the Pope. These met in sessions of independent groups (theologians, professors of medicine, demographers and sociologists, pastoral agents), and in combined sessions of two or more groups. Only at the end there were plenary sessions. It was in the course of this fifth session that the split in the "majority" and "minority" experts was consolidated. The sessions of the new PC of Cardinals and Bishops were initially informative; they later became deliberative with intense debates, followed by the vote which, finally, decided in favor of the opinion of the majority of the experts, maintaining that the traditional doctrine was reformable. The PC was dissolved once by Riedmatten, the Secretary General who delivered the complete documentation to the Pope on June 27, 1966.

7.2. The medico-biological notions in the sessions of the Pontifical Commission

Overall, the work of the PC was highly diversified as befits the multidisciplinary nature of its members who were divided into groups in Sessions IV and V. There were three groups in the IV Session: Demography, Economics and Sociology; Medicine and Psychology; and Theology; and four in the V Session: Theology, Medicine, Pastoral and, finally, Demography and Sociology. In the course of the last two sessions, the group of theologians which was the most numerous, enjoyed more time for their presentations and debates and was responsible for preparing most of the study documentation and conclusions. In the final phase of the PC, the theologians were the ones who had the greatest role: they offered the last word to the Cardinals and Bishops.

In this chapter, attention will be focused on the way in which the PC and particularly its medical members[238] treated the biological and clinical aspects of contraception, a topic which would serve as the starting point for the debates and conclusions of the other groups and of the entire PC. It was not, however, the main topic of the deliberations of the medical group. On the contrary, its attention centered mainly on evaluating the weaknesses of the rhythm method which led to the conclusion that such

---

[238] The fifteen members of the medical-biological group of the COP were Doctors Bertolus, Cavanagh, Férin, Gaudefroy, Görres, Hellegers, Lemaitre, López Ibor, Marshall, Moins, Moriguchi, Potvin, Rendu, van Rossum and Thibault.

method could not be offered as an acceptable solution to the problem of birth control.

It is generally admitted that the medical-biological section played an essential role as a source of information and as a leading actor in the debates of the PC. The members of the PC participated in the idea that it would not be possible to offer a correct solution to the doctrinal problem of contraception without supporting it in a solid biology. Paul VI himself had said so to the PC[239].

Consequently, it was up to the medical group to assume the responsibility of offering the PC an up-to-date documentation on the physiology of human reproduction; on the biology and uses of contraception, especially of the pill (and also of the IUDs); and, finally, a detailed information on the mechanism of action of the contraceptives, being this last issue indispensable for the moral evaluation the theologians would have to perform. The medical group was an advisory body; it did not have to pronounce the final word of the PC which was the duty of the Commission of Cardinals and Bishops, with the counsel of the experts of the PC, especially of the theologians.

In any case, in spite of the subordinate situation of the medical group within the PC, its expert opinion was of the utmost importance for the Pope who wanted to take into account scientific information when issuing his judgment on the morality of the new contraception. The Pontiff felt the

---

[239] "These are, dear sons, the planes in which your research is situated: on the one hand, a better knowledge of the physiological laws, the psychological and medical data [...]; on the other hand and above all, the plane of the superior light that the data of the Faith and the traditional teaching of the Church project on those facts." Pope Paul VI. Allocution à la Commission d'Étude sur les Probèmes de la Population, de la Famille, et la Natalité, Samedi 27 Mars 1965. Available at: http://w2.vatican.va/content/paul-vi/fr/speeches/1965/documents/hf_p-vi_spe_19650327_demographic-commission.html.

urgency of the matter that he has had to express it to the members of the PC[240]. One of those most urgent questions was to determine whether the pill acted through an anovulatory effect or it could do so as an abortifacient.

Based on the information provided by the doctors, the PC adopted the following positions:

7.2.1. Affirmation of the value of human life and exclusion of abortion

The members of the PC manifested without exception a seamless adherence to respect for human life and many of them expressly stated that such respect and protection must extend from the beginning of life in fertilization. Two examples are enough for evidence:

Testimony of de Riedmatten: "All the members have firmly stated that it is necessary in the first place to protect human life. Consequently, in doubtful cases such as the IUD and in the case of problems posed by the beginning of human life, it will be necessary to adopt and maintain vigorously a tutiorist position. For this purpose, in practice it will be considered that life takes its origin with the fertilization of the ovule."[241]

Report of the Majority: "In grave language, Vatican Council II has reaffirmed that abortion is altogether to be excluded from the means of responsibly preventing birth.

---

[240] "We urge you not to lose sight of the urgency of a situation that demands precise indications from the Church and its Supreme Authority. The conscience of the people can not be left exposed to uncertainties that today, too often, prevent the conjugal life from unfolding according to the design of the Lord." Paul VI, Ibíd.

[241] de Riedmatten H. Introduction du Secrétaire Général au Rapport de la session commune des professeurs de médecine et des théologiens, 2 au 8 mai 1966: 3. (Marshall Papers).

Indeed, abortion is not a method of preventing conception but of eliminating offspring already conceived. This affirmation about acts which do not spare an offspring already conceived is to be repeated in regard to those interventions as to which there are serious grounds to suspect that they are abortive."[242]

Thus, the unanimous position of the PC in favor of the principle of respect for life should apply not only when there is tangible evidence that certain contraceptives involve the loss of newly conceived embryos but also when there are suspicions that they can be abortive.

---

[242] Report of the Majority of the Papal Commission. Chap. IV. Objective criteria of morality, 2.

7.2.2. The possible abortifacient effect of certain contraceptives

This firm position of respect for the nascent life put on the shoulders of the medical members of the PC the burden of reviewing and evaluating critically and without bias the bibliography on the abortifacient effect of contraceptives[243] which was published before 1966; a complex and arduous task particularly when it must be carried out under the tension of finishing it as soon as possible[244]. It could be not ignored that some authors had expressed their suspicion, more or less founded, that the mechanism of action of certain contraceptives (some types of the pill, IUDs) included the possibility of causing the death of the newly conceived embryo. Such a suspicion could only be discarded after a serious and detailed analysis of the bibliography since everyone was aware that from a Catholic perspective, the well-founded suspicion of abortion could not be part of the morally correct prevention of conception.

What did the members of the medical group find in the scrutinized publications that referred to a possible or proven abortifacient effect? To reduce the search to its minimum dimensions, it suffices to mention what was published or said by some of the participants in the sessions of the PC.

Cavanagh, an American psychiatrist and personal

---

[243] Given that the fifth session of the PC was held in the months of April, May and June of 1966, it seems logical to limit the critical study of the medical group to the bibliography published before the end of 1965.

[244] According to Kaiser, the collective duty of the PC was to fulfill the task entrusted to it by the Pope, that is, offering a reasoned solution to the problem of the morality of contraception. But "... none of the subsections provided a definitive 'answer'. Those who attempted to force answers won no admiration from the rest [...] John Marshall said, 'Most of us were there in a kind of fact-finding mode." Kaiser, The Encyclical ..., p. 119.

physician of Cardinal Cicognani for many years, was very interested in the problems of marriage and sexuality. He published a book in 1965 in which he devoted a section to discuss the mechanism of action of contraceptives[245]. He referred to several articles that expressed the opinion that part of the effectiveness of the contraceptives had to be attributed to the lack of suitability of the endometrium which, modified by the medication, became inadequate for the implantation of the embryo. He deduced that the bibliography reviewed was inconclusive and left the question open. However, Kaiser, in his history of the PC, notes that Cavanagh claimed that the specialists he had asked about the particular could not rule out that the pill acted as an abortifacient and as well as an anovulant, a circumstance of the singular importance for the PC[246]. This point is confirmed in the documentation of the IV session of the PC in which it is said that Cavanagh "added an important contribution to the discussion. He himself had undertaken an investigation into the so-called abortive effects of the pill and found no [published] evidence of such effects although he could observe that when he asked this question directly to the specialists, they could not agree on the way in which the pill acts."[247]

Noonan, a consultant to the PC and later a firm opponent of the Encyclical Humanae Vitae[248], in discussing

---

[245] Cavanagh J. The Popes, the Pill, and the People. A Documentary Study. Milwaukee: The Bruce Publishing Co; 1965: 33-37.

[246] Kaiser, op. cit. p. 121.

[247] Report of the 4th session of the Commission. p. 28. Documents disseminated by Grisez on the Internet. Accessible at:

http://www.twotlj.org/BCCommission.html.

[248] As already mentioned, Noonan, who was not a member but a consultant to the COP, inaugurated the IV Session of the CP with a long historical exposition

the pill's mode of action, points out that "the progesterone taken by the pill seemed to make the endometrium unfavorable to implantation of the egg". And, immediately, it tries to discredit such an assertion: "Hence, if the pill failed to prevent ovulation, it might still prevent pregnancy either by preventing fecundation or by preventing nidation. Prevention of nidation would be described by most modem Catholic theologians as abortion. That, in fact, an abortive effect occurred was not proved". In support of his position, Noonan reiterates twice a purely imaginary argument by conjecturing that "if the pill failed to affect a particular woman's ovulatory responses, it might be equally ineffective in affecting her endometrium". Thus, he absolved the pill of its possible antinidatory effect. He honestly concludes, however, that at the moment he writes only one thing is certain: we ignore what happens when the pill fails as anovulator[249].

---

on the changes of the Catholic doctrine (canonical and theological) on contraception. His intervention was a summary of his prestigious book which waspublished on that same year (1965) about the history of contraception (see next note). Noonan has been criticized because his interpretation of the canonical texts suffers from extreme legal rigidity and lacks the flexible mentality of the historian. Consequently, Noonan tends to confuse the originality and adaptability of the canonical discipline of the Church with the fallibility and mutability of a Magisterium which Noonan thinks incoherent. Vid.: Rouche M. La Preparation de l'encyclique «Humanae Vitae». La Commission sur la Population, the Famille et la Natalité. Actes du Colloque de Rome (2-4 juin 1983). Rome: École Française de Rome; 1984. Accessible at: www.persee.fr/doc/efr_0000-0000_1984_act_72_1_2419.

[249] Noonan Jr JT. Contraception A History of Its Treatment by the Catholic Theologians and Canonists. Cambridge, Mass: The Belknap Press; 1965: 461. Noonan provides the references of some articles which authors suspect or accept the abortifacient effect of the pill: Tyler ET, Olson HJ. Fertility Promoting and Inhibiting Effects of New Steroid Hormonal Substances. JAMA 1959; 169: 1843-1854; Bishop PMF. Oral Contraceptives. Practitioner 1960; 185: 158-162; Goldzieher JW et al. Study of Norethindrone in Contraception. JAMA 1962; 180: 359-361; Guttmacher AF. Oral Contraception Postgr Med 1962; 32: 552-558; Anonymous. To day's Drugs. Br Med J 1963; 2: 488-491; AMA's Council on Drugs. An Oral Contraceptive: Norethindrone with Mestranol (Ortho-Novum). JAMA

On the other hand, Noonan registers an important point: in the discussions on contraception held by theologians between 1957 and 1964, it was assumed that the pill acted exclusively as an anovulant[250]. Nevertheless, in a footnote Noonan cites a review article in which Ayd gathers and analyzes practically all publications on the mode of action of oral contraceptives appeared until July 1965. According to Ayd several researchers affirm that part of the high effectiveness of the pill in the prevention of pregnancy is due to its action, as a contraceptive, on the cervical mucus to impede the passage of sperm and also as an abortifacient that modifies the endometrium, making impossible the implantation of the blastocyst[251].

7.2.3. Doubts about the abortifacient effect in sessions of the PC

In the *Relatio Generalis*[252], de Riedmatten reports that the following question was put to the vote of the group of theologians: "If the condemnation of any direct abortion should be extended to all methods of artificial intervention

---

1964; 87: 664.

[250] Ibíd.

[251] Ayd published two different versions of his review of oral contraceptives both dated July 1964. The shorter one (Ayd FJ, Jr. The Oral Contraceptives, Their Mode of Action, Rome, Pontifical Gregorian University, July 13, 1964, 29 pp. typewritten), appeared as a Report prepared for the Family Life Bureau of the National Catholic Welfare Conference. The other, which was more detailed, dated July 31 and circulated as the first issue of a publication edited by Ayd himself (Ayd FJ, Jr. The Oral Contraceptives. Their Mode of Action. Med Newslet Religious 1964; 1: 1-64).

[252] It is a report to inform the Cardinals and Bishops of the PC in its final session in which de Riedmatten summarized the work and opinions of then known as PC experts. It can be found at:

http://www.twotlj.org/De%20Riedmatten%2020%20June.pdf. The citation is in page 12.

on which there would be some serious reason to claim that they are abortive". The proposal was approved by an overwhelming majority. Consequently, the demonstration or the well-founded suspicion of the abortive effect of contraceptives thus became a question of great moral importance which placed a serious responsibility on the shoulders of the experts of the medical group. They were thus obliged to examine critically the medical literature on the mechanism of action of the contraceptives then in use and then offer to the PC a reasoned opinion on the matter. Obviously, they could not be content with echoing the dominant opinion in society and among practitioners that the pill acted exclusively through an anovulatory effect.

The exclusivity of the anovulatory mode of action of oral contraceptives was a notion of John Rock who defended this concept with extraordinary tenacity[253]. But the "strong" notion of Rock's anovulant effect was a consequence of the high hormonal content of the first-generation pill as the Enovid 10 which caused many users an annoying symptomatology, similar to that presented by many pregnant women in the first months of pregnancy. When, some pharmaceutical laboratories reduced the hormonal content of oral contraceptives[254] in order to avoid these bothersome side effects, it could be observed that in many cases ovulation was not inhibited while the maximum contraceptive efficacy was nevertheless maintained. They had to admit then that the pills with reduced hormonal content not only acted by inhibiting ovulation but also by

---

[253] See, for example, Rock J. The Time Has Come. A Catholic Doctor's Proposals to End the Battle over Birth Control. New York: Alfred A. Knopf, Inc; 1963.

[254] The marketing of the low-hormone pill began in 1963 (Ovulen, Ortho-novum 2 mg) and 1964 (Norlestrin 1 mg, Norinyl 1).

complementary mechanisms, among which was the incompetence of the endometrium for nesting (abortifacient effect) and the densification of the cervical mucus (contraceptive effect). The recognition of the abortifacient effect is demonstrated in a reaction of John Rock: when his colleagues Pincus and Chang asked him to cooperate in the clinical trials of the new pills, Rock strongly refused because he considered them endowed with an abortifacient effect[255].

For reasons easy to understand, the pharmaceutical industry showed no interest in investigating the frequency and fine mechanism of the abortifacient effect of lower-dose oral contraceptives so that the literature on the subject went into eclipse: it turned out to be very scarce and inconclusive. Such behavior did not cause scientific concerns or ethical discomfort among doctors and researchers: the behavior of scientists was then dominated by what could be called the "anovulatory prejudice". The articles and books published in those years systematically repeated that hormonal contraceptives acted as anovulants. The literature of the early 1960s that expressed doubts about the exclusivity of the anovulatory effect or the probability of an anti-nidatory effect fell in oblivion. It was only until many years later that such suspicions were accepted.

In this complex situation, the medical section of the PC was faced with a serious dilemma: either it accepted as a fact the inexistence of the abortifacient effect and informed the PC of such an extreme or it drew the attention of theologians to the suspicion expressed by some authors

---

[255] Lader L. Three Men Who Made a Revolution. New York Times Magazine, April 10, 1966: 8-9, 55-56, 63-64, at 55. Also: Abell B. The Pill. A Biography of the Drug that Changed the World. New York: Random House; 1995: 348-349.

that the pill could act with an undetermined frequency by means of an anti-implantation (abortifacient) mechanism.

From what can be gathered from the information about the sessions of the doctors of the PC, they paid some attention to the matter but they did not seem to have focused in depth and critically the crucial problem of whether the inhibition of implantation was a reality, a fiction, or a serious and founded suspicion. The medical section simply opted for accepting the anovulants effect as sufficient explanation of the efficacy of oral contraceptives and decided not to go deeply into the matter. Consequently, the Holy Father was not warned of the suspected abortifacient effect and was left in ignorance of some crucial information for the moral judgment he wished to perform.

Why did the medical group not respond or could not respond to the expectations placed on it? There is no evidence in the PC documents known until now that a study of the problem was commissioned to any of its members. However, in the sessions of the medical group, some members expressed doubts on anovulation as the only explanation the efficacy of oral contraceptives and suspected that the zygote could be affected by the contraceptive medication during its preimplantation stage[256]. The opinions of Hellegers, the only professor of obstetrics and gynecology at the PC, were particularly important on this issue. In his general information document on contraceptive methods, he noted that "the pill acts by

---

[256] Thus, Gaudefroy said: "It seems that a line that separates the different methods has to be placed on the border of what is not yet a human life and what is already. It is a blurry area in which science does not yet know exactly where the border is to be located." Response of Doctors to Conclusions of Theologians, May 7, 1966.

inhibiting ovulation. Some opinions have been expressed that its efficacy is due to the impenetrability of cervical mucus and the prevention of nesting due to alteration of the endometrium. But there is no scientific evidence today."[257]

In the course of the V session, Hellegers reported that the American College of Obstetricians and Gynecologists had prepared a definition that places implantation as the moment after which an intervention becomes an abortion. He also pointed out that part of the fertilized egg was destined to form the placenta which led him to wonder if the soul infused in fertilization animated the placenta[258]. Hellegers, after recognizing that a sufficient dose of progestins was anovulant but not abortive, said that lower doses did not block ovulation but are capable of preventing pregnancy. He was then interrogated by the moral theologian Fuchs about whether an intervention before implantation was contraceptive or abortive. Hellegers replied that he did not think doctors could answer that question. He added that he agreed that a human life is present after implantation and not before fertilization. The problem lies in the interval between the two (eight days or so). Prudence does not allow us to affirm that there is no life in that phase[259].

Three days later, Hellegers offered a more complete version of his thought. We can observe that there is a split between his moral vision and his scientific opinion. He said: "As to abortifacient actions of method, I would prudentially call abortifacient all actions which lead to the loss of a

---

[257] Hellegers A. Document CBCC 2/06 M-4. Survey of Contraceptive Methods [12] XI. The Pill.

[258] Hellegers A. Report of the Medical Session. The significance of the stages in the development of life. May 4th 1966.

[259] Hellegers A. Ibíd.

fertilized ovum. This is so because the value of life is best protected by placing the starting point there [in fertilization] for the present. Scientifically I am more inclined to place the dividing line at the point where the *conceptus* is divided into fetus and placenta, i.e. at implantation."[260]

7.2.4. The abortifacient effect in the final documents of the PC

In the stories that have been written until now, the role played by biology in the reflections of the PC is usually reduced to inform of the existence of a medical-biological section and of its participation in some meetings of the Commission. The section had as its main function the delivery to the other members of the Commission, especially to the theologians, of an accurate and up-to-date information on two points: the physiology of human reproduction and on the types and effects of contraceptive methods. The very existence of the section is a permanent testimony to Paul VI's interest in biological knowledge as a firm support for the building of a moral teaching on human marriage and contraception[261].

However, Paul VI did not see his expectations fulfilled. Once the encyclical *Humanae Vitae* was published, he was strongly criticized for not making any reference to the biology of human procreation or to modern contraceptives. Among those who expressed that disenchantment with the

---

[260] Hellegers A. Response of Doctors to Conclusions of Theologians, May 7, 1966, p. 12 (emphasis in the original). (From the Marshall's archive).

[261] Paul VI exhorted the members of the CP with these words: "The planes in which your investigation is located are: on the one hand, a better knowledge of the physiological laws, of the psychological and medical data of the demographic movements and of the social overturns; on the other hand and above all, the plane of the superior light that on these events project the data of the Faith and the Church." Paul VI. Allocution à la Commission, cited in note 14 above.

encyclical were some members of the medical-biological section of the PC. In his view, cruelly expressed by Hellegers, all the efforts of the section had been useless and even mocked[262].

As already stated, the topic that dominated the meetings of the doctors was the insistent and detailed consideration of the weaknesses of the rhythm method especially during lactation or premenopause, two important situations in the life of women. In fact, it can not be said that the biology of hormonal contraception was the star theme in the group's work. Certainly, it was the object of considerable attention during some sessions but it hardly occupies a place in the final documents of the PC. It is not even alluded to some of them.

In the final documents of the PC, four writings are understood. On one hand, the summaries that the Secretary of Riedmatten wrote as an informative summary of what was discussed in the sessions of the PC. These are two, namely: the *Relatio Generalis*, destined for the Commission of Cardinals and Bishops[263]; and the *Final Report*, for the

---

[262] "For the scientist the encyclical presents a number of puzzling aspects: in the first place comes the absence of scientific evidence for, or indeed of scientific thought in reaching, the conclusions which the encyclical draws. Secondly, the scientist is struck by the absence of biological considerations in the entire encyclical [...] nowhere acknowledges that there might have been new biological facts of importance discovered since the encyclical *Casti Connubii*. Thus paragraphs 2 and 3 of the encyclical are written as if no biologist had ever been appointed to the Papal Commission. Equally interesting but more ominous in this context is paragraph 6. Here is made clear that nothing that a precedent and future scientists could possibly contribute in terms of scientific data could have any pertinence to the subject, if certain criteria of solutions would emerge which departed from the moral teaching of marriage proposed with constant firmness by the teaching authority of the church." Hellegers AE. A Scientist's Analysis. In: Curran CE. Contraception: Authority and Dissent. New York: Herder and Herder; 1969: 216.

[263] The *Relatio Generalis* can be accessed on the Internet in the Grisez

Holy Father[264]. On the other, the two famous papers, the Reports of the Majority and of the Minority which were leaked to the press in 1967.

The writing of the *Relatio Generalis* and the *Final Report* was almost exclusively the responsibility of de Riedmatten[265]. The *Majority Report* was commissioned by de Riedmatten himself to a group of six theologians (Joseph Fuchs, Raymond Sigmond, Paul Anciaux, Alfons Auer, Michel Labourdette and Pierre de Locht), to serenely and reasonably summarize the dominant position among the members of the PC. The *Minority Report* was written on the initiative of the American Jesuit John Ford who was assisted by Germain Grisez and with the encouragement of Card. Ottaviani. It was presented to the Pope with the signature of the theologians John Ford, Jan Visser, Marcelino Zalba and Stanislas de Lestapis who reviewed the final draft[266].

7.3. The Relatio Generalis

It is a document almost exclusively theological, centered primarily on the consideration about the Church's judgment on the intrinsic malice of contraceptive acts and about the possibility that the Magisterium may issue a new

---

archive: www.twotlj.org/De%20Riedmatten%2020%20June.pdf.

[264] The *Final Report* can also be found at: www.twotlj.org/Final-Report.pdf.

[265] In the letter of reference to the Pope that accompanies the Final Report, de Riedmatten indicates that in application of the Regulations of the PC, he presented the Report in a schematic manner to the President and the Vice-Presidents of the Commission and that after listening to his observations, he was authorized to write the final version of the document. It can be assumed that the same procedure was applied to the Relatio Generalis.

[266] The four commented documents speak "for themselves": they do not include bibliographical references nor guarantee their affirmations using sources of recognized authority, may they be: biblical, magisterial, theological, or, what is of greater interest here, biomedical.

decision on the matter. It deals also with the role that the *Sensus fidelium* has to play in the discernment of the new doctrine and in the determination of the state of doubt about the morality of contraception that seems to reign within the Church. Lastly, it proposes some suggestions on how to present the new doctrine to the People of God and the pastoral problems attached to its practical application.

The biological considerations in this document are minimal and subordinated to its main purpose of advocating before the Cardinals and Bishops of the PC in favor of the reformability of traditional doctrine.

The *Relatio* affirms that the natural ordering of every conjugal act to procreation, reaffirmed by *Casti connubii*, must adapt itself in the framework of responsible fatherhood to the obligation of parents to raise and educate their children with dignity in a harmonious home. On the other hand, spouses need to express their mutual love through the sexual act which is a human act, good and dignified, since it is the object of a free decision. Consequently, the moral demands of sexuality within the framework of responsible fatherhood are not, by principle, of a biological nature; their morality is framed instead by the good of the procreative and responsible marital community. Therefore, it is not acceptable to affirm that such a good –which is higher, more human and more important in the history of the couple's salvation– must be subordinated to the demands of the physiological integrity of the conjugal act.

In addition, the *Relatio* affirms that contraception does not damage the absolute value of the new life, an inviolable element, against which one cannot attempt at any price. The wastage of gametes and the cyclical infertility of women sustain the scientific certitude that most conjugal acts are not ordered to procreation[267]. On the other hand, admitting the morality of periodic continence forces us to accept that man directs through his intervention and his power of decision the procreative force of his life of conjugal intimacy[268]. The morality of the diverse contraceptive methods is to some extent indifferent. In the opinion of many physicians, the chronological intervention characteristic of the rhythm method is the exact analogue of whatever contraceptive mechanical or biochemical intervention.

The *Relatio* does not mention that some members of the PC manifested that some oral contraceptives of low hormonal content and the IUDs, were under suspicion that part of its effectiveness was to be attributed to an abortifacient effect. On the contrary, the *Relatio* states that contraceptives do not violate the absolute value of new life.

---

[267] Arises here the argument that Thomas Hayes presents in his article entitled The Biology of the Reproductive Act, which is discussed later in this book (Hayes and the "reproductive act", in Chapter VIII).

[268] Relatio generalis, p. 8.

7.4. The Final Report

The biological content of the *Report* is broader than that of the *Relatio*. It is guided by the intention of persuading the Pope, to whom the document is addressed, of the need to introduce into the Church a position of greater tolerance regarding contraceptive methods. It includes a first chapter to describe the composition, objectives and work program of the PC. The next chapter deals with the works and conclusions of the theologians. The third chapter is devoted to describing the scientific facts in three sections: medical and biological facts, psychological facts and, finally, demographic and sociological facts. It ends with a final chapter dealing with the final session of the PC (Cardinals and Bishops).

The document affirms that almost all of the experts of the PC, relying on the scientific knowledge acquired in the last thirty years, declared themselves in favor of reforming the magisterial current teaching on contraception. Unanimously, the experts considered it inappropriate to affirm that every conjugal act had to be naturally ordered to procreation since science had shown that only a small proportion of conjugal acts are naturally fertile. Consequently, and contrary to what *Casti connubii* teaches, it seems senseless to affirm that it is immoral to divest the conjugal act from its own natural procreative virtue[269].

The *Final Report* contains a strong condemnation of abortion as a procedure to practice responsible fatherhood because it destroys a human life and has nothing to do with contraception or sterilization. The doctors of the PC discussed the problem on the time from when there exists a human life that could be aborted. In their unanimous

---

[269] Again, we find here Thomas Hayes's theory.

response, they affirmed that it was at the moment when "the fertilized egg could not but become a human being. Certainly, this stage is reached with the implantation and it is not before fertilization. In the interval of about six days between those stages, it reigns, for scientific reasons, the doubt". The doctors of the PC do not explain the reasons or proofs behind such affirmation.

To soften this response, too similar to the proposition formulated shortly before by the experts of the British Council of Churches[270], and in agreement with the theologians of the PC, the doctors proposed, to opt for another solution until more extensive and sounder data are available. Given that the life of a third party could be at stake, they decided that in practice, "human life will be considered to begin with the fertilization of the ovule". The medical group attached great importance to the establishment of the beginning of human life by the wide diffusion of the IUD as a contraceptive, whose mechanism of action was still uncertain, although it was believed that it acted after fertilization.

With regard to hormonal contraceptives, the *Final Report* indicates that the medical group avoided responding to the pressing question of its mechanisms of action and thus contributing to the solution of the theological-moral problem of the lawfulness or illegality of its use.

---

[270] "Our conclusion is that a distinction must be made between biological life and human life and that, in the absence of more precise knowledge, it can be assumed that it is best to choose nesting as an event in which the first becomes the second." Working Party of the British Council of Churches. Human Reproduction. A Study of Some Emergent Problems and Questions in the Light of the Christian Faith. London: British Council of Churches; 1962.

7.5.   The Majority Report

This Report, entitled in Latin *"Schema Documenti de Responsabili Paternitate"*, was delivered to de Riedmatten by the theologians who drafted it on May 26, 1966. It was revised and approved at the Plenary Session of the PC which took place from June 4 to 9.

It is basically a theological document. It includes a few general and abstract allusions to the role that biological science could play in the practical aspects of responsible parenthood, such as, for example, that scientists can design decent and human means of contraception; or that, in accordance with the demands of human nature and the progress of science, it is to be hoped that more and more apt and adequate means may be discovered so the regulation of births can be carried out in a manner worthy of man (Part I, Chap. II, 2). It declares that new knowledge in biology, psychology, sexuality and demography, along with other contemporary events (social changes in marriage and family, and decline in infant mortality, new insights on human sexuality, and, above all, better vision of man's duty to humanize and perfect human life as it is granted by nature), does not contradict either the genuine concept of Christian tradition or the previous doctrinal condemnations (Part I, Chapter III).

The *Report* points out that the interventions on physiological processes to regulate responsible parenthood must respect the essential values of marriage and especially the good of children and must adhere to the fundamental principles and objective criteria of morality. It condemns, in addition, the acts that do not respect the life of the already conceived child, as is the case of abortion and of those interventions raising a serious suspicion of acting as abortive (Part I, Chapter IV).

But, unfortunately, the Report does not enumerate or describe the contraceptive methods then in use nor informs on the mechanisms of their physiological action. Consequently, it falls short of establishing a tentative moral judgment on these procedures. Thus, it leaves unanswered the pressing request Paul VI had forwarded to the PC that was to provide the necessary data that would allow him to establish a magisterial judgment on contraceptives, especially on the pill.

7.6. The Minority Report

Its title in Latin (*Status Quaestionis: Doctrina Ecclesiae eiusque Auctoritas*) is actually the title of its first chapter. It was delivered to the Secretary General of the PC on May 23, 1966, two weeks earlier than the Majority Report. Like this last one, its content is theological. Its first chapter reviews the history of the doctrine on the morality of contraception as it has been established over the centuries, paying attention to the reasons both for the teaching of the Church which states that contraception is always a moral evil as of the immutability of that position in the Church. Finally, it summarizes the recent doctrinal evolution. The report recalls that the Fathers, the theologians and the Magisterium of the Church have always taught that sexual relations and generative processes are in some way especially inviolable precisely because they are generative. This inviolability was always attributed to the sexual act and the generative process which are biological acts or processes; not because they are simply biological, but because they are human, that is, insofar as they are human acts, destined by nature for the good of the human species.

It is in the review of the recent doctrinal evolution that the Report refers to the different types of contraceptive methods. It places the pill among interventions that affect the natural function (opus naturae) without mutilation which acts before the beginning of every new human life. The Report does not allude to the possibility that the pill could act through an abortifacient mechanism which underscores the suspicion that this question was not treated openly in the sessions of the PC. The Minority Report adds that post-fertilization interventions could reignite medieval doubts about whether the animation occurs at the time of fertilization or later, or perhaps when, after nesting, differentiation of the placenta begins and of the embryo. At no time, the Report refers to IUDs.

As can be seen, the minority coincided with the Majority in ignoring the suspicion that the pill could act through an abortifacient effect, an effect that some authors had denounced. Not only does it not take it into account, but it also seems to deny it when it frames the pill between interventions that act before the beginning of a new life. He thus provided an indirect response to Paul VI's request on the mode of action of oral contraceptives.

7.7. Did the Pontifical Commission fulfill the task requested by the Pope?

As already noted, the PC not only varied in the number and condition of its members; it underwent also important changes in the task requested of it by the Pope or in the intermediate objectives assigned to itself by its Secretary General.

The first assignment received –to offer an answer to a United Nations questionnaire– gave rise to the question about what population control policies could be authorized by the Church. In this way, with the consent of the Pope, the PC found itself confronted with the study of birth control methods, both in their technical and theological-moral aspects. This last task raised the question on the reformability of the teachings of the preceding Magisterium of the Church, intensely and lengthly debated, a matter that, logically, did not figure on the agenda of the PC but which turned to be one of its principal concerns.

Thus, the course of the PC's deliberations moved away from its initial objective assigned by the Pope and derived towards theology, both fundamental and moral. Consequently, that unforeseen shift delayed the response urgently requested by the Pontiff who asked only for a multidisciplinary analysis of two contraceptive techniques: that of rhythm, which the Church accepted; and that of oral contraception with steroid hormones (the pill), on which the Pope wished to take a stand. The Pope was under the pressure of the many petitions of Bishops, priests and laymen for an authoritative answer to the question of whether or not it was lawful to use the pill, which had already in that moment an immense popularity.

How the medical-biological Section of the PC did respond to the requests of the Pontiff? To answer this question, it would be necessary to know the whole documentation produced and received by the Section. In the absence of such information, it is only possible to offer some suggestions.

In the first place, one must underline the efforts and the success of the Section in criticizing and even discrediting the method of rhythm. Rhythm enjoyed the approval of the Magisterium along the pontificate of Pius XI and, above all, of Pius XII; certainly nothing was more alien to Paul VI's intention than to offer a negative vision of the morality of the natural methods of birth control. But, curiously enough, the purpose of the PC turned out to be the opposite: it decided to bring into disrepute the rhythm as a trustworthy method and with such purpose it presented not only biological arguments (menstrual cycle variability, high failure rate in the critical times of premenopause and lactation) but also very moving and dramatic sociological testimonies of families and women destroyed for having relied on such an ineffective method. The Section invoked also philosophical reasons to show that the so-called natural methods are in fact artificial because voluntary human intervention (the selection of the days of abstinence) breaks the natural random character of the spontaneous sequence of sexual acts. As seen from the perspective of many members of the PC, the rhythm method was as artificial as pharmacological or mechanical methods.

Logically, the good-will acceptance of so many negative reasons led many commissioners who had entered the sessions with a strong conviction of the effectiveness of the rhythm method and the positive effects it exerted on the human values of marriage to abandon their initial adherence and to recognize that the use of the method could seriously damage relationships between spouses. The rejection of the rhythm method by most of the members of the Section and the whole PC was radical, without nuances, despite the efficiency recognized to the correct practice of the method in many international statistics.

In the second place, it is very likely that the medical-biological Section reached such an extreme position towards natural methods of fertility control with the purpose in mind of preparing a privileged place for the new contraceptive procedures specifically for the pill. That explains the great interest of the Section to emphasize the high biological effectiveness of the pill which, together with its exclusive performance through a supposed anovulatory mechanism and its lack of interference with the conjugal act itself, made hormonal contraception the method of choice.

In the third place, the medical-biological Section discarded as irrelevant the possibility of an abortifacient (antinidatory effect) of the pill, especially when low-hormone pills were used. This circumstance had been pointed out in the medical literature prior to 1966. But in none of the final documents of the PC is there any mention of the anti-implantatory effect of contraceptive methods, although it alluded to, to be cursorily denied in the debates of the Section. Therefore, it is unavoidable to ask for the motive of that silence on a point of the utmost importance for the Pope's moral evaluation of the pill. Was it an involuntary oblivion? or a deliberate concealment? Or a scientific judgment based in available evidence? It was in any case an omission of very serious consequences: the Pope was thus deprived of the knowledge of a particularly significant issue.

Chapter 8. Protagonists in the Shade

In this chapter, attention is paid to four relatively unknown doctors and scientists who played a notable role in diverse aspects of the professional and social acceptance of contraception. Although the specific contributions of each one of them to the 'cause' of contraception differ widely, it must be emphasized that such contributions exerted a remarkable influence in the development and diffusion of contraception into society. The fact that the passage of time has diluted their meaning and reduced it to insignificance is a sufficient and valid reason to recover their memory and to raise a question of historical justice.

8.1. Edward C. Hughes and obstetric-gynecological terminology

The figure of Edward C. Hughes is closely linked to the change of obstetric-gynecological terminology, an event of capital importance in the introduction and acceptance of contraception and abortion in modern society. Hughes' academic career began in 1928 and was spent entirely at the University of Syracuse (later converted into the Upstate Medical University), where in 1944 he became Professor of

Obstetrics, and in 1961 Professor of Obstetrics and Gynecology. His most salient activity developed, however, not in the academic world but in the field of professional associations. In 1951 he was one of the creators of the American Academy of Obstetrics and Gynecology, which soon after was renamed American College of Obstetricians and Gynecologists (ACOG). He chaired the ACOG in the period 1962-1963, and from 1965 he presided over its Terminology Committee[271].

8.1.1. Hughes and his interest in obstetric-gynecological terminology

It is beyond doubt that the terminological changes advocated by Hughes, and specifically the new definitions of conception and gestation, have provoked a remarkable ethical impact not only on the minds and behavior of many physicians but also on a large part of the public.

It seems clear, however, that the intention that guided the first efforts of Hughes in the field of the obstetrical and gynecological vocabulary was educational and professional, rather than ethical. Apparently, his initial intention was not to provoke changes in the dominant ethical status, but simply to create a new nomenclature better adapted to the needs of medical education and the improvements in the statistical studies of the clinical activity[272]. A prime example

---

[271] This biographical information is taken from Mengert WF, Pearse WH. History of the American College of Obstetricians and Gynecologists. The First Quarter Century 1950-1976. Washington; ACOG; 2001: 189-190. It has not been possible to find in the bibliography other data (biography, obituary) about Hughes.

[272] In 1963, Hughes published two articles on prenatal life (Hughes EC. Life in Inner Space, Oxygen and nourishment are primary survival factors for the fetus in utero in inner space and the astronaut in a capsule in outer space. Am J Nurs. 1963; 63: 92-94; and Hughes EC. Comparison of Intrauterine and Outer Space Life, New Physician 1963; 12: 57-59), in which he manifested his wonder at the

to this is found in his inaugural address as President of ACOG in April 1962, when he recommended that teachers in medical schools ought to use uniform terms, so that the results of their educational efforts could not only be better evaluated and compared, but also could help to develop more solid pedagogical principles[273]. He also announced that the ACOG had already begun the pertinent terminological studies in which he was personally involved. Hughes stated finally that it was his intention to create a committee whose purpose was to clarify definitions and nomenclatures as a step towards improving statistical analysis and coding systems[274].

In another article, published shortly thereafter, he referred again to the ACOG's plans to standardize the nomenclature used in the specialty, and announced that a committee to study the problem had been created, whose work was already in progress; and reported that he had discussed the matter with representatives of other agencies interested in having accurate statistics, and who had expressed their support for the project[275].

The Terminology Committee, under the chairmanship of Hughes, produced two publications that deserve a comment. The firstone to note was its Bulletin of

---

physiology of the pregnant uterus, which he compared with a capsule space. According to a final note in the first of these articles, both were based on a talk addressed to nurses delivered in 1962. In it, Hughes agrees with the idea that human life begins with fertilization. He said: "We have all lived in a capsule for at least nine months of our lives, because we think that life begins with the union of the sperm and the oocyte (The Chinese say that their children have, on the day they are born, one year old)."

[273] Hughes EC. To Sow is to Reap. Inaugural Address. Obstet Gynecol 1963; 21: 639-645, at 641.

[274] Ibíd., 644.

[275] Hughes EC. Noblesse Oblige. Obstet Gynecol 1962; 20: 821-825, at 825.

Terminology Number 1, dated 1965, only one sheet printed on both sides, which dealt with the *Terms Used in Reference to The Fetus*[276]. Inserted in the September issue of *Obstetrics and Gynecology* (the journal of the ACOG) the Bulletin was sent to the members of the College "for information and consideration". Its content appeared divided into four sections (Introduction, The Fetus, Stages of Labor, Abortion). Most of the definitions contained in the Bulletin did not offer sensible changes compared to the usual ones then and now. The Introduction welcomed the suggestions that ACOG members would like to send to the Committee, and at the same time informed its readers that it was preparing a series of Bulletins with the definitions of other obstetric-gynecological terms[277]. Although presented under the simple appearance of a loose leaf, the Bulletin introduced, as we shall see, an ethical revolution through the redefinition of some terms.

The second publication, issued in 1972, was the book *Obstetric-gynecologic Terminology*[278], born from the initiative of Hughes. It contained in 731 pages the definitions of nearly 10,000 terms of the obstetric-gynecological specialty, of neonatology and of developmental disorders. At the front of the volume appear the lists of the members of the Committee of Terminology and of the 43 experts who collaborated in the preparation

---

[276] Terms Used in Reference to the Fetus. ACOG Terminology Bulletin No. 1. September, 1965. The authorship appears to correspond to The Committee on Terminology of the American College of Obstetricians and Gynecologists. No place of publication is indicated.

[277] Apparently, the Terminology Committee did not publish any further issue of the Bulletin.

[278] Hughes EC, ed. Obstetric-Gynecologic Terminology with Section on Neonatology and Glossary of Congenital Anomalies. Philadelphia: F.A. Davis Co.; 1972.

of the work. The book presented itself as a very ambitious work. Both the Prologue of M. Newton, then President of the ACOG, and the Preface of Hughes himself, insisted that this modern, uniform and well-defined compilation would serve to enhance the quality and precision of the language used in teaching, statistics and research, and would help overcome communication difficulties present at local, national and international levels. And, what is most important in our context, *Terminology* maintained and reinforced the ethical revolution introduced by the *Bulletin* with its new definitions.

8.1.2. New definitions with ethical implications

The vast majority of the terms contained in *Bulletin* and in *Terminology* are simply technical, in the sense that they lack relevant ethical implications. But this does not happen in the case of a few terms, whose definitions appear endowed with a meaning that is not only new, but ethically highly questionable, for which they deserve special consideration. These terms are 'conception', 'gestation', 'embryo' and 'fertilized egg'. *Bulletin* and *Terminology* offer more or less coincident definitions of each of them. It seems that the Committee when preparing the Bulletin did not give maximum precision to its definitions; so, when the Committee drafted *Terminology,* it was forced to amend and complete what appeared in the *Bulletin*. The corresponding pairs of definitions are transcribed below.

CONCEPTION. *Bulletin* says: "It is the implantation of a fertilized ovum. This definition has been selected deliberately because union of sperm and ovum, cannot be detected clinically unless implantation occurs." The corresponding entry in *Terminology* says simply: "Conception is the implantation of the blastocyst. It is not synonymous with fertilization. SYNONYMOUS:

Implantation."

PREGNANCY. *Bulletin* says: "is the state from conception to expulsion of the products of that conception." For *Terminology*, "it is the state of a female after conception and until termination of the gestation. SYNONYMS: Gestation, Cyophoria, Cyesis, Gravidity."

EMBRYO: *Bulletin* says: "the term applied from the time of implantation until the end of the eighth week, when organogenesis is largely completed". In *Terminology* it is said: "is a term applied to a human fetus from the time of conception until organogenesis is largely completed (10 gestational weeks). Embryo is an embryological term and should not be used for purposes of statistical reporting."

FERTILIZED OVUM: *Bulletin* says "the stage of development from fertilization until implantation at the end of the first week." The term does not appear in Terminology.

The differences that are established between the definitions of 1965 and 1972 deserve a brief remark.

CONCEPTION. For *Terminology*, conception is 'implantation of the blastocyst', which technically improves 'implantation of the fertilized egg' of *Bulletin*. There was no justification offered by *Bulletin* for the radical change implied by the new meaning granted to conception as implantation, and so cancelling the classical equivalence of conception with fertilization. Despite the importance of this change, *Terminology* does not give any justification for the new and misleading decision. To emphasize the new order of things, it insists that conception is not synonymous with fertilization, but with implantation. Logically, the new definition attracted some strong criticism from Rock and Ramsey.

GESTATION. The two versions coincide in affirming that the beginning of pregnancy is implantation. However, they have notable differences in style. *Terminology* is more 'human': it refers to women and the end of pregnancy; *Bulletin* is rather 'zoological', because it designates the fetus and its contents as 'products of conception'.

EMBRYO: *Bulletin* and *Terminology* insist on their disdain for the time before implantation and leave the preimplantation conceptus in a limbo of ignorance: the new being in its first days of development is non-existent. *Bulletin* extends this time until the end of the eighth week, without specifying what measurement (gestational, fetal) it had used; *Terminology* specifies that the embryonic period concludes with the tenth gestational week. Somewhat disappointing is the unjustified claim by *Terminology* that the term embryo should not be used for statistical purposes.

FERTILIZED OVUM. It would be interesting to know the reasons that led the Committee to eliminate this term, the only one that, according to *Bulletin*, made reference to the pre-implantation period. Obviously, with the transfer of the beginning of gestation from fertilization to implantation, the first days of the developing embryo are ethically emptied of meaning. Consequently, the 'fertilized ovum' stage, besides being superfluous, could become embarrassing when dealing with its ethical status. Apparently, the Committee chose to remove the problem by deleting the term. 'Fecundated Ovum' disappeared without leaving traces, although in *Terminology* the terms close related terms 'Zygote', 'Morula' and 'Blastocyst' survived.

8.1.3.   The authority of Hughes' Terminology

The foregoing considerations cause a certain uneasiness, because it is inevitable to suspect that the new meanings assigned to the terms 'conception' and 'gestation' were not motivated by demands of scientific advances or professional efficiency but by the ideological convenience of leaving in the penumbra the abortifacient effect, real or hypothetical, of oral contraceptives and IUDs. No reasons are given for the changes, except the one *Bulletin* offers to justify the new definition of conception (the impossibility of detecting conception clinically unless implantation occurs). It would not be improper to describe the justification adduced as naive.

It should be borne in mind that the new definitions are products, not of the ACOG itself, but of its Terminology Committee. The Committee acted in this case as an autonomous entity under the initiative and direction of its president E.C. Hughes[279]. In fact, contrary to what could be expected, ACOG did not endorse the achievements of the Committee. In fact, the ACOG did not appear in the *Terminology*'s title page. Moreover, after recognizing the tentative and debatable nature of the work, M. Newton, President of the College, in the Prologue he wrote for the bookmerely expressed good wishes for it: "The Executive Commission [of the ACOG] believes that the publication of this book and the discussions that are certain to follow, will eventually get a generally accepted and standardized nomenclature in obstetrics and gynecology."[280]

For his part, in the Preface Hughes tells the story of Terminology as an ambitious endeavor: "Before starting the adventure, the opinions of many obstetricians, gynecologists, statisticians, public health administrators,

---

[279] "The first edition [...] was published in 1972 as a cooperative effort between the Terminology Committee and the F.A. Davis Company publishing house." Mengert WF, Pearse WH. History ..., cit. in note 1.

[280] Newton M. Foreword. Hughes, Op cit, in note 8, p. vii.

medical librarians, state and national health officials, and world-wide authorities from other related organizations and societies were obtained. Meetings were held with maternal welfare committees and state health officers and authorities around the world to obtain their support and suggestions [...] In completing this work, the Committee has winnowed the current literature, textbooks, dictionaries, and all other sources of reference for new terms and for new uses of old terms."[281]

Despite these praises, it is necessary to investigate whether *Terminology* was recognized as an arbitrator of the lexical discrepancies in obstetrics and gynecology. As a dictionary, what authority did it enjoy? It does not seem to have been very strong.

It hardly received applause or censorship on the part of the bibliographical reviewers, since it seems that only one critical appraisal was published in the medical bibliography[282]. Certainly, the book was not very successful among translators as there is only one translation of *Terminology* into a foreign language, the one made in 1975 to Spanish[283].

Hughes' work has not been cited frequently. A search

---

[281] Hughes EC. Preface, Op cit in note 8, pp. ix-x. A very eloquent and laudatory version of the Hughes' Preface was part of a statement to the United States Senate, made by Nolan-Hale, in which the author states that, at the time of the Supreme Court decision Roe vs. Wade on the abortion, perhaps the most authoritative source for the definition of obstetric terms was the Terminology edited by Hughes: Nolan-Haley J. Statement. In: Proposed Constitutional Amendments on Abortion: Hearings before the Subcommittee on Civil and Constitutional Rights of the Committee of the Judiciary, House of Representatives, Ninety-fourth Congress, Second Session. Serial No. 46, Part 1. Washington, D.C.: U.S. Printing Office; 1976: 256.

[282] Coleman HH. Obstetric-Gynecologic Terminology. J Obst Gynecol Neonat Nurs 1973; 2: 71.

[283] Hughes EC. Terminología en Obstetricia y Ginecología. Revisada por J.M. Carrera. Barcelona; Salvat Editores; 1975.

in Pubmed provided a little more than 300 citations accumulated over four decades, citations that correspond mainly to articles on hypertension linked to pregnancy, eclampsia and malformative fetal syndromes.

In what concerns us most directly, the new definitions of conception and pregnancy, it must be concluded that they have been scarcely cited. Those referring to the existence or nonexistence of an abortifacient effect of contraceptives are not very numerous. They appear in articles dealing with the mechanisms of action and can be assigned to two different positions. One is that of those who repeatedly claim that these contraceptives are not abortifacient, argue that they act before implantation and emphasizing that "it is a biological fact that pregnancy begins with implantation and not with fertilization."[284] The other is defended by those who profess that the life of the individual begins with fertilization, so any attack to the human embryo, the same before as after its implantation, is ethically unacceptable.

It seems legitimate to conclude that the authority of *Terminology* is not properly or exclusively scientific. It is rather a social one. It comes from the credit each one wants to give to Edward Hughes and his Committee. It is not, after

---

[284] For example, Grimes DA, Cook RJ. Mifepristone (RU486). An Abortifacient to Prevent Abortion? N Engl J Med 1992; 327: 1088-1089. The authors state that gestation begins when the implantation is complete, and cites Terminology as the authority for such a firm and gratuitous affirmation. But in Terminology that is not said. In the response Grimes and Cook offer a letter to the Editor on the matter (Grimes DA, Cook RJ. Mifepristone (RU486). An Abortifacient to Prevent Abortion? N Engl J Med 1993: 328: 254-355), they show a condescendent attitude towards those who maintain discrepant ideas about the beginning of gestation, stating that their beliefs "can not change the biological process involved." And again, they invoke Terminology as final authority when affirming that the biological fact is that gestation begins in implantation and not in fertilization. But, again, Terminology does not use so energetic language.

all, an independent, public, and institutional authority as someone has proposed[285]. Its strength lies in the quality of the definitions it presents. It would not be legitimate to sustain that *Terminology* is an oracle of the obstetric language, especially in terms with important ethical implications. It never has been a consensual glossary. It is not known if the *Bulletin*'s request for opinions to ACOG members received a statistically significant answer. In fact, many obstetricians disavow the dictum that conception is implantation. According to a relatively recent survey, carried out by Chung et al., the obstetricians and gynecologists who maintain that gestation begins with conception-fertilization are more numerous (57%) than those who believe (28%) that pregnancy starts with implantation (15% were not sure)[286].

8.2. Alan S. Parkes and the simile of the chicken egg

Sir Alan S. Parkes (1900-1990) was one of the most remarkable figures in the 20th century Biology of Reproduction, to which he made important contributions, especially in the areas of endocrinology, cryobiology of gametes and tissues, role of pheromones, and, finally, of comparative physiology. He also devoted a lot of attention to the control of fertility in the human species. He was appointed to the Royal Society at age 33, held the Mary Marshall Chair of Reproductive Physiology at Cambridge, founded and directed major reproductive science journals,

---

[285] Fleming AS. Statement. In: Proposed Constitutional Amendments, cit. above, in note 11: 155.

[286] Chung GS, Lawrence RE, Rasinski KA, et al. Obstetrician-gynecologists' beliefs about when pregnancy begins. Am J Obstet Gynecol 2012; 206: 132.e1-7.

and served on countless committees. He was a great promoter of contraception and actively participated in the population programs of the International Planned Parenthood Federation, the Royal Commission on Population Control and the Advisory Committee of the World Health Organization[287].

8.2.1. The simile of the chicken egg

Parkes, in his purpose of spreading birth control in society, tried very hard to discredit pro-life activists' claim that some contraceptives could act through an abortifacient effect. To this end, he defended the idea that conception and implantation are equivalent expressions that designate the same phenomenon, a concept of which he was one of his most energetic and effective propagators.

For Parkes, the identity between conception and implantation was an indisputable axiom, which did not need to be demonstrated. Supported by this intuition, he firmly rejected the qualification of abortifacient that different authors had applied to certain hormonal contraceptives and intrauterine devices. He had no problem recognizing that these procedures interfered not only with fertilization, but also, and frequently, with implantation. But for him, that did not mean they could be called abortifacients. And what is more, in his view, it was wholly incorrect to label them so, since, according to Parkes, conception was a complex and long process and from which implantation was the final stage. In his mind, anti-implantation agents acted during conception and would have to be recognized as contraceptives.

---

[287] Polge C. Sir Alan Sterling Parkes: 10 September 1900 – 17 July 1990. Biogr Mem Fellows R Soc 2006; 52: 263-283.

It was in defense and clarification of the thesis that the conception includes, as an integral part, the implantation of the fertilized egg where Parkes adduced his analogy of the hen's egg, a simile that he used repeatedly in his articles and lectures in the first half of the 1960s.

He did it for the first time in an article on the threat of overpopulation, published on June 8, 1961 in New Scientist. These were his words: "The *Oxford English Dictionary* is cautiously vague about the meaning of the word conception, but biologically there is little doubt that the word should be applied not to fertilization of the egg, but to nidation, the implantation of the fertilized egg in the uterus, which in Man takes place about a week after fertilization. (A hen is not said to conceive when her egg is fertilized, or to abort when she lays it). According to this view, contraception could properly be exercised up to the time of implantation and would have the very great advantage of being retrospective rather than anticipatory."[288]

Although put in parentheses, as if it were an idea that suddenly comes to mind, the analogy of the hen's egg is presented here as part of an argument that wants to be persuasive, almost evident since it neither arouses doubts nor needs proof. It leads the reader to believe that the proposal to extend the time limit of contraception to implantation is convincing and reasonable.

A few days later, on June 20, 1961, in his Oliver Bird Lecture, Parkes reiterates more firmly the argument: it gives more prominence, strength and extension to the simile of the chicken egg, and highlights the decisive role that the identification of implantation with conception was playing in the acceptance of new forms of contraception: "There is

---

288 Parkes AS. The Menace of Overpopulation. New Scientist 1961; 10: 566-570, at 570.

no generally accepted definition of the word conception, but in my biological view it must refer not to fertilization but to the implantation of the fertilized egg in the uterus. For instance, a hen is not said to conceive when her egg is fertilized, or to abort when she lays it. On this view, contraception can properly be practised up to the time of implantation. This is a most important point because much interesting work is now being carried out on the control of implantation."[289]

The analogy of the hen's egg appears now, not as an example that clarifies, but as the underlying reason for the identification of conception and implantation. In the general discussion of a Seminar on Human Fertility and Population Problems, held in Cambridge, Massachussetts, at the end of 1963, Parkes observed: "The first point here is whether preventing the implantation of an already fertilized egg can strictly be called contraception and that of course depends on what you mean by conception. I have said this before and I shall undoubtedly say it again, that in my view as a biologist, conception means implantation of the fertilized egg and that contraceptive methods therefore can properly be applied up to that stage. I base my opinion on the very simple fact that no one says that the hen conceives when her egg is fertilized or that she aborts when she lays it."[290]

In 1964, Parkes published in the journal *Nature* a summary of his speech delivered a few months before at

---

[289] Parkes AS. Biological Control of Conception. The Fifth Oliver Bird Lecture. J Reprod Fertil 1962; 3: 159-172, at 162. Previously, Parkes had published a summary of his Lecture, in which he makes no mention of his simile (Parkes AS. Biological Control of Conception. Nature 1961; 191: 1256-1257).

[290] Parkes AS. The Biology of Fertility. Discussion. In: Greep RO, ed. Human Fertility and Population Problems. Proceedings of the Seminar Sponsored by the American Academy of Arts and Sciences with the support of the Ford Foundation. Cambridge, Mass: Schenken. Co.; 1963; 238.

the British Association for the Advancement of Science[291], in which he reaffirmed, almost in the same terms, that presented the previous year in the United States. The simile of the chicken egg is constituted in the cornerstone of the ethical legitimization of implantation as the time limit of contraception. "This raises the important question of what constitutes conception in man – the fertilization of the egg or its implantation in the uterus some days later. My own view is that implantation not fertilization constitutes conception, and I base this view on the biological analogy that no one maintains that a hen conceives when her egg is fertilized or that she aborts when she lays it. On this view contraception can properly be exercised up to the time of implantation."[292]

As of 1965, Parkes, for reasons that he did not explained, stopped using the simile of the chicken egg. He continued insisting, however, on the identity of conception and implantation, and tenaciously maintained that implantation's inhibition does not imply ethical problems for the practice of contraception. "I am prepared to argue the point with biologists, bureaucrats, bishops or any others who wish to take issue on the matter."[293] Moreover,

---

[291] Parkes AS. Biological Aspects of the Population Explosion. In: Parkes AS. Sex, Science and Society. Addresses, Lectures and Articles. Annotated by the author and illustrated by A.G. Wurmser. Newcastle upon Tyne: Oriel Press Ltd; 1966: 170-181, in 177.

[292] Parkes AS. Biological Aspects of the Population Explosion. Nature 1964; 204: 320-322, at 321. This is an extensive summary of the speech, delivered in September 1964 before the British Association for the Advancement of Science. It was published later as: Parkes AS. Biological Aspects of the Population Explosion. In: Parkes AS. Sex, Science and Society. Addresses, Lectures and Articles. Annotated by the author and illustrated by A.G. Wurmser. Newcastle upon Tyne: Oriel Press Ltd; 1966: 170-181.

[293] Parkes AS. The Future of Fertility Control. In: Meade JE, Parkes AS. Biological Aspects of Social problems. A Symposium held by the Eugenics Society in

according to Parkes, antinidatory methods had, through ignorance on whether or not a fertilization has taken place, the added "advantage" of deadening the moral responsibility, "so that in any particular occasion it would be impossible to say or not an egg has been fertilized. In my view it would be entirely wrong to apply the words 'abortifacient', 'abortion' or 'miscarriage' to such a situation."[294]

"On a more philosophical plane, with the use of the IUD it is not known in any particular cycle whether an egg has been fertilized or not, because the menstrual rhythm is not disturbed, and I do not think you can abort a hypothetical embryo."[295]

October 1964. Edinburgh: Oliver & Boyd; 1965: 205-212, in 210.

[294] Parkes AS. Biological Aspects of the Control of Human Fertility. The Practitioner 1965; 194: 455-462.

[295] Ibíd., 209.

8.2.2. Is the Parkes simile scientifically sustainable?

As the quotes collected above show, Parkes did not offer any biologically based evidence in favor of his assertions. He limited himself to proposing it as something obvious. He tried, however, to support it with the authority of general biological science *per se* and the weight of his expertise in the field. From this it can be deduced that the Parkes analogy, not being sustained by objective evidence, must be considered as a mere argument of authority. Probably, Parkes created his simile as a brilliant improvisation, not devoid of humor, and capable of winning the adhesion not only of many of his readers, but of himself, as evidenced by the repeated publication of the analogy over a five-year period.

In science, however, an authority-based argument is not valid in itself. It is valid insofar as it is congruent with the science of the time; otherwise, it would risk becoming a case of illegitimate use of authority. It is required, therefore, to pose the question: did the Parkes simile agree with the science of human reproduction of the 1960s?

The answer to that question is negative. In the first place, the simile is a trick. It is not, as it might seem, a pedagogical resource that clarifies the problem under consideration. It is a rhetorical clause that distracts the attention of the listener or reader and leaves the problem unclear. Secondly, the Parkes' comparison does not seem legitimate from a scientific perspective. In fact, it ignores the basic difference that exists between the internal gestation of mammals and the oviparity of birds. When he states that it is not said of a chicken that conceives when its egg is fertilized, or that it aborts it when it is laid, Parkes seems not to have paid due attention to certain traits that differentiate avian and human reproduction. In general terms, the expressions 'conception', 'gestation' and 'abortion' (or parturition) apply exclusively to the reproduction of mammals; they are strange and inappropriate when they are applied to the reproduction of birds. There is in the birds internal fertilization of the oocyte, as there is in mammals; there is formation of envelopes (albumen, shell membranes, shell and cuticle) along the migration of the egg through the different sectors of the oviduct, the uterus and the vagina, and, finally, there is followed by the external incubation; but there is no conception (in the original sense of retention in the genital tract), nor implantation, nor placentation, nor intrauterine development, which are necessary prerequisites for talking about abortion as the interruption of pregnancy. The processes in mammals and birds are so different that it is not possible to establish equivalences or homologies.

There is, however, a detail that should be noted and that corroborates the unsustainable nature of the equation "conception is equal to implantation", as well as the inappropriateness of the Parkes simile. In the hen, internal fertilization is not followed by diapause, but immediately gives place to the starting of the embryonic development (segmentation, blastulation, formation of the endoderm), stages that are carried out during the hours of the transit of the egg (embryo) along the genital tract (oviduct, uterus, vagina and cloaca), a development that occurs without implantation. At the time of laying the fertilized egg, i.e., the embryo has already reached a stage close to gastrulation, so that the primitive streak is fully formed at 16 hours of external incubation[296].

---

[296] Patten BM. The Early Embryology of the Chick, 4th ed. New York: McGraw-Hill Book Co; 1951: 58-59.

The simile of the chicken egg had a short life. As previously stated, it was abandoned by Parkes without giving us his reasons. Probably he realized that his brilliant witticism suffered from an extreme logical and scientific weakness.

8.3. Thomas L. Hayes and the "reproductive act"

Biophysicist Thomas Hayes was an important "character in the shade". He barely appeared in public in the Catholic debate on contraception. But, as shown below, he exerted a very important influence on the Papal Commission by means of an article in which he introduced a new concept (that of "the reproductive act", as opposed to "the singular sexual act") with which the author intended to discredit the moral doctrine about sexuality based on the natural law that the Church professed.

8.3.1. The story of Maurovich

On July 25, 2013, the day of the 45th anniversary of the Encyclical Humanae Vitae, Frank Maurovich revealed an unpublished story[297]. One day in 1964, in his editor's office of *The Catholic Voice*, the weekly newspaper of the Diocese of Oakland, California, he was visited by Thomas Hayes, a biophysicist from the neighboring University of California at Berkeley. Hayes told him that he had the solution to the problem of birth control in the Church, which he went on to explain briefly. Maurovich was convinced by the arguments

---

[297] Maurovich F. Humanae Vitae at 45: A Personal Story. Nat Cath Reporter 2013 Jul. 25, 2013. Accessible at:

https://www.ncronline.org/news/vatican/humanae-vitae-45-personal-story.

of the scientist and thought it was necessary to make them reach the Papal Commission for the Study of Birth, Population and Family (PC). He asked Hayes to draft his ideas in an article to be published in a national magazine. Maurovich mediated for the Hayes manuscript, entitled *The Biology of the Reproductive Act*, to be accepted for publication in the Fall 1965 issue of *Cross Currents*[298] magazine, and immediately sent it, through some contacts, to Cardinal Suenens. The Cardinal passed the article to the Executive Committee of the PC[299], which found it so interesting that, according to Maurovich's testimony, sent an invitation to Hayes to visit Malines to discuss the article. The meeting took place in March 1966[300].

Hayes's article, it must be admitted, went virtually unnoticed both among the general public and the cultivators of the biological sciences or moral theology. In 1965, the magazine *Cross Currents* had a reduced diffusion. It does not appear that the republication of the article two years later in the magazine *Insight*[301] contributed much to its wider dissemination. A thorough search on the Internet confirms this[302]. It exercised, however, as shown below, a

---

[298] Hayes TL. The Biology of the Reproductive Act. Its Application to Various Methods of Birth Control. Cross Currents 1965; 15: 393-406.

[299] The Executive Committee of the PC was formed by the Dominican Henri de Riedmatten, Secretary, and two of its members: Canon Pierre de Locht, a theologian from Brussels, and Dr. John Marshall, neurologist from London.

[300] Maurovich, op. cit.

[301] Hayes TL. The Biology of the Reproductive Act. Insight 1967; 6: 12-19. This article was reprinted in a special issue dedicated to birth control, as indicated by Springer RH. Current Theology. Notes on Moral Theology: July-December, 1967. Theol Stud 1968; 29: 275-300, at 292.

[302] Hayes's article was not recorded by Medline Plus. Google Acholar incluyes two citations only: one of them (Léonard, 1976) is about a marginal point; the other, (Hilgartner CA, Randolph JF. Psycho-logics: An axiomatic system describing human behavior, J Theoret Biol 1969; 23: 285-338) seems to be a false

notable impact on the deliberations and conclusions of the PC. According to Maurovich's view, the influence of Hayes's article could have been much greater, since it offered the CP arguments capable of changing the traditional doctrine about contraception. In particular, they could make it "virtually impossible for Pope Paul to ignore changing the Church's current birth control policy, or conversely, if used today, make it relatively easy for Pope Francis to correct the church's second "Galileo affair"."[303]

8.3.2.   Hayes' thesis

In order to appreciate Maurovich's praiseworthy judgment, it is important to evaluate the ideas that Hayes included in his article. The content of this is complex but, in what it concerns here, it seems sufficient to limit these considerations to its concept of the "reproductive act" as a biological and moral unit for judging the various methods of birth control. The new concept is proposed to replace the "act of sexual relationship", which until then had played that role.

Hayes does not offer a formal definition of the reproductive act but implies that it comprises the whole set of component acts (male, female, co-sexual) that are required for fertilization to take place. Given the periodicity with which the ovary releases fertilizable oocytes, the reproductive act usually takes a month to complete. Thus understood, this act may include a more or less elevated number of acts of sexual intercourse, each and every one of which is subordinated to the corresponding reproductive act. This one is, according to Hayes, the one that properly

---

attribution.

[303] Maurovich, op. cit.

tends to procreation as to its natural end, and therefore has a reasonable probability of achieving it. On the contrary, most acts of sexual intercourse, distributed randomly throughout the menstrual cycle of the woman, lack such probability, do not tend *per se* to reproduction, since they occur mostly when there is no oocyte susceptible to be fertilized, only a small number of acts of sexual relationship tend to reproduction. They are those performed in the few days of the cycle in which an oocyte is available and can be fertilized[304].

Hayes maintains that when the human free will intervenes to limit the performance of the sexual act to the infertile periods, the rhythm method ceases to be a natural method and becomes a procedure of artificial contraception. At the beginning of his article Hayes announces that in the light of his concepts of the reproductive and sexual act, the rhythm method is not distinguishable from other methods of birth control (diaphragm, coitus *interruptus*, condom, anovulatory pill). For this reason, Hayes arrives at the decisive conclusion that the rhythm method, because it lacks biological naturalness, can not be considered as a natural method of birth control.

8.3.3. Hayes and the Papal Commission

Maurovich laments that Hayes's article had gone almost unnoticed among the members of the PC[305]. An

---

[304] For Hayes, this random nature is of paramount importance to establish the somewhat artificial nature of the natural methods of birth control authorized by the Church: "Randomness in the realization of physical union under natural conditions is a real part of the sexual relationship. The alteration of that random temporary program constitutes a human act that can alter the result of the reproductive act." Hayes, op. cit, p. 395.

[305] Maurovich writes: "In all honesty, however, since no other commission member made mention of the female cycle or its consequences, it is quite possible

attentive reading of the Minority Report reveals, however, that Hayes's ideas are unmistakably included in it, which proves that they were taken into serious consideration by at least some members of the PC[306]. Hayes' proposal appears, although nuanced, in the Majority Report[307]. The documentation of the PC records that Cardinal Suenens divulged the Hayes article among the members of the CP, at least among those of the medical group[308].

On the other hand, it seems clear that the concepts of Hayes were included in the two documents of the highest

---

that Hayes' paper never made it from Malines to general circulation among commission members. Then again, perhaps his paper was a victim of information overload and ended up buried in the 12-volume commission material given to Pope Paul along with the Final Report." Maurovich, op. cit.

[306] The Minority Report reads: "Some say that the teaching of the Church was founded on the false supposition that all conjugal acts are procreative by their very nature, whereas the facts of physiology show that very few of them are actually fertile or productive of new life. In answer to this, it must be said that the older thinkers knew that many conjugal acts are actually sterile, e.g., during pregnancy and old age. Moreover, a legitimate conclusion from the facts now known would be this: there are fewer acts which are as a matter of fact capable of producing new life; therefore, there are fewer acts against which a person in acting contraceptively would incur the specific malice of contraception. But the facts do not invite us to intervene contraceptively, now that we have a more accurate knowledge about fertility; rather they invite us to have a greater respect for them." To be found in: http://endowgroups.org/wp-content/uploads/2012/10/HV-Minority-Papal-Commission-Report.pdf.

[307] "[…] the morality of sexual acts between married people takes its meaning first of all and from the ordering of their actions in a fruitful married life, that is one which is practiced with responsible, generous and prudent parenthood. It does not then depend on the direct fertility of each and every particular act." Majority Papal Commission Report. Ibíd., 149-173.

[308] "Cardinal Suenens then drew attention to an article by Thomas Hayes that saw the reproductive act as a series of acts over a period." When the paper by Hayes was discussed in the meeting of the medical group, Hellegers praised its content and, in particular, the notion that the use of the rhythm method interfered with the random succession of sexual acts; Marshall, on the other hand, criticized Hayes concept, since in his opinion the reproductive act should include not only the time necessary for conception, but also the time required for gestation and lactation. Report of the Medical Session, 2nd May 1966.

level produced by the PC. They are the final reports that Riedmatten wrote as a summary of what was presented in the communications and discussions held: the *Relatio generalis*, for the Commission of Cardinals and Bishops[309], and the *Final Report* delivered to Pope Paul VI[310]. Logically, neither of them expressly mentions Hayes' article, since the documents of the PC do not include direct references to works and authors, except those from Scripture, the Magisterium or the Holy Fathers. But the coincidence between the ideas that Hayes expressed in his article and those that are present in the *Relation* and the *Report* of the Secretary general of the PC is so remarkable that any reasonable doubt about the connection between them could be easily dissipated. For example, the most revealing text is practically identical in both Final Reports, where it is not difficult to identify the unmistakable ideas of Hayes (highlighted in italics) enveloped into Riedmatten's rhetoric and persuasive exposition:

"In contraception, where is the inviolable element, the absolute value against which it cannot proceed at any price? Modern science teaches us that nature squanders sperm and oocytes. The cyclical infertility of women forbids us to affirm scientifically today that most conjugal acts are naturally ordered to procreation. What life is being talked about when *vita in fieri* is mentioned to characterize the good that has to be protected against any contraceptive intervention? In most cases, none. If things are examined in the light of contemporary science, it would not be more

---

[309] de Riedmatten H. *Relatio generalis*, presented to the Commission of Cardinals and Bishops the 20th June 1966.

[310] de Riedmatten H. Report Final des Travaux de la Commission Pontificale pour l'étude des problèmes de la famille, de la population et de la natalité, presented to the Pope Paul VI the 27th June 1966.

than a very distant preparation. In other words, where it was believed with confidence to be before an *"intentio naturae"*, a complex reality is discovered which is still formless, morally indifferent in itself. That [reality] is given to man so that, as a good administrator of his body and of his organic functions, he makes it serve the human good of the person: of his own, of his spouse, of the children born or to be born. Many add here that from the day when the moral correctness of periodic continence was admitted, it was admitted that man directs, through his intervention and his power of decision, the procreative force of his life of conjugal intimacy. For many doctors, on the other hand, a chronological intervention is exactly the analogue of a mechanical or biochemical intervention."[311]

Nor is it difficult to find Hayes ideas reflected, albeit somewhat veiled, in the Majority Report, when it affirms that "the morality of sexual acts between married people takes its meaning first of all and specifically from the

---

[311] The original French in pp. 13-14 of the Final Report (in p. 9 of the Relatio) reads so: "Dans la contraception, par contre, où se trouve l'élément inviolable, la valeur absolue contre laquelle on ne saurait procéder à aucun prix? La science moderne nous apprend que la nature gaspille sans compter les spermatozoïdes et les ovules. L'infécondité cyclique de la femme défend de parler scientifiquement aujourd'hui pour la plupart des actes conjugaux, d'actes naturellement ordonnés à la procréation. On mentionne la "vita in fieri" pour caractériser le bien à protéger contre toute intervention contraceptive. Mais il n'y a pas de vie dans la plupart des cas, il ne se prépare aucun devenir. En d'autres termes, là où on croyait être à coup sûr devant une "intentio naturae", on découvre une réalité complexe, encore informe, indifférente moralement d'elle-même.' Elle est, comme tant d'autres, donnée à l'homme pour que, bon administrateur do son corps et de ses fonctions organiques, il les fasse servir au bien humain de toute la personne. La sienne, celle de son conjoint, celle des enfants nés ou à naitre. Beaucoup ajoutent ici que du jour où on admettait la licéité de la continence périodique, on admettait que l'homme règle par son intervention et son pouvoir de décision la force procréatrice de sa vie d'intimité conjugale. Pour de nombreux médecins également, une intervention chronologique est exactement l'analogue d'une intervention mécanique ou biochimique."

ordering of their actions in a fruitful married life, that is one which is practiced with responsible, generous and prudent parenthood. It does not then depend upon the direct fecundity of each and every particular act."[312]

In these words, the ideas of Hayes came to the knowledge of the Commission of Cardinals and Bishops and, finally, to that of the Pope. In the Final Report that Riedmatten delivered to the Supreme Pontiff, Hayes's thesis is used as a starting point for two proposals of great importance. The first, that of depriving the singular conjugal acts of substantive ethical meaning and reducing them to the condition of epiphenomena morally subsumed in the inclusive reproductive act. The second, to declare that there is no moral distinction between natural methods of birth control and artificial methods, whether mechanical or chemical.

Both proposals clashed heads with the doctrine until then proclaimed by the Magisterium of the Church, which is the reason why they presented to Paul VI this disjunctive seemingly without exit. The Pope would have to choose between ignoring the voice of science and maintaining the current doctrine on contraception or accepting the opinion of scientists and abandoning the condemnation that the Church had up to then. This had been ratified by Pius XI in *Casti connubii*[313], and reaffirmed twenty years later by Pius XII[314].

----

312 Papal Commission Majority Report. Chapter II: Responsible Parenthood and the Regulation of Conception.

[313] "Any use of marriage, in which maliciously remains the act destitute of its own natural procreative virtue, goes against the law of God and against the natural law, and those who commit such, are guilty of a serious crime." Pius XI, Litt Encycl Casti Connubii, 31 dec 1930. Acta Apost Sedis 1930; 22: 560.

[314] "Any attack by the spouses in the performance of the conjugal act or in

8.3.4.   Hayes after the Humanae vitae

Excluding its anonymous influence on the PC, Hayes's article would have gone unnoticed if it had not been invoked as an argument in the debates that followed the publication of the Encyclical *Humanae Vitae*. As it is well known, Paul VI reformulated in his encyclical with reinforced energy the traditional doctrine of the Church on the matter: that any marital act should be open to the transmission of life.

It is interesting to observe the increasing strength with which the successive texts of the Magisterium expressed the moral condemnation of contraception, especially from *Casti connubii* onwards. In his letter, Pius XI declared that "any use of marriage (*quemlibet matrimonii usum*), in which maliciously remains the act destitute of its own natural procreative virtue, goes against the law of God and against the natural law, and the ones they commit, they are guilty of a serious crime."[315] Pius XII interpreted this text in his famous 1951 address to the midwives, concluding that contraception is intrinsically immoral: "all attempts by spouses in the performance of the conjugal act or in the development of its natural consequences, an attempt to deprive it of the inherent force to prevent the procreation of a new life, is immoral; and no 'indication' or necessity can change an intrinsically immoral action into a moral and lawful act."[316] Finally Paul VI *in Humanae vitae* reaffirms the

---

the development of its natural consequences, an attempt to deprive it of the inherent force and prevent the procreation of a new life, is immoral." Pius XII. Speech to the Congress of the Italian Catholic Union of Midwives, 29 Oct 1951.

[315] Pius XI. Littera Encyclica Casti Connubii. Acta Apost Sed 1930; 22: 560.

[316] Pius XII. Discorso alle Partecipanti al Congresso della Unione Católica Italiana Ostetriche. In: Discorsi e Radiomessaggi di Sua Santità Pio XII. Vol. 13: 333-353.

doctrine with new force, formulating it in the affirmative sense, when he says that the Church "teaches that it is necessary that any use of marriage remain open to the procreation of human life."[317]

Detractors of the encyclical tend to offer a radicalized version of this reaffirmation of Paul VI and do not hesitate to describe it as absurd, when contrasting it with the ideas of Hayes. They assign to the Pope the notion that every conjugal act must be *de facto* open to fertilization which, in their view, only takes place in the reproductive act defined by Hayes. But in reality, what Paul VI affirms is simply that the use of marriage must be open to procreation. Critics of the encyclical turn the moral requirement of the Pontiff into a physiological one, to which the encyclical does not even allude, or accuse the encyclical of being based on a naturalistic and biologistic interpretation of natural law[318].

A text by Hellegers expresses with extreme vividness the strong physicalist, or rather physiological, inclination of Paul VI's critics. In an interview given a few months after the publication of *Humanae Vitae*, Hellegers argued: "The biology of the encyclical has not been thoroughly thought. It says that the conjugal act *should* always be open to the transmission of life, and then ask us to perfect a method -

---

[317] This is the most literal translation of the official Latin text of point 11 of the encyclical Humanae vitae, 1968, which says: "Ecclesia [...] docet necessarium esse, ut quilibet matrimonii usus ad vitam humanam procreandam per se destinatus permaneat."

[318] Rhonheimer has highlighted the errors (interpretative and moral theological) of the critics of the encyclical and clarifies that it does not teach, as they claim, that the biological patterns inherent in the human generative faculty have normative value, so that never they can be broken. Rhonheimer M. Ethics of Procreation & The Defense of Human Life. Contraception, Artificial Fertilization, and Abortion. Ed. By WF. Murphy Jr. Washington, DC: Catholic University of America Press; 2010: 40. Also: Pardo JM. Rationality of Openness to Life and Contraception. Scripta Theol 2009; 41: 113-141.

that of rhythm- closed to the transmission of life. This implies that when a woman is sterile, the marriage act is open to the transmission of life. That is not true. When there is no oocyte that can be fertilized, the act is closed to reproduction. How to explain why a sexual act that can not generate a child is a sexual act open to the transmission of life? A scientist would say that it is closed. And we ask: why is a sterile act fertile, why is a closed act open?"[319] Finally, Curran incurs the same position in a book published in 1969. Besides accusing the encyclical of being based on an obsolete biology, he resorts to Hayes as a scientific arbiter: "The conception can not occur unless a sperm is able to fertilize an oocyte. But the fertilizable oocyte is only present in the woman during a comparatively short time of the menstrual cycle. From a biological point of view, many acts of sexual intercourse are not truly open to procreation, since no oocyte is present. Perhaps, as one author suggests, the natural law in this matter would require the randomization of sexual acts, a principle that would be specifically violated by rhythm."[320]

Humanae vitae has been accused both of ignoring the biology of human sexuality, and of relying on a naturalist and biologist interpretation of natural law. Hellegers has been particularly energetic in this regard, when he points out the "absence of scientific evidence for, or indeed of scientific thought, in reaching the conclusions which the

---

[319] From an interview with Hellegers published in a report entitled Catholics and Their Agony over Birth Control Issues. Look Magazine, Dec.10, 1968. The quotation is taken from Dvorak J. Natural Family Planning and the Christian Moral Code, which can be accessed at:

http://lapidesclamabunt.angelfire.com/nfpwinters.htm.

[320] Hayes's article is cited for this purpose by Curran et al.: Curran CE, Hunt RE, and the "Subject Professors" with Hunt JF and Connelly TR. Dissent In and For the Church. Theologians and Humanae Vitae. New York: Sheed & Ward; 1969: 165.

encyclical draws"; the "absence of biological considerations in the entire encyclical [...] as if no biologist had ever been appointed to the Papal Commission"; and "that nothing that a present or future scientist could possibly contribute in terms of scientific data could have any pertinence to the subject, if certain criteria or solutions would emerge which departed from the moral teaching of marriage proposed with constant firmness by the teaching authority of the Church."[321]

At the same time and paradoxically, the encyclical has been accused of professing a physicalist (or rather, physiological) view of sexual relationships in marriage, with its excessive emphasis on the biological aspects of those relationships as ethically normative[322].

8.4. Raymond T. Holden and the activation of the Resolution of 1937

As has been told previously, the Resolution adopted in 1937 by the AMA in Atlantic City, was left unfinished: the responses of the various Committees from which specific reports were required were never received. In consequence, the Resolution could not be ratified, and what is more, it was partially retracted in the AMA Session held in San Francisco in 1938. Despite such serious irregularities, the 1937 Resolution received the adhesion of many members of the AMA who in the following years adopted the Resolution's criteria in their contraceptive practice, cautiously in the early 1940's, regularly in the 1950's, and

---

[321] Hellegers AE. A Scientist's Análisis. In: Curran CE, ed. Contraception: Authority and Dissent. New York: Herder and Herder; 1969: 216-237, in 216.

[322] Latkovic, MS. Is the Teaching of Humanae Vitae Physicalist? A Critique of the View of Joseph A. Selling, Linacre Quart 1995; 62: 39-58.

almost massively after the approval of Enovid by the FDA in 1960. In this way, the Resolution of 1937, despite its obsolescence, was for almost thirty years a kind of blank check for the practice of contraception. In fact, for all these three decades, contraception was a free medical activity, non-regulated by the organized profession.

8.4.1. The Human Reproduction Committee

To overcome this anomalous situation and aware of the problems posed by the accelerated population growth and perceiving the important role that the doctor was called upon to play as a counselor in the sphere of human reproduction, the AMA created a new Committee in 1964 with the task of preparing, in view of the resolutions previously adopted by the AMA on the subject, a new declaration on contraception and other aspects of human reproduction[323].

The new committee was called the Human Reproduction Committee (HRC). Among its members,

---

[323] AMA Proceedings. House of Delegates Miami Beach, Florida. 18th Clinical Convention, Nov 30-Dec 2, 1964. New Committees of the Board of Trustees: 27. The previous Committee on Contraceptive Practices had been dissolved by the AMA's Council in 1948. It was typical of the AMA Committees to include among their members doctors, who, although not outstanding in the academic or institutional world, were experts in the matter that the Committee had to consider, beside other doctors who were not experts, but who enjoyed public prestige. Those on the Human Reproduction Committee were of proven pro-contraceptive attitude, apart from their President, Raymond Holden, four other members: C. Lee Buxton, who had played a decisive role in the annulment of the restrictive legislation on contraception in Connecticut and that opened the first Planned Parenthood clinic in that state; Mary S. Calderone and Janet T. Dingle, who held high positions in Planned Parenthood; and H. Close Hesseltine. The other members were George M. Fister, urologist, who had just finished his term as President of the AMA; Henry D. Lederer, psychiatrist, who had been associate director of the National Institute of Mental Health and Dean of the School of Medicine at Georgetown University; and Mark H. Lepper, professor of preventive medicine and infectious diseases at Rush Medical College, Chicago.

predominated those who had already shown their support for the spread of contraceptive practices, starting with its president, Raymond T. Holden[324], an active supporter of fertility control, since he was convinced that the accelerated rate of population growth in the world was terrifying.

The HRC set for itself as its main objective the redaction and distribution among the members of the AMA of a publication that described and updated the methods of fertility control then in use. The initial project intended to give the book the form and extension of a manual dealing with "all phases, methods and aspects of reproductive control." The final product was, however, as far as its extension is concerned, well below what was projected, reduced to the modest dimensions of a review article, which was approved by the Board of Directors of the AMA and its House of Delegates in the Clinical Convention of Miami Beach (November 1964)[325]. This approval was considered a historical milestone that marked the change of the AMA policy with respect to human reproduction and demography. From a neutral position and strictly limited to medical practice, the Association went on to declare itself an active and concerned agent for economic and social problems.

The referred article, entitled *The Control of Fertility,*

---

[324] Raymond T. Holden (1904-2007) worked as an obstetrician in several hospitals in Washington and acted as a teacher at Georgetown University. He was very active in the AMA from whose Board of Directors he became a member. Some biographical data can be seen in Sullivan P. Raymond T. Holden, 102; Longtime District Obstetrician. Washington Post, March 22, 2007.

[325] AMA's Committee on Human Reproduction. The Control of Fertility. JAMA 1965; 194: 462-470. It was published also as Exhibit 22, in: Population Crisis. Hearings Before the Subcommittee on Foreign Aid Expenditures of the Committee on Government Operations. United States Senate, Eighty-Ninth Congress, Second Session on S. 1676. Washington: U.S. Government Printing Office; 1966: 135-147

was published shortly after in the JAMA[326]. It was addressed exclusively to members of the Association, since it was not part of the duties of the AMA to promote educational programs on sexuality or birth control aimed at the general public. Such an education was the individual responsibility of the doctors, while the role of the Association was to provide sufficient information to its associates[327].

In its first paragraphs, *Control of Fertility* defines the principles, certainly ambitious if not utopian, that the AMA will respect in the following matters[328]. Namely, that the control of the population should not be considered simply as a responsible parenthood problem, but also as a matter of responsible medical practice; that the medical profession has to adopt a serious attitude with respect to human reproduction, as it affects the entire population as well as the individual family; that the doctor must offer advice and guidance at the demand of his or her patients, or refer them to an appropriate counselor; that the AMA assumes the responsibility to disseminate information among physicians and by the most appropriate means concerning all phases of human reproduction, including sexual behavior.

The following year, *Control of Fertility* was reproduced in its entirety in the documentation of the hearings held in the United States Senate on the crisis of the population[329].

---

[326] Committee on Human Reproduction. The Control of Fertility. JAMA 1965; 194: 462-470.

[327] Medical News. AMA's Population Control Program Keyed to Physician Role as Counselor. JAMA 1965; 191: 31-33, in 31.

[328] The general press registered explicitly the new AMA's policy on contraception. See, for example, Bruner R. Neutral Stand Dropped. Doctors to Aid in Population Curbs. The Blade, Ohio, January 22, 1965: 5.

[329] Population Crisis. Hearings Before the Subcommittee on Foreign Aid Expenditures of the Committee on Government Operations. United States Senate, Eighty-Ninth Congress, Second Session on S. 1676. Part 1. Exhibit 22. "The Control

Despite the important institutional support received, the document did not get much resonance judging by the number of citations it got[330].

A second assignment made to the CRH by the Board was the preparation of a teaching program that would serve as a guide to educate medical students about human reproduction. The document was sent to the Medical Education Council of the AMA and to the deans and department heads of all medical schools in the United States. Given the silence of the recipients, no further decisions were made on this matter. This teaching guide was not published in the JAMA although, as happened with the Control of Fertility, Holden referred to it when he deposed before the Senate Commission on Population Crisis. The Commission's President decided to include it in the corresponding minutes, thanks to which we know today about this document[331]. It offers an exhaustive list of the topics that the different disciplines of the medical curriculum could include in their lessons in order to promote the most complete education of students on human reproduction. It does not contain, however, a single allusion to the ethical aspects of the subject.

With the publication of *Control of Fertility* and other recommendations of lesser importance, the process of

---

of Fertility," a monograph prepared by the AMA Committee on Human Reproduction. Washington: U.S. Government Printing Office; 1966: 135-147.

[330] Surprisingly, Control of Fertility was not included in Medline (now Pubmed). It appears with confusing authorship in Google Scholar, where no mention is made of the fact that it has never been cited in the biomedical literature.

[331] Population Crisis, op. cit. Exhibit 21. Inclusion of Basic Material to the Physician's Professional Role in Problems of Human Reproduction in the Undergraduate Medical Curriculum. Washington: U.S. Government Printing Office; 1966: 132-135. This Government publication is the only that reproduces the study of the CRH.

acceptance by the AMA of the contraceptive practices and their dissemination among physicians could be terminated[332]. It was a long task, which, with various alternatives, the Association had sponsored from 1937. But, for various reasons, the Control of Fertility did not achieve the desired objectives. The CRH was criticized for not being properly multidisciplinary, since, for example, it did not include any endocrinologist among its members, while hormonal contraception directly involves the endocrine system[333]. The HRC was also accused of lack of objectivity because, perhaps overly concerned to highlight the benefits of oral contraception, he referred in silence to the adverse phenomena attributed to oral contraceptives, including circulatory and metabolic disorders. Holden himself acknowledged that there was not enough emphasis on the unwanted effects of the contraceptives, because in the CRH they considered that the approval of the FDA was sufficient to guarantee the safety of the 'pill'[334].

8.4.2. Contraception and Catholic conscience

Once again, the problem which affected many Catholic doctors (such as Kosmak, Rock, Hellegers and many others), on how to make their Catholic faith compatible and their

---

[332] The Resolutions of the AMA were addressed exclusively to physicians, since it was not part of the Association's functions to offer directly such information to the general public, or to initiate programs on sexual and contraceptive education aimed at non-physicians. AMA's Population: 31

[333] Mintz M. Are Birth Control Pills Safe? In: Katz J, ed. Experimentation with Human Beings. The Authority of the Investigator, Subject, Professions and State in the Human Experimentation Process. New York: Russell Sage Foundation 1972: 751-754, in 752-753.

[334] In *Control of Fertility*, p. 232, when dealing with the mechanism of action of oral hormonal contraceptives, it is stated somewhat cryptically: "The associated production of a hostile cervical mucus or the acceleration of endometrial changes may also be factors of antifertility."

professional medical attitude favorable to contraception is repeated here. It was well known that Holden, though divorced and remarried, was a Catholic and professed himself as such. He could not ignore, therefore, the teaching of the Catholic Magisterium on contraception. In addition, he knew that an abortifacient effect of oral contraceptives could not be excluded. As President of the CRH he wished "to find methods that are acceptable in a human sense, and acceptable also to the various religious and ethnic groups."[335]

From these words of Holden, it follows that he did not lack good intentions, even though they might seem somewhat utopian in regard to the Catholic Church. Although in 1964 there was widespread dissent among moralists and common people about the moral legality of the use of contraceptives among the married, the Catholic doctrine on this matter was still valid[336].

Holden, however, was convinced, as well as many scientists, ordinary people and numerous ecclesiastics, of the very grave threat to humankind that the growth of the world's population constituted. "The statistics," he said repeatedly, "leave one terrified. It is appalling to realize that, if the current trend were allowed to continue unchecked, the world population would double in 40 years and in another 40 it would double again." He added that it was "the responsibility of physicians to provide guidance to

---

[335] AMA's Population, 33.

[336] Pius XI. Littera Encyclica Casti Connubii. Acta Apost Sed 1930; 22: 539-598, in 560; Pius XII. Allocutio iis quae interfuerunt Conventui Unionis Catholicae Italicae inter Obstetrices Romae habito. Romae die 29 Octobri mensis a. 1951. Acta Apost Sed 1951; 43: 835-860, at 853-854; Paulus VI. Allocutio ad E.mos Patres Purpuratos, fausta et felicia ominatus Beatissimo Patri nominalem diem celebranti, anno ex quo ad Summum Pontificatum est evectus. Die 23 mensis Iunii a. 1964. Act Apost Sedis 1964; 56: 581-589, in 588-589.

their patients in this matter."[337] Holden also shared the widely publicized opinion that the only effective weapon against abortion was the wide dissemination of contraceptives. The ethical reason for such a position does not seem entirely clear. The social rejection of abortion was still very strong, and the rejection and contempt toward abortionist doctors an imperative of professional morality, but the repudiation of abortion was also a tactical weapon to make contraception ethically tolerable. Although he declared himself personally opposed to the termination of pregnancy, Holden argued however, that doctors had the right to decide for themselves about abortion[338].

It is therefore logical to ask: How did Holden reconcile his Catholic status with his role of chairman of a Committee whose recommendations dissented or were frontally against the teachings of his Church? It seems clear that Holden resolved the conflict between his two loyalties –the one due to his Catholic creed and its morality, and the other due to his institutional and professional commitments– establishing a complete separation between both fields. His religious commitments and professional engagements belonged to two separate worlds, independent of each other. With this, the conflict ceased to exist. In an interview, he declared: "When I was asked to be president of a committee that had to consider the problems of human reproduction and population control, I thought of my position as a Catholic. But an AMA Committee would have to study its material in a broad and objective way from a medical point of view. It seemed to me that there had to be no conflicts for religious reasons in relation to a material

---

[337] AMA's Population: 31.

[338] Ibíd.

that the committee had to consider professionally."[339]

This double loyalty (to religion and to the profession) was not a recent phenomenon. Veatch has described it when dealing with the situation of Catholic doctors in 1847 who had enrolled in the AMA after its constitution[340]. They found that the medical ethics contained in the Association's Code of Ethics, based on the uses, customs and traditions doctors had developed to regulate their reciprocal relationships and relationships with their patients, ignored the principles of moral theology, a discipline which centered its reasoning on the consideration of God's commandments, Church sacraments and Christian virtues. As a result, Catholic physicians faced two systems of medical ethics that, while imposing widely coinciding norms, also showed notable normative discrepancies that have been increasing in number and entity as time has gone by. Veatch wonders how it could be that Catholic doctors did not live in a terrible permanent crisis, caught in conflicts of double loyalty; or how could Catholic patients submit to the prescriptions of doctors who followed a code that solved certain questions in ignorance of what was taught by the moral theological tradition, or even in contradiction with it.

Veatch suggests that these conflicts did not arise simply because the two traditions did not enter into communication, furthermore, they ignored each other. In the nineteenth century, the world of medicine and the world of the humanities were so far away that they could not perceive the contradictions involved in their respective moral systems. From this, Veatch deduces that "Catholic

---

[339] Ibíd., 32.

[340] Veatch RM: Disrupted Dialogue. Medical Ethics and the Collapse of Physician-Humanist Communication (1770-1980). New York: Oxford University Press; 2005: 149-153.

doctors" considered that "as medical professionals" they could believe in a set of ethical secular norms they had to apply, while "as Catholics" they had to apply another set of norms of a different nature. Since practically all believing Catholic physicians were lay people in the theological field, they did not feel able to enter the realm of moral theology. And, in turn, theologians kept careful distance from the professional morality of doctors.

Chapter 9. The *Ethos* of Scientific Research on Contraception: Dominance mentality and Zoological vision of Women

This chapter aims to review some ethical aspects of the clinical trials conducted by researchers who developed hormonal contraception. Obviously, we cannot judge the conduct of these investigators in the light of the ethical and legal regulations in force now at the end of the second decade of the 21st century. We must apply the criteria considered valid in the 1950´s, which, although much more rudimentary than the current ones, established already a notable set of ethical demands on the researcher. The 1950's norms derive on one hand from the non-codified tradition, expressed in the ethos of humanity proper to medical ethics. And, on the other hand, from the guidelines of conduct contained in the deontological codes of the medical profession and especially of a few ethical codes on human experimentation and research that had begun to be enacted by then.

When reviewing the clinical studies on contraception in women, it is possible to observe in many of them the commission of irregularities of varied nature and intensity, both in matters of method and ethics. The faults in method are easily understood, given the poor development of medical research regulative bodies and the scarcity of official regulations approved and enacted by scientific societies or governments. In the 1950's the legal and ethical regulation of clinical research was a relatively new field.

The ethical conflicts could be grouped into two general types or patterns. The first type would include those studies distinguished by the strong control, even dominance, of scientists over research subjects as the prevalent feature of their relationship. Here we will use the expression 'dominance mentality' to describe this power and influence of the researchers overe women subjects. The second corresponds to papers whose authors exhibit what could be labeled as zoological prejudice, in virtue of which the researcher tends to consider the women participating in clinical trials as if they were laboratory animals.

For a better understanding of the problem, it seems convenient to present first of all the regulation and ethos of biomedical research in the mid-twentieth century, in order to have a frame of reference against which to contrast the errors and omissions incurred by the authors of the first modern contraceptive trials. Next, we will offer some samples of the mentality of dominance expressed by the pioneering promoters and researchers. Finally, some cases will be briefly presented to show how the reductionist mentality operated and arrived to consider the procreative function of women as a purely zoological function.

9.1. The ethics of biomedical research in the mid-20th century

The ethical rules on biomedical research were then few and little observed[341]. In the time before 1950, any reference to the ethics of biomedical research was absent from the codes of ethics and deontology of the national medical organizations[342]. Nor was there any legal norm in any country about experimentation on human beings[343], a situation which contrasted with the existence, in several nations, of laws on animal protection and animal experimentation, inheritance of the vigorous antivivisectionist movement of the last quarter of the 19th century[344]. In turn, very little or no attention was devoted to

---

[341] The American Medical Association had published some Requirements for Experiments on Human Beings (JAMA 1946; 132: 1090), with the immediate purpose of presenting a document to the Military Court of Nuremberg that bear witness of the existence of some ethical standards in which to support the accusations against the Nazi doctors. It was a document improvised for the occasion, poor in content and made known in a precarious way. At the Nuremberg Trial it was challenged by the defense lawyers of the accused Nazi doctors. The Requirements were ignored by American doctors.

In 1954, at its General Assembly, the World Medical Association prepared a resolution, called by some "Declaration of Rome", which, although never given the consideration of an authoritative document, is remembered as a remote precursor of the Declaration of Helsinki. World Medical Association. Principles for Those in Research and Experimentation. World Med J 1955; 2: 14-15.

[342] The first to do so was the Code of Ethics of the Order of Physicians of Belgium, 1950, which, in its art. 22, advised that the doctor "should avoid any form of reckless experimentation" and that "it is forbidden to cause diseases or morbid states for the sole purpose of scientific observation, except the formal consent of the subject duly warned of the risks to which it is exposed". Only since 1975, the European codes included a chapter on human experimentation, inspired, in general, by the guidelines of the World Medical Association contained in the Declaration of Helsinki.

[343] Usually the so-called 'German Norms' (Ministry of Culture, Prussia, 1900, German Reich, 1931) are cited as legal documents. But those norms were not obligatory legislative decrees, but simple guidelines of advisable behavior to protect the patients admitted in public institutions; they included advice on informed consent, documentation, research on minors and exploitation of vulnerable and dependent patients. Roelcke V. The use and abuse of medical research ethics. The German Richtlinien/guidelines for human subject research as an instrument for the protection of research subjects and of medical science, ca. 1931-1961. In Weindling P, ed. From Clinic to Concentration Camp. Reassessing Nazi Medical and Racial Research, 1933-1945. London: Routledge; 2017: 46.

research and experimentation on humans by the few medical ethics manuals published before 1950[345].

There were, however, some isolated writings by some doctors, especially in France, who in the nineteenth century remembered the basic principles of a truly human and respectful research of people[346]. In the middle years of the following century, two documents of high ethical significance were published, but they were barely known, and still less assimilated, by the medical profession: the now famous Nuremberg Code (1948)[347] and the Discourse on the limits of experimentation on humans that Pius XII addressed to the International Congress of Histopathology of the Nervous System (1952)[348].

David Rothman has described in detail the ethical

---

[344] Bates AWH. Anti-Vivisection and the Profession of Medicine in Britain. A Social History. The Palgrave Macmillan Animal Ethics Series. London: Palgrave Macmillan; 2017.

[345] A worth to mention exception is the chapter on Science and Medical Research, in Moll A. Aerztliche Ethik. Die Pflichten des Arztes in allen Beziehungen seiner Thätigkeit. Stuttgart: Verlag von Ferdinand Enke; 1902: 474-596.

[346] In the 19th century, the French Max Simon and Georges Surbled affirmed the need for informed and free consent of the subjects and defended energetically the supremacy of the interests of the individual over those of society (Vid. Herranz G. The Ethics of Medical Research: A Christian View. Bull Med Ethics 2004; 200: 13-19 + bibliography and notes at: http://www.bullmedeth.info/). In the 20th century, was published a very remarkable editorial by the American physiologist Walter Cannon (Cannon W. The Right and Wrong of Making Experiments on Human Beings. JAMA 1916; 67: 1372-1373. Reproduced in JAMA 2016; 316: 2680).

[347] United States Adjutant General's Department. Trials of War Criminals Before Nuremberg Military Tribunals Under Control Council Law No. 10 (October, 1946 - April, 1949), The Medical Case. Vol. 2. Washington, U.S. Government Printing Office; 1947: 181-183.

[348] Pius XII. Speech to the Participants in the First International Congress of Histopathology of the Nervous System. The Moral Limits of Medical Methods. September 14, 1952. Accessible at: http://w2.vatican.va/content/pius-xii/es/speeches/1952/documents/hf_p-xii_spe_19520914_istopatologia.html.

environment of biomedical research in the decades immediately following World War II, a period he called "the golden age of research"[349], a time enjoying the contentment by the victory in the WWII. The American public was convinced that the war had been won in large part by the contributions of science to the war effort and professed an almost unlimited trust in scientific research and its amazing ability to solve problems. The biomedical researchers participated in that optimistic mentality and almost without realizing it, developed in the course of a few years an *ethos* that could be described as triumphalist.

Among the elements of this *ethos* are the following: to give as axiomatic the autonomy of the researcher in the design and execution of clinical trials; to consider that ethical control of research should be left in the hands of scientists and their sponsors, so that the point of reference marking the ethical limits of the research projects was the conscience of researchers, not the institutional guidelines; to prioritize the potential benefits of clinical trials and experimental studies, so that the rights and freedoms of research subjects should be subordinated to those expected benefits; to maximize the expectations and confidence of healthy patients and volunteers in the promises of research which would allow physicians to undertake high-risk trials. That was precisely the ethical environment where the studies that led to hormonal contraception began.

That *ethos* ignored the ethical criteria of the humane treatment of research subjects (respect for life and personal integrity, voluntary consent, principle of no harm) that had been outlined by Claude Bernard, the French deontologists[350],

---

[349] Rothman DJ. Strangers at the Bedside. A History of how Law and Bioethics Transformed Medical Decision Making. New York: Basic Books; 1991: 51-69.

Moll[351], Walter Cannon[352], the regulations of the German Reich of 1900, or the Directives of the State of Prussia of 1931[353]. The latter, very advanced for their time, regulated issues of informed consent, documentation, research on minors and exploitation of vulnerable and dependent persons and introduced the distinction between therapeutic and non-therapeutic research[354]. Thus, it was inevitable that in such scientifically and ethically uninhibited *ethos*, there would be abuses wherein the subjects of research were victims.

The first complaints appeared at last presented both by patients who felt mistreated, as well as from a very small number of physicians, offended by the behavior if their colleagues. The principal of these protesting doctors, Henry Beecher[355], denounced a set of aberrations in which numerous medical investigators, some of them very prestigious, had fallen under the intoxicating effect of the

---

[350] See to this effect: G. Herranz, note 6 above.

[351] Moll A. Op. Cit. In note 5 above.

[352] Cannon W. The Right and Wrong of Making Experiments on Human Beings. JAMA 1916; 67: 1372-1373.

[353] The text of these regulations, along with some comments, can be seen in: Grodin ME. Historical Origins of the Nuremberg Code. In: Annas GJ, Grodin MA, ed. The Nazi Doctors and the Nuremberg Code. Human Rights in Human Experimentation. New York: Oxford University Press; 1992: 121-144.

[354] Roelcke V. The use and abuse of medical research ethics. The German Richtlinien / guidelines for human subject research as an instrument for the protection of research subjects - and of medical science, ca. 1931-196. In Weindling P. ed. From Clinic to Concentration Camp. Reassessing Nazi Medical and Racial Research, 1933-1945. London: Routledge; 2017: 46.

[355] In 1966, Beecher published a report of enormous impact which in a certain way was the trigger that set in motion the serious consideration of the ethical aspects of clinical experimentation (Beecher HK. Ethics and Clinical Research, New Eng J Med 1966; 274: 1354-1360). Four years later, he published a book (Beecher HK. Research and the Individual: Human Studies. Boston: Little, Brown, 1970), which analyzed the subject in depth.

triumphalist *ethos*. Some of the episodes reported by Beecher, along with others that had got a resounding echo in the general media, were included for many years among the examples of research misconduct provided to students of biomedical research ethics[356].

9.2.   The researcher's dominance mentality in contraceptive research

When reading the works published by Pincus, Rock and their collaborators on their first field trials to demonstrate the effectiveness and safety of the pill, one is astonished by the way women were treated. The researcher's mood is dominant; the women's attitude is submissive. In most studies, the women, belonging to a low socioeconomic and educational level, were intensely anxious to limit the number of children and in fact they showed little interest on being informed about the nature and risks of the clinical trials. As will be shown later, the authors hardly lend attention to the ethical aspects of the experiments in the papers they published in scientific journals. Consequently, it is necessary to resort to external sources to obtain information about the ethical aspects of these trials which not always is correct and frequently biased or contradictory. In addition, at a distance of almost seventy years, there is the added difficulty of evaluating behaviors that were guided by moral and professional criteria that today seem

---

[356] In a typical anthology of "scandalous" research trials were frequently included the tragedy of Thalidomide (1957-1959), the abuses committed at the Jewish Chronic Disease Hospital in New York (1963), the vaccinations of hepatitis in Willowbrook (1971), the egregious Tuskegee's social experiment (1932-1972), the Milgram's studies on obedience to authority, and the radiation experiments related to atomic energy. Included in this anthology of ethical errors was the Goldzieher's clinical trial of contraceptives known as the San Antonio, Texas experiment which will be discussed briefly below.

rudimentary. As already indicated above, in the 1950s, the application of legal and ethical regulations on human experimental studies was a question of the investigator's personal choice.

Two important manifestations of the ethos which informed the behavior of the researchers who carried out the first experimental studies of hormonal contraception in women are presented below.

9.2.1. A paradigmatic precedent of the dominance mentality

One of the most salient cases of the researcher's domain over human sexuality occurs when for the convenience of the methodology of the experimental study, the researcher enters the highly private area of the spousal love exercise and submits it to the requirements of scientific design.

In contraceptive experimentation not a few occasions are found in which the researcher invades, in the name of science, the intimacy of the conjugal act and imposes a precise programming of the moment in which couples have to have sexual intercourse.

It is worth paying attention to an important precedent, well known and commented. This is the case of the famous "embryo hunt" carried out by Hertig and Rock[357] between 1938 and 1954 which resulted in the exceptional collection of human embryos from 2 to 17 days. These specimens, conserved at the Carnegie Institution, have served for more

---

[357] Morgan LM. Icons of Life: A Cultural History of Human Embryos. Berkeley: University of California Press; 2009. A section, entitled Egg Hunting (pp. 125-133) is devoted to referring the history of the collection from hysterectomy specimens of human early embryos. The expressions "egg hunting" or "embryo hunting" are due to Hertig and Rock.

than three quarters of a century as the universally accepted guide of the temporal and morphological development of the earliest stages of the human embryo.

Hertig and Rock were aware that in order to obtain the embryo collection for the first two weeks of development, they should set the woman's ovulation day as precisely as possible and, from that date, schedule the day on which hysterectomy should be performed to obtain specimens from each of the days of postconceptional development. Their patients were fertile, married women who lived with their husbands and to whom the uterus had to be removed for various reasons (fibromyomas, prolapse, disorders of position, etc.). While they were on the waiting list, they were asked to provide the investigators with a double information: on one hand, on the chronology of their cycles in order to calculate the date of ovulation using the thermometric data; and on the other, the dates on which they had maintained marital relations without using any contraceptive method. Apparently, after much thought, Hertig and Rock concluded that the ethics of this study was correct although in none of the successive articles they published on this project made further reference to the ethical problems involved[358].

Some bioethicists, however, have seen ethical problems in the study of Hertig and Rock[359] and specifically

---

[358] Nothing is stated about the ethical implications of this research in the articles published in the Anatomical Record, the American Journal of Obstetrics and Gynecology or the "Contributions to Embryology of the Carnegie Institution". There is even no allusion to ethics in Rock's brief reference to this study in his book "The Time Has Come", p. 184.

[359] Several authors have offered interesting observations on the ethics of this study, for example, McLaughlin L. The Pill, John Rock, and the Church. A biography of a Revolution. Boston: Little. Brown and Co.; 1989: 63-64; Marsh M, Ronner W. The Fertility Doctor. John Rock and the Reproductive Revolution.

inquiring if women could be ethically pressured to perform the conjugal act on the days set by the researcher or, on the contrary, if they were left in total freedom in this regard. McLaughlin[360] thinks it would have been advisable to recommend women to refrain from sexual intercourse before the operation, to eliminate the possibility that they were pregnant the day they would be operated on. Hertig insisted that "the patients had not been instructed on when to have intercourse but in case they had done it without taking precautions [contraceptives], they should communicate this fact to the researchers through a postcard."[361] From a long conversation with Hertig, McLaughlin refers that he "vehemently maintained that women were not commanded to maintain or not maintain relationships; only that, if they had had them, they would register and communicate. He asked if those women were sufficiently intelligent and informed to know that it was possible that they had conceived a child, Hertig replied: 'I do not think they had the slightest doubt about that. But I never discussed that issue with them.'"[362] McLaughlin also notes that Hertig remembered the first embryo they found: "Well, the woman's name was Mrs. –, […] he began to tell the story and was glad to do so. He spoke with infinite care, scientific precision and selective language. In 1938, when they brought him the tissue in which he discovered the first embryo, he already had a lot of experience and the necessary skills to bring it to light."[363]

Baltimore: Johns Hopkins University Press: 2008: 101-194; Morgan LM. Icons of Life. Op cit in note 17, pp. 128-133.

[360] McLaughlin, op. cit. in note 19 above: 64.

[361] Hertig AT. A Fifteen-Year Search for First-Stage Human Ova. JAMA 1989; 261: 434-435.

[362] McLaughlin, op. cit., note 2: 64.

In contrast to these affirmations evoked from memory many years after the events took place, there is a contemporaneous and objective testimony in which Hertig himself states exactly the opposite with respect to the instructions given to that participating woman. In the letter Hertig sent to Streeter[364] accompanying the first specimen (an embryo of a few days), Hertig, in contradiction with what he afterwards affirmed, pointed out that the woman "had been ordered to maintain conjugal relations daily during her theoretically fertile period, which she did. The uterus was removed in what was probably her eleventh postovulatory day, that is, the 24th day of the cycle."[365]

Hertig's letter to Streeter is cited here for the first time. It brings strong doubts on the freedom and willingness of the women who participated in the Hertig and Rock's investigation. It must be retained in mind that the Free Hospital was free and, therefore, favored a peculiar doctor-patient relationship which, on the side of the women, tended to be charged with dependence and submission. Finally, the Hertig and Rock's ethics fails on the side of the embryos collected: in some way, "embryo hunting" is based in an ethics that is blind to the value of the embryo itself, as a human being, an ethic that authorizes to sacrifice them

---

[363] Ibíd.

[364] George Streeter was at the time (1938) Director of the "Carnegie Institution of Embryology, Baltimore". In this institution worked a technical team of exceptional quality to perform the histological preparation, photography, drawing and conservation of the embryos. For that reason, once fixed and dehydrated, the embryos were sent from Boston to Baltimore.

[365] Letter from Hertig to Streeter, dated October 22, 1938. This letter has been included in the presentation of a graphic story of the pill, entitled 'Conceiving the Pill' and produced by the Center for the History of Medicine, of the Francis A. Countway Library, Boston: 2013. Accessible at:

https://collections.countway.harvard.edu/onview/exhibits/show/conceiving-the-pill.

for the benefit of science[366].

9.2.2. The dominance mentality in the first clinical trials of oral contraceptives

Although the situation in which the first clinical trials on hormonal contraceptives were carried out involved very different factors and interests, it seems inexcusable to admit that the dominance mentality informed the work of many of their protagonists. In the first place, the promoters of the study -Katherine McCormick, above all, but also Margaret Sanger- urged the researchers to obtain immediate and positive results, so as to allow the introduction without delay of the pill in society. That urgency induced scientists to design trials poor in methodological quality and even poorer in ethical rigor. Although John Rock was able to resist for a while the promoters' pretensions and was able to design some technically correct trials, Gregory Pincus yielded almost without resistance to McCormick's demands, and, to satisfy her, he did what some have called "small trials".

Although they were never published in scientific journals, it is interesting to pay some attention to such small trials. Some authors have written about them, echoing the

---

[366] It is worthwhile to note at this point that, in the experiments that led to human in vitro fertilization, Steptoe asked the patients he was to hysterectomize to have sex with their husbands in the days preceding the operation. They did it with the purpose of recover from the tubes 'capacitated' sperm with which to fertilize oocytes matured in vitro. Edwards RG, Steptoe PC. A Matter of Life, The Story of a Medical Breakthrough, London: Hutchinson, 1980: 59. Occasionally, Steptoe deposited during surgery matured oocytes and sperm in the tubes of women in order to obtain, in the expression of Mandelbaum, in vitro "intratubal" fertilization. Mandelbaum J. Histoire de la fecundation in vitro. In: Poncelet C, Sifer C, eds. Physiologie, pathologie et thérapie de la reproduction chez l'humain, Springer Science, 2011: 65. More on this point in: Johnson MH. Robert Edwards: the path to IVF. Repr Biomed Online 2011; 23: 245- 262, in 256.

revelations that McLaughlin advanced in 1989 in her biography of Rock[367]. These minor clinical trials are two, carried out at the initiative of Pincus: the first is a study of the effects of norethynodrel on the menstrual cycle of medical students in Puerto Rico; the second was carried out at the Worcester State Hospital on the effects of the new progestins in psychiatric patients of both sexes[368].

The ethical aspects of both essays have been the subject of commentary and disapproval by many authors[369]. Both essays incur a varied set of ethical transgressions, such as vices in obtaining the consent of incapable participants; threats of academic reprisals to the students to force them to enter the trial; a pressing need to follow a very onerous set of analytical practices (basal temperature and vaginal smear everyday, endometrial biopsy and determination of pregnanediol in urine, once a month); poor design that did

---

[367] McLaughlin, op. cit: 118-120.

[368] Apparently, there were other attempts of "small trials" in Puerto Rico (on nursing students from the San Juan City Hospital, and on women detained at the Correctional Institute of Vega Baja), but there is hardly any data available about them.

[369] The unsuccessful essay on medical students in Puerto Rico has been commented on tried repeatedly. The most complete description is found in Seipp C, Ramirez de Arellano AB. Colonialism, Catholicism, and Contraception: A History of Birth Control in Puerto Rico. Chapel Hill, NC: University of North Carolina Press; 1983: 107-110. Other descriptions in: McLaughlin (op. cit., pp. 118-119); Marsh and Ronner (op. cit., p. 174); and Oudshoorn N. Beyond the Natural Body: An Archaeology of Sex Hormones. New York: Routledge; 1994: 123. The trial on psychiatric patients of the Worcester State Hospital, which May has described as "one of the most hurtful episodes of the pill's development" (May ET. America and the Pill, A History of Promise, Peril, and Liberation, New York: Basic Books, 2010: 19), has been commented on by McLaughlin (op. cit., pp. 119-120); Marsh and Ronner (op. cit., p. 159); Mark LV. Sexual Chemistry: A History of the Contraceptive Pill. London: Yale University Press; 200: 100; Eig J. The Birth of the Pill. How Four Crusaders Reinvented Sex and Launched a Revolution. New York; WW Norton; 2014: 177-180; Speroff L. A Good Man: Gregory Goodwin Pincus. The Man, his Story, the Birth Control Pill. Portland, Or: Arnica Publ., Inc; 2009.

not allow a sound statistical analysis; and, finally, the unexplained absence of the control groups. They could not in any way be considered pilot tests.

Moving on to the most solid field of the printed materials, we find that the first article published in the Journal *Science* contains a varied sample of ethical errors induced by the dominance mentality. This study, designed by Rock to determine to what extent three new progestins could remedy unexplained sterility, carries the neutral title of "Effects of certain 19-Nor steroids on the normal human menstrual cycle"[370]. In fact, the fifty women entered in it were searching an opportunity to have descendants, thanks the so-called "rebound effect" of Rock. But the trial was used to make a collateral investigation: to determine the anovulant (contraceptive) efficacy of the three compounds tested, two of them at different dose levels. The trial plan could not provide satisfactory statistical data, given the small number of patients per compound and dose level. To improve the statistical appearance (there is no statistical analysis, only absolute data, percentages and some standard deviations of the mean), the computations do not refer to the participating women but to the menstrual cycles studied (50 control cycles, 112 cycles with medication)[371]. The data obtained from each woman during the first cycle without treatment served as a control. The methods used were: the basal temperature and a daily

---

370 Rock J, Pincus G, García CR. Effects of Certain 19-Nor Steroids on the Normal Human Menstrual Cycle. Science 1956; 124: 891-893.

371 The use of the references to the total of menstrual cycles studied (or to the "woman-years" index), although habitual since the 1930s in contraceptive research, allowed the authors certain licenses in the use of statistical evaluations. See, on the subject of the study of Puerto Rico, the commentary of Briggs L. Reproducing Empire: Race, Sex, Science, and U.S. Imperialism in Puerto Rico. Berkeley, CA. University of California Press, 2002: note 102, p. 233.

vaginal smear; an endometrial biopsy between days 19 to 24 of the cycle; and, finally, the urinary level of pregnanediol between days 17 to 23 of the cycle measured from 48-hour samples.

The women entered the trial to remedy their sterility, but nothing is said about their desire to participate in a study on contraception. Mastroianni, who collaborated in that work as a clinical assistant, recalled that Rock had a special ability to persuade his patients to enter as research subjects in their clinical trials, although following his own rules of the play, not the formal guidelines in force[372].

On the other hand, the article refers, as if by chance, to an extra group of seven women (not included among the fifty of the main group), who for some or other reason required a laparotomy. They were treated with one of the new 19-Nor steroids for a period of one to three months before the intervention[373]. The important thing for the authors was to observe in the ovaries of these women the absence of recent luteal bodies which was interpreted as visible evidence of the anovulant effect of the progestins. This is a further example of the dominance ethic: on their own initiative the researchers impose to their patients a significant delay of the surgery and force them to pharmacological treatment that was not necessary for them. For reasons never explained, no credit was recognized in the work published to Dr. Angeliki Tsacona, who was responsible for monitoring, operating and performing histological examinations of these seven women[374].

---

[372] McLaughlin, op. cit: 116-117.

[373] Briggs says that laparotomies were done in women who were already scheduled for a hysterectomy. Briggs L. Reproducing Empire: 134.

[374] McLaughlin, op. cit: 117.

Such a study, the first to show the anovulant effect of the new 19-Nor steroids in women, was published in the selective journal Science. Interestingly, its lead author, John Rock, had opposed the publication of the article as premature, believing that no firm conclusions could be drawn from a single study of fifty patients; for that purpose, more clinical trials were needed[375]. However, the work was published probably to make sure its authors of the historical priority of their findings, as well as to satisfy the impatience of Katharine McCormick. Despite all its weaknesses, the same findings were republished more than once[376].

9.2.3. The dominance mentality and the approval of the pill by the FDA

The dominance mentality was exercised by researchers not only over the women who participated in subsequent trials, but also in their relations with the FDA with the purpose of obtaining the authorization to put in the market the new hormonal contraceptives. That behavior is revealed in two episodes, of which there are contradictory versions.

The first one refers to the participation of John Rock in the final phase of the approval by the FDA of the pill (specifically the Enovid, by G.D. Searle & Co.). The story of this episode is well known, as it has been related with minor variations by McLaughlin[377], Marsh and Rooner[378], Asbell[379],

---

[375] Ibid: 118. In total, the study comprised 50 control cycles and 112 medication cycles.

[376] The same findings were re-published in more extensive articles immediately after: Rock J, García CR, Pincus G. Synthetic progestins in the normal human menstrual cycle. Rec Progr Horm Res. 1957; 13: 323-339; García CR, Pincus G, Rock J. Effects of three 19-nor steroids on human ovulation and menstruation. Am J Obstet Gynecol 1958; 75: 82-87.

[377] McLaughlin, op. cit: 143.

Speroff[380] and Eig[381]. Its origin seems to be in the interviews that McLaughlin maintained with Winter, top manager of the Searle, and with John Rock[382]. Rock was surprised by the youth and apparent inexperience of Dr. deFelice. He came to assume that the postponement of the decision depended from the fact that deFelice had not made a thorough study of the documentation submitted by Searle. The climax of the interview is manifested, as Rock himself recalls, when he, furious at the objections deFelice opposed to the fast approval of Enovid, intimidated the man from the FDA to sign the immediate authorization. Rock remembers "I got up, grabbed him by the lapels of his jacket and said: 'No, you will not take this matter home. You will solve it right now'. DeFelice replied: 'Oh, very good'. I think he [deFelice] did not realize the importance of what it meant what he

---

[378] Marsh, Ronner, op. cit., pp. 218-219.

[379] Asbell B. The Pill. A Biography of the Drug that Changed the World. New York: Random House: 1995: 167.

[380] Speroff, op. cit., pp. 226-228.

[381] Eig, op. cit., pp. 288-289.

[382] The interview with Rock is confirmed by Marsh and Rooner: "Rock recorded McLaughlin's interview in his diary, March 18, 1979. He wrote that he thought his name was Loretta McDonald. 'Well, she, whatever her name, came and spent four whole hours asking me all kinds of questions, some very personal'. Although he responded to everything she asked, he wrote that he did not know what she intended to do with the interview." Marsh, Rooner, op. cit., note 99, p. 345. It is curious that McLaughlin does not include any specific reference to her long interview with Rock in his book. She says in the section of Acknowledgments: "There are many others of whom I am indebted, in particular those who, thanks to their interviews, filled many empty spaces. They made the book possible" (McLaughlin, op. cit., p. unnumbered). But McLaughlin does not name them. Certainly, in the book the quoted fragments abound that are, obviously, taken from interviews (with Rock and other individuals). There is another interview (author unknown) with Rock in which it is related how Rock intimidated deFelice so that Enovid approval from the FDA was immediately granted. That interview can be accessed at the Kentucky University Oral History collection:

https://kentuckyoralhistory.org/catalog/xt7d251fmx35.

was doing."[383] It was, of course, an attitude of dominance in which the weight of Rock's prestige imposes itself overwhelmingly on the inexperience of his colleague, whom he deemed incompetent for the task that the FDA had entrusted him.

However, deFelice offers a very divergent version to that reported by Rock. It was taken by McLaughlin during an interview with deFelice himself[384], which Marsh and Ronner later referred to[385]. In essence, deFelice realized that he was before a new situation and it was necessary to assess with precision its risks. The hormonal contraceptive was not intended to treat a disease or pathological symptoms but rather healthy women; and not for a short time, but for many months and even years. He rightly judged that Searle's request was inadequate and the documentation presented incomplete, since the number of subjects included in the trials was insufficient to assess possible risks. He demanded, in particular, that the effect of Enovid on the mechanisms of blood coagulation be studied. DeFelice's attitude was not that of an ignoramus. The delay of Enovid's approval was not an obstructionist maneuver, but a responsible decision.

9.2.4. The dominance mentality and the Río Piedras trial control cases

---

[383] McLaughlin, op. cit., p. 143. In another interview given by Rock to Dale Deaton, on June 15, 1979, preserved in the Louie B. Nunn Center for Oral History, Library of the University of Kentucky, Rock represents deFelice as a young general practitioner, who ignored the content of the application for approval of Enovid by the FDA, and who was intimidated to sign the authorization for the marketing launch of the contraceptive. The oral file can be heard at: https://kentuckyoralhistory.org/catalog/xt7d251fmx35.

[384] McLaughlin, op. cit., pp. 143-144.

[385] Marsh, Ronner, op. cit., p. 217.

Barbara Seaman, who devoted much of her investigative journalism work to reporting the adverse effects of the pill, is the author of a serious accusation of fraud with respect to the controls used in the Rio Piedras experiment.

Seaman's complaint appeared in an article published in the New York Times in 2000, when forty years had passed since the approval of the Pill as a contraceptive by the FDA. After consulting the Pincus file, deposited in the Library of Congress of the United States, Seaman denounced that, "... already advanced the study, the FDA informed Pincus of the need for a control group. As the recruiter of the Family Planning Association of Rio Piedras (Puerto Rico) could not incorporate new volunteers, Pincus ordered her to remove the label from the files marked as 'lost cases' - which corresponded to the women who had abandoned the trial- and mark them again as 'control cases'". Seaman added the accusation that in May 1959 the provisional norethinodrel-only pill was changed to the definitive pill of norethinodrel added with estrogen. Seaman concluded that the so-called "control group" by Pincus was not only a group of women who had previously been excluded from the trial, but also who had converted into a control group receiving successively pills of different composition[386]. Seaman summed up his impression of Pincus' file with these words: "They reveal an awesome scientific and entrepreneurial brinkmanship and make one wonder why Pincus didn't burn the evidence."[387] Regrettably, Seaman did not indicate the precise reference of the Pincus document on which she bases her complaint.

---

[386] Seaman B. The Pill and I: 40 Years On, the Relationship Remains Wary. New York Times, June 25, 2000: 15-19.

[387] Ibíd.

Seaman's accusation did not go unanswered. Marsh and Ronner confess that, in a thorough review of the entire Pincus file in search of the source invoked by Seaman, he was not able to find any basis for her accusation and suggests that the suspicions of the latter are based on a false interpretation of a letter sent to Pincus by Dr. Rice-Wray, the person who directed the trials at Rio Piedras[388].

Would it be possible to find some light on the Seaman/Marsh conflict in the publications of Rock, Pincus and their collaborators? The articles that expose their first clinical trials on the pill do not help, however, to clarify the problem; on the contrary, they contribute rather to maintaining doubts.

The works published on the initial studies of Puerto Rico and Haiti make little or no reference to control groups: they merely refer generically to the constitution of these groups but they tell us nothing on the criteria applied for the selection of subjects nor on the interventions they were subjected. Thus, for example, in the Rio Piedras study the values used as controls (daily basal temperature, daily vaginal smear, a determination of pregnanediol in the urine collected between days 19 and 21, and an endometrial biopsy taken ordinarily day 21) were obtained in the cycle immediately prior to the start of the contraceptive treatment so that each woman acted as a control of herself[389] as it had been done before with the fifty women in the trial that Rock had performed at his Massachusetts clinic[390].

---

[388] Marsh, Ronner, op. cit., p. 190, and particularly note 15, p. 340.

[389] Pincus G, Rock J, Garcia CR. Effects of Certain 19-Nor Steroids upon Reproductive Processes. Ann N Y Acad Sci 1958; 71: 677-690; García CR, Pincus G, Rock J. Effects of three 19-nor steroids on human ovulation and menstruation. Am J Obstet Gynecol 1958; 75: 82-97.

[390] Rock J, Pincus G, Garcia CR. Effects of Certain 19-Nor Steroids on the

In the Humacao trial, it is indicated that the controls were recruited as matched controls (by age of the woman, number of children, number of pregnancies and years of marriage) with the experimental cases. But it resulted very difficult to gather a control group so designed, which is not surprising, because the women had been told that it was simply a study of the size of families in that local community[391]. In later publications, including some review papers, no reference is made to the control groups[392].

This lack of data on the control groups, the variants of the method followed in the different trials and, in particular, and the low appreciation in which the participants' complaints about the collateral effects of the medication had raised the suspicion that the researchers granted very little relevance to the design and monitoring of the control groups. In fact, their prevailing, if not exclusive, interest was the demonstration of the absolute efficacy of hormonal contraception.

9.2.5. The persistence of the dominance mentality

Throughout the years from 1955 to 1975, there were many episodes that showed the recurrence of the dominance mentality. They presented in practically all possible situations: in the way in which the women who

---

Normal Human Menstrual Cycle. Science 1956; 124: 891-893.

[391] Rice-Wray E. Field Study with Enovid as a Contraceptive Agent. Proc Symp on 19-Nor Steroids. Chicago: GD Searle & Co; 1957: 78-82, 92-93. Reprinted in: Katz J. Experimentation with Human Beings. New York: Russell Sage Foundation; 1972: 742-745.

[392] Pincus G, Rock J, Chang MC, Garcia CR. Effects of Certain 19-Nor Steroids on Reproductive Processes and Fertility. Fed Proc 1959; 18: 1051-1056; Cook HH, Gamble CJ, Satterthwaite AP. Oral Contraception by Norethynodrel. A 3-Years Field Study. Am J Obstet Gynecol 1961; 82: 437-442, 444-445. Reprinted in Katz, op. cit. 739-742.

participated were harmed in their rights and dignity, in the relations of some researchers with others, and even in the authorization by government agencies of procedures for human use of contraceptives.

Some of these episodes have reached the dubious prestige of being paradigms of research misconduct. It is the case, for example, of Joseph Goldzieher[393] and his notorious "contraceptive study of San Antonio"[394]. The study, carried out in 1971 in Texas, was along with other scandalous events (Willowbrook, Tuskegee, Jewish Hospital of Brooklyn) in the manuals for the teaching of the ethics of biomedical research in order to sensitize students and future scientists against the temptation of abuse of power.

The contraceptive study of San Antonio is very instructive; first of all, because Goldzieher showed a behavior far below what one could expect from someone who had recently published an extensive article about the correct ways to design and evaluate the different types of clinical trials[395]. In his case, knowledge of the theory did not

---

[393] For many years, Joseph W Goldzieher headed the Department of Endocrinology at the Southwest Foundation for Research and Education in Texas, San Antonio. He was very active in the investigation of contraception and its diffusion especially among the Chicano population. Two short biographies have been published about him. One, written by himself, appears in: Bettendorf, ed. Zur Geschichte der Endokrinologie and Reproduktionsmedicine. Berlin: Springer-Verlag; 1995: 177-180. The other is due to Benagiano: Benagiano G. Joseph W. Goldzieher and the birth of hormonal contraception. Contraception 2010; 82: 119-124.

[394] Goldzieher JW, Moses LE, Averkin E, Scheel C, Taber BZ. A Placebo-controlled Double-blind Crossover Investigation of the Side Effects Attributed to Oral Contraceptives. Fertil Steril 1971; 22: 609-623. Another complementary communication from the same authors about the same patients was published a few months later: Goldzieher JW, Moses LE, Averkin E, Scheel C, Taber BZ. Nervousness and depression attributed to oral contraceptive: A double-blind, placebo-controlled study. Am J Obstet Gynecol 1971; 11: 1013-1020.

[395] Hines DC, Goldzieher JW. Clinical Investigation: A Guide to its Evaluation.

protect him against practical error. The study had a very complex design: it was a double-blind clinical trial with a placebo control group and a double cross-over with four experimental groups receiving different oral contraceptives. The main objective was to determine whether the annoying side effects of the contraceptives had an objective physiological basis or were a consequence of psychogenic factors. All women were ordered to use a vaginal cream as a complementary protection as the pills may not be totally effective (especially the dummy ones given to women in the placebo group). The trial, in which participated 398 women, largely of Mexican descent, was seriously damaged when the FDA banned the use of one of the contraceptives under investigation. As a result, the statistical strength of the trial collapsed. In spite of this, Goldzieher preferred to finish the ill-fated project to give an appearance of solidity to his intuitions and to finally conclude that the collateral symptoms suffered by the users of oral contraceptive depended on mere subjectivity (placebo effect).

What gave fame, however, to the contraceptive study of Saint Anthony was the contempt with which, in general, the women who participated in it were treated. That mistreatment provoked an intense reaction in the media. The study was a grievance to women, mostly poor and illiterate, who had enrolled in the trial not because of their interest in helping the progress of science but to avoid new pregnancies. Their consent was dubiously valid; they were not informed of the use of placebo nor on the risk of becoming pregnant, an event that affected 10 of the 76 women in the groups who received placebo at some stage of the trial. Goldzieher completely disregarded them. And so did the other sponsors of the research (Planned

---

Am J Obstet Gynecol 1969; 105: 450-487.

Parenthood of Texas, Syntex Laboratories, and the Agency for International Development of the Government of the United States). These women did not receive any compensation.

The criticisms of the scientists did not wait; some of them were even divulged before the study was published. The first protests occurred in March 1971 when the work was presented to the Annual Meeting of the American Fertility Society in New Orleans. In June 1971, based on the information provided by Medical World News[396], Robert Veatch published a sharp criticism in the inaugural issue of the Hastings Center Report[397]. Above all, the popular protests among the Chicano community of Texas stood out which led to the creation of groups of activists who advocated for pregnant women and their children[398].

Goldzieher was accused of committing serious failures in obtaining the consent of the participants both in regard to the content of the information given and in the attitude of assuming that it was legitimate to omit consent because he considered them incapable of understanding the complex design of the study; many of them were not informed that they would receive a placebo instead of the active pill. In essence, it must be concluded that the study was based on deception and the exploitation of a vulnerable and destitute population.

And one of the most remarkable things is that the investigators were not censored or received any sanctions;

---

[396] Anonymous. Placebo Stirs Pill "Side Effects". Med World News, 1971, April 16. The article has been reproduced in: Katz J. op. cit: 791-792.

[397] Veatch RM. 'Experimental' Pregnancy. The ethical complexities of experimentation with oral contraceptives. Hastings Cent Rep 1971; 1 (Jun): 2-3.

[398] See, for example, Hume M. Maybe Baby. Texas Monthly 1973; 1 (9): 43.

they continued to receive the support of the sponsoring agencies (Planned Parenthood, USAID, and the South Central Texas and Southwest Foundation for Research and Education) and enjoying remarkable prestige in the world of biomedical science[399].

9.3. The zoological mentality in some researchers of contraception

Modern contraceptive research was devised from the beginning -and still it is today- as feminine contraception, that is, a study of procedures applicable to women. By contrast, male contraception, although receiving some attention in recent years, has remained in a secondary place[400].

As already noted at the beginning of this chapter, the strategy of scientists in their search for hormonal contraceptives for human use was based on the scheme of

---

[399] Benagiano G. Joseph W. Goldzieher and the birth of hormonal contraception. Contraception 2010; 82: 119-124.

[400] There are several reasons pointed out by Briggs for which male contraception has not entered the agenda of experimentation in the 1950s and 1960s. On one hand, Pincus renounced to it despite the fact that his study of psychotic patients of the Worcester State Hospital had shown that steroids could stop spermatogenesis'; there was then a widespread suspicion that progestins could exert a feminizing effect in men. On the other, Pincus was influenced by the decision of the promoters of the essays, McCormick and Sanger, to limit himself exclusively to search exclusively methods that could control fertility in women. In addition, in those years, women were regarded as the objective to which efforts should be directed to put an end to overpopulation. Briggs L. "The Pill" in Puerto Rico and the Mainland United States: Negotiating Discourses of Risk and Decolonization. In: Reed L, Sankko P, eds. Governing the Female Body. Gender, Health, and Networks of Power. Albany: State University of New York Press; 2010: 159-184, at 182. It is very likely, however, that other factors influenced that decision: as some feminists point out, the research was conducted by men for whom experimenting on women was more comfortable than doing it on men. Finally, there is a fundamental physiological reason: the much greater complexity of the male gametogenesis compared to the female one (Asbell B. The Pill, pp. 345-346).

pure physiological control of the female reproductive system. To do this, they tried to identify in women the factors and processes homologous to those known from experimentation in domestic and laboratory animals. This research strategy reinforced, on one hand, the legitimate methodological reductionism that experimental science requires: isolated the problem under study and formulated it in its simplest and most abstract terms in order to eliminate as much "background noise" due to interference with the physiological environment. On the other hand, it responded to the purpose of many researchers to make the study of reproductive physiology scientifically respectable, divesting it from subjective and anthropological contaminations. It was this approach, which did not take into account the genuinely human of human procreation that presided over the investigation of contraceptives[401].

One of the main consequences of such an approach was the development among researchers of modern female contraception of a mentality that could be described as "zoologist", a term used here to imply that women were deprived, as experimental subjects, of the intrinsic dignity of human beings and reduced to the status of laboratory animals. It was not a new phenomenon, because the idea of women as reproductive animals was, to a large extent, a legacy of the 19th century[402] which survived, as will be shown below, until the following century. It is, from the

---

[401] "Men who aspired to a scientifically respectable study of sex recognized that their basis would have to be largely biological and independent of human interests or subjective experiences ... It was a liberal position, a biology liberated as an autonomous science." Hall DL. Biology, Sex Hormones and Sexism in the 1920s. Philosophical Forum 1974; 5: 81-96.

[402] Smith-Rosenberg C, Rosenberg C. The Female Animal: Medical and Biological Views of Woman and Her Role in Nineteenth-Century America. J Am Hist 1973; 60: 332-356.

anthropological point of view, an impoverished vision, as much as it is Manichean spiritualism, which denies the positive value of the body[403]. The ideology of the overpopulation of planet Earth contributed to consolidate this approach with its characteristic downgrading of the value of the individual and his or her particular reproductive projects and with its no less characteristic drive to take into account almost exclusively the anonymous mass and its collective reproductive potential.

The zoologist vision of human reproduction was incubated and developed at the shadow of Darwinian evolutionism and under a materialist view of biology. Darwin and many of his followers were convinced of the physical and intellectual inferiority of women with respect to men[404]. Pincus, on the other hand, had been a disciple of Jacques Loeb who professed that all biological processes (including human procreation) could be reduced to physics and chemistry, so that they could be "reingenierized" and applied to the control of breeding in the human[405]. This led to a notion of the merely animal nature of human sexuality in which human procreation is deprived of any anthropological and moral sense[406].

---

[403] Kaiser points out that, at a certain moment, the psychologists and psychiatrists of the Papal Commission need to make it clear to some of its celibate [theologians] members that sexuality was not simply a part of the "animal nature"nature' of the human being, but that it was something positive in itself, part of the divine plan about man. Kaiser RB. op. cit: 127-128.

[404] Darwin, C. The Descent of Man and Selection in Relation to Sex, 1896 edition, D. Appleton and Company; New York, 1871: 561-3. The subject has been recently exposed in: Saini A. Inferior. How Science Got Women Wrong, and the New Research That's Rewriting the Story. Boston: Beacon Press; 2017: 13-18.

[405] Clarke A.E. Disciplining Reproduction. Modernity, American Life Sciences, and "the Problems of Sex". Berkeley: University of California Press; 1998: 24.

[406] Benagiano G. Reproductive strategies for human survival. Repr Bio Med Online 2001; 4, suppl 1: 72-76.

The influence that such a zoological view exercised on the scientists who designed the strategy of the contraceptive clinical trials was very great. Moreover, such a strategy was accepted without much opposition by a society extraordinarily receptive to science because it was convinced that biomedical research could solve all the problems that affect the health and well-being of the human being[407]. As observed above, this research was also carried out at a time when the related ethical and legal regulations had barely begun to be created, a time in which researchers were habituated to be the authority who autonomously and discretionally put an ethical limit to experimentation on human beings. Those scientists believed firmly that the ultimate goal of science was to acquire new knowledge and to solve problems, an objective to which the interests of individuals should be subordinated. In such circumstances, they did not consider it especially offending that women, especially those of a low socio-economic and cultural level, were included in research projects that were clearly harmful to their dignity and freedom.

It seems appropriate to consider two of the main manifestations of the zoologist bias in contraceptive experimentation: one is to equate the woman, as a subject of experimentation, to a mere animal, to a "human guinea pig"; the other consists on the reduction of the woman's body to a manageable system of hormonal molecules.

9.3.1. The equalization of women, as a subject of experimentation, to a mere animal, to a human guinea pig

The simplest manifestation of the phenomenon

---

[407] Rothman DJ. Strangers ..., pp. 51-59.

appears in the biomedical language. Scientific speech abounds in simple, "naturalistic", non-pejorative, neutral expressions used in the parlance of scientists when they refer to matters of comparative biology. In the literature, one finds phrases such as: "Some observations have also been made in women and monkeys after ovariectomy."[408] On other occasions, it is stated that there are no differences between the woman and the inferior female animal in terms of reproductive processes[409]. Although this identification can be interpreted "aseptically", analogies of this type depending on the context, can be degrading for women[410].

The phenomenon has been captured in the image of the human guinea pig. The expression guinea pig had been used long before the 1950s to designate various types of human experimental subjects; from the volunteers who usually were paid for submitting to different types of interventions ('professional' human guinea pigs), to doctor's minor children on whom new vaccines or medicines were tested[411].

However, it was in contraceptive research that the

---

[408] Dixon WE. The Action and Uses of Ovarian Extracts. Br Med J 1927; 2: 1070-1074, in 1071.

[409] "Everything we know about the menstrual cycle of primates suggests that its hormonal control is the same as in lower animals and it is extremely probable that the factors governing the implantation of a fertilized egg are fundamentally similar in women and in lower animals." Parkes AS, Dodds EC, Noble RL. Interruption of Early Pregnancy by Means of Orally Active Oestrogens. Br Med J 1938; 2: 557-559, at 559.

[410] Mitchinson W. The Nature of Their Bodies. Women and Their Doctors in Victorian Canada. Toronto: University of Toronto Press; 1991: 91.

[411] Lederer S. Subjected to Science. Human Experimentation in America Before the Second World War. Baltimore: The Johns Hopkins University Press; 1955.

condition of women as experimental animals reached its greatest notoriety, thanks to Katharine McCormick and her expression "a cage of ovulating women". The phrase had achieved great diffusion. This is why is interesting to know its history. It appeared for the first time in a letter McCormick wrote to Sanger in May 1955 wherein McCormick complained about the slowness with which Pincus was carrying out the tedious clinical trials with oral contraceptives on women which contrasted with the speed with which Pincus himself had performed the experiments on animals. He wrote that full of impatience and asked Pincus, "How could we get a cage of ovulating women to experiment?"[412]

The expression, ingenious but inappropriate, remained unpublished in the correspondence of Sanger for almost a quarter of a century until 1978, when it was cited by Reed[413]. It is surprising that despite the ethical and sociological conflict and the degrading nature of the phrase, Reed did not offer any comment on it. After a few years, other authors interpreted it in different ways. In 1983, Ramírez de Arellano and Seipp took the simile of the ovulant women's cage as an image that they applied to Puerto Rico as a whole, to underline the character of social laboratory that the Caribbean island had acquired after hosting the first large-scale clinical trial of hormonal contraception[414]. In

---

[412] Letter of Katherine McCormick to Margaret Sanger, May 31, 1955. Margaret Sanger Papers, Sophia Smith Collection, Smith College, Northampton, MA. "Before my energetic complaint to Dr. Pincus about our lack of clinical results ("How can we get a 'cage' of ovulating women to experiment? - that is our bottleneck")". The letter can be read in: The Pill: Birth of a New Woman. Correspondence between Margaret Sanger and Katharine McCormick: http://93778645.weebly.com/letters-between-sanger-and-mccormick.html.

[413] Reed J. From Private Vice to Public Virtue. The Birth Control Movement and American Society Since 1830. New York: Basic Books; 1978: 358.

1994, the image of the cage was again used by Oudshoorn as a metaphor for the stability of the population in the isle of Puerto Rico that was a guarantee that women would not easily withdraw from the project[415]. Preciado used it as a symbol of the connection between incarceration and the demands of scientific precision[416]. In its most literal sense of women as human-guinea pigs, the metaphor of the cage of ovulant women has recently become commonplace and has been cited "on almost every occasion that someone has written about the development of the pill."[417]

It was necessary to wait until 1998 to see published the first ethical evaluation of the conflicting phrase of McCormick. We owe it to Marks, who emphasized that the most salient of that expression is "the suggestion that women could be reduced to their reproductive physiology and be seen as mere 'ovulating females'."[418] Such a reductive vision was, according to Marks, not a random and isolated speculation, but the very foundation on which the

---

[414] Ramírez de Arellano AB, Seipp C. Colonialism, Catholicism, and Contraception: a history of birth control in Puerto Rico. Chapel Hill, NC: University of North Carolina Press; 1983: 175.

[415] Oudshoorn N. Beyond the Natural Body: An Archeology of Sex Hormones. New York: Routledge; 1994: 124-125. The same author reiterates the idea years later in Oudshoorn N. Drugs for healthy people: The culture of hormonal contraceptives testing for women and men. In: Gijswijt-Hofstra M, van Heteren GM, Tanse EM, eds. Biographies of Remedies: Drugs, Medicines and Contraceptives in Dutch and Anglo-American Healing Cultures. Amsterdam; Rodopi; 2002: 123-140, at 127.

[416] Preciado B. Testo Junkie: Sex, Drugs, and Biopolitics in the Pharmacopornographic Era. New York: Feminist Press at the City University of New York; 2008: 180.

[417] Marsh M, Ronner W. op. cit: 158.

[418] Marks L. "A Cage of Ovulating Females": The History of Early Oral Contraceptive Pill Clinical Trials, 1950-59. In Chadaverian S, Kamminga H, eds. Molecularizing Biology and Medicine: New Practices and Alliances, 1910s-1970s. Amsterdam: Harwood Academic Publishers; 1998: 208.

researchers designed the first clinical trials of the pill[419]. The following year, Marks further hardened her criticisms: she claimed that McCormick admitted that women could be treated as mere animals and that she considered acceptable that in the trial of the pill on psychiatric patients in the United States, as well as the studies done in Puerto Rico, Haiti and Mexico, were included preferably women easy to be manipulated and who "did not consider themselves as human beings endowed with the ability to think and feel."[420]

Clarke, in turn, has emphasized the concept that manipulation is at the heart of mechanistic rationalization of reproduction. She adduces as evidence that Austin and Short entitled *Manipulating Reproduction*[421], a book dealing with the techniques of such manipulation in humans and domestic animals. She concludes that the human / non-human distinction has been made every time less relevant to the science and technology of reproduction[422]. But such a manipulation, as seen from a scientific perspective, is mere biologism, the product of a scientistic bias, because it is based on the idea that only the biological science can bring us a total understanding of reproduction in man. But this is not the case: it is not simply the reproductive function that is at stake in research on contraception but the full human condition, the nature of the human being. As Janet Smith points out, the biological process of human generation is something far superior to the parallel process in animals; it

---

[419] Ibíd.

[420] Marks L. Human Guinea Pigs? The History of the Early Oral Contraceptive Clinical Trials. Hist & Technol 1999; 15: 263-268.

[421] Austin CR, Short RV. Manipulating Reproduction, 2nd ed. Vol. V, in Austin CR, Short RV, eds. Reproduction in Mammals. Cambridge, Cambridge University Press; 1986.

[422] Clarke, A.E. op. cit., p. 26.

requires a completely different way of study and evaluation: the generative process in human beings "has to do directly with the value of the human person and with the importance of the actions that have to respect the fullness of his dignity as a human person. Treating man as if he were just another animal would justify contraception, not condemn it."[423]

9.3.2. The woman's body, a manageable system of hormonal molecules

The comparison to a laboratory animal did not mark the ultimate limit of the depreciation of women in which incurred, for methodological reasons or cultural prejudices, the pioneering researchers of hormonal contraception. In the course of their experiments on the selection, administration and effects of hormonal contraceptives, they fixed their preferential, if not exclusive, attention on the physiological modifications induced by the compounds used and, consequently, they greatly reduced their interest on the human and personal implications of the women who participated in the trials. They recognized them simply as interesting and manageable systems of hormonal molecules and ended up forgetting about their peculiarities as human beings. This ontological eclipse of women had already been initiated years before in the discussions about the "physiological control of reproduction" by devising which types of molecules or interventions could be designed with contraceptive purposes for each of the vulnerable points of the female reproductive process.

The reduction of women to a manageable hormonal

---

[423] Smith J. Humanae Vitae. A Generation Later. Washington, DC: The Catholic University of America Press; 1991: 177.

system was not the result of the initiative of an individual or an isolated group; it was, rather, the result of a mentality that was widely spread among the biologists of the late nineteenth century, which has rightly been called "molecular vision of life", the most radical and extreme form of biological reductionism[424]. In the first decades of the 20th century, the Rockefeller Foundation became the focus from which this mentality expanded. Clarke has drawn attention to the concern of the directors of that Foundation to create and disseminate a biochemical/endocrinological perspective of life and, especially, of reproduction, in order to "promote a mechanistic biology as a central element of the new science of man and whose purpose would be social engineering".[425]

An outstanding effect of this molecular vision was the promotion of hormones, especially of sex hormones, to the status of dominant protagonists in life and sexuality. As Harding says, "it was discursively proclaimed that sex hormones embodied the essence of sex."[426] According to Pfeffer[427], the idea of considering the female reproductive body as a chemical factory was introduced in 1905 when Heape proposed that a secretion of the ovary governed the activity of the other generative organs[428]. Consequently, the female organism went from being a "reproductive body"

---

[424] Kay LE. The Molecular Vision of Life: Caltech, the Rockefeller Foundation and the New Biology. New York: Oxford University Press; 1993: 45-50.

[425] Clarke A.E. op. cit., p. 26.

[426] Harding J. Sex and Control: The Hormonal Body. Body & Society 1996; 2: 99-111, in 99.

[427] Pfeffer N. The Reproductive Body. In: Cooter R, Pickstone J. Companion to Medicine in the Twentieth Century. Abingdon, UK; Routledge; 2013: 277-290, in 281.

[428] Heape W. Ovulation and Degeneration of Ova in the Rabbit. Proc Roy Soc Lond B 1905; 76: 260-268, at 265-266.

(Pfeffer) to being a "hormonal body" (Harding).

In the history of hormonal contraception, we find examples of how molecular vision was imposed on human vision.

One is what Marsh and Ronner tell us on the reaction of Pincus to the report that Dr. Rice-Wray presented on the Rio Piedras trial. Rice-Wray concluded in her report that the pill, when ingested according to the instructions established by the researchers, provided 100% protection against pregnancy. But the women had numerous side effects, causing Dr. Rice-Wray to discourage its general use. Pincus turned a deaf ear to the conclusion that unwanted effects were a serious drawback. "The expert on rats and rabbits," Marsh and Ronner point out, "diagnosed that the reactions in women were psychosomatic. He ignored the bad news and reacted with exultant joy to the good ones: the pill worked and that was the only thing that mattered to him."[429] From his molecular view of life, Pincus considered that women's complaints were irrelevant; what really mattered were the molecules, the Enovid 10. A short time later, Rice-Wray was forced to renounce to the supervision of the trial and left Puerto Rico.

The second example is offered by Rock. Rock, who had fame of treating with great delicacy all his patients whatever their social class, was strongly opposed to the use of reduced doses of hormones in contraception. On the contrary, he tenaciously struggled to maintain the Enovid 10 with its high content of steroids and its sequelae of intense, and sometimes unbearable, unwanted effects. This behavior was motivated by his determination to ensure that the primary and exclusive mechanism of action of the pill

---

[429] Marsh M, Ronner W. op. cit. p. 196.

was the anovulant effect induced by that pill's high hormonal content. Rock considered that the reduced hormonal content pill did not always exert an anovulant effect and, consequently permitted ethically questionable or negative mechanisms of action (in particular, the inhibition of the implantation of the embryo). In addition, and above all, Rock understood that the anovulant effect was essential to maintain the contraceptive's supposed character of natural method imitating pregnancy, a figuration on which he intended to legitimize the legality of the pill in the eyes of Catholic moral theology. For Rock, enduring the annoying side effects of the high-dose pill was the price women had to pay for safeguarding the moral innocence of the medication.

The reduction of women to a manageable system of hormonal molecules is, in a certain sense, the culmination of a process that, depriving the human body of its existential unity, transforms it into separable pieces which, in turn, are fragmented into smaller units no longer referable to a human subject. This process of molecularization has marked indelibly the ethical course of contraceptive research.

Bibliography

Abell B. The Pill. A Biography of the Drug that Changed the World. New York: Random House; 1995.

Albright JP, Byrne PB, Crooks NP. Church-State Religious Institutions and Values: A Legal Survey 1960-1962, Notre Dame L Rev 1962; 37: 649-719.

American Medical Association. Proceedings Kansas City Session. JAMA 1936; 106: 1911.

American Medical Association. Minutes of the 76th Annual Session of the AMA, in Atlantic City, May 25-29, 1925. JAMA 1925; 84: 1635-1667.

American Medical Association. Minutes, House of Delegates, Seventy-Seventh Annual Session, Held at Dallas, Texas, April 19-23, 1926: 39.

American Medical Association. Resolution on Contraception. Minutes, House of Delegates. Seventy-Eighth Annual Session of the American Medical Association, Held at Washington, D.C., May 16-20, 1927: 60.

American Medical Association. Resolution on Contraception. Minutes, House of Delegates, Seventy-ninth Annual Session, Held at Minneapolis, Minn., June 11-15, 1928: 27.

American Medical Association. Resolutions on the Appointment of a Committee to Study Birth Control. Minutes, House of Delegates. Eighty-third Annual Session, Held at New Orleans, La., May 3-13, 1932: 45.

American Medical Association. Resolutions on Creation of the Committee for the Study of Birth Control. Minutes, House of Delegates.

Eighty-fourth Annual Session, Held at Milwaukee, Wis., June 12-15, 1933: 50-51.

American Medical Association. Resolutions on Contraceptive Methods. Minutes, House of Delegates. Eighty-fifth Annual Session, Held at Cleveland, Ohio, June 11-15, 1934: 42.

American Medical Association. Editorial. Policies Adopted by the House of Delegates. JAMA 1935; 104: 2351.

American Medical Association. Resolutions on Contraception. Minutes, House of Delegates, 86th Annual Session, Atlantic City, June 10-14, 1935: 34.

American Medical Association. Editorial. Organized Medicine Dodges the Issue. Birth Control Rev 1936; 3 (10) (n.s.): 1-3.

American Medical Association. Report of Committee to Study Contraceptive Practices and Related Problems. Minutes, House of Delegates. Eighty-Seventh Annual Session, Held at Kansas City, Mo., May 11-15, 1936: 53-55.

American Medical Association. Report of Reference Committee on Executive Session. JAMA 1936; 106: 1911.

American Medical Association. Editorial. The Atlantic City Session. JAMA 1937; 108: 2124-2125.

American Medical Association. Editorial. Contraceptive Advice, Devices and Preparations still Contraband. JAMA 1937; 108: 1179-1180.

American Medical Association, Proceedings of the House of Delegates. Eighty-Eighth Annual Session, Held at Atlantic City, N.J., June 7-11, 1937.

American Medical Association. Report of the Reference Committee on Executive Session. Proceedings of the House of Delegates, AMA. Eighty-Ninth Annual Session, Held at San Francisco, Calif., June 13-17, 1938: 73.

American Medical Association. Report on the Use of Roentgen Rays for Contraception. JAMA 1938; 111: 1767.

American Medical Association. Councils' Committee on Contraceptives. Proceedings of the House of Delegates. Ninetieth Annual Session, Held at St. Louis, Mo, May 15-19, 1939: 18.

American Medical Association. Book Notices. New and Nonofficial Remedies, 1944. Chicago: American Medical Association; 1944. JAMA 1944; 125: 1000.

American Medical Association. Requirements for Experiments on Human Beings (JAMA 1946; 132: 1090).

American Medical Association Proceedings. House of Delegates Miami Beach, Florida. 18th Clinical Convention, Nov 30-Dec 2, 1964. New Committees of the Board of Trustees: 27.

American Medical Association. Report of Reference Committee on Miscellaneous Business. Supplementary Report G American Medical Association. Proceedings of the House of Delegates, 18th Clinical Convention. Miami Beach, Florida. Nov. 30-Dec 2, 1964: 95.

American Medical Association's Council on Drugs. An Oral Contraceptive: Norethindrone with Mestranol (Ortho-Novum). JAMA 1964; 87: 664.

American Medical Association's Committee on Human Reproduction. The Control of Fertility. JAMA 1965; 194: 462-470.

American College of Obstetricians and Gynecologists (ACOG). Terminology Bulletin no. 1: September 1965.

American Law Institute. Model Penal Code. Tentative Draft No. 9, May 8, 1959. Philadelphia: American Law Institute, Executive Office; 1959.

American Law Institute. Model Penal Code. Tentative Draft No. 9. Submitted by the Council to the Members for Discussion at the Thirty-sixth Annual Meeting, May 20, 21, 22 and 23, 1959. Philadelphia: The Executive Office, The American Law Institute; May 8, 1959: 161-162.

American Law Institute. Model Penal Code Proposed Official Draft (May 4, 1962). Philadelphia, PA: The American Law Institute; 1962.

American Law Institute. Model Penal Code. Official Draft and Explanatory Notes. Philadelphia, PA: The American Law Institute; 1985.

Ames O. Massachusetts Doctors Take the Initiative. Birth Contr Rev 1932; 15 (2): 51-52.

Anonymous. Placebo Stirs Pill "Side Effects". Med World News, 1971, April 16. The article has been reproduced in: Katz J. op. cit: 791-792.

Anonymous. To day's Drugs. Br Med J 1963; 2: 488-491.

Asbell B. The Pill. A Biography of the Drug that Changed the World. New York: Random House; 1995.

Austin CR, Short RV. Manipulating Reproduction, 2nd ed. Vol. V, in Austin CR, Short RV, eds. Reproduction in Mammals. Cambridge,

Cambridge University Press; 1986.

Ayd FJ, Jr. The Oral Contraceptives, Their Mode of Action, Rome, Pontifical Gregorian University, July 13, 1964, 29 pp. typewritten

Ayd FJ, Jr. The Oral Contraceptives. Their Mode of Action. Med Newslet Religious 1964; 1: 1-64.

Ballard F.A et al. Contraceptive Advice, Devices and Preparations. JAMA 1937; 108: 1819-1820.

Barnard Jr. TH. An Analysis and Criticism of the Model Penal Code Provisions on the Law of Abortion. Cas W Res L Rev 1967; 18: 540-564.

Bates AWH. Anti-Vivisection and the Profession of Medicine in Britain. A Social History. The Palgrave Macmillan Animal Ethics Series. London: Palgrave Macmillan; 2017.

Beecher HK. Ethics and Clinical Research, New Eng J Med 1966; 274: 1354-1360.

Beecher HK. Research and the Individual: Human Studies. Boston: Little, Brown, 1970.

Benagiano G. Joseph W. Goldzieher and the birth of hormonal contraception. Contraception 2010; 82: 119-124.

Benagiano G. Reproductive strategies for human survival. Repr Bio Med Online 2001; 4, suppl 1: 72-76.

Benjamin H.C. Lobbying for Birth Control. Publ Opin Q 1938; 2: 48-60, at 57.

Bettendorf, ed. Zur Geschichte der Endokrinologie and Reproduktionsmedicine. Berlin: Springer-Verlag; 1995: 177-180.

Beyer HS. Model Penal Code Selected Bibliography. Buff Crim Law Rev 2000; 4: 627-639.

Bishop PMF. Oral Contraceptives. Practitioner 1960; 185: 158-162.

Blasingame F.J.L, ed. AMA Digest of Official Actions, Vol. I: 1846-1958. Chicago: American Medical Association; 1959: 69.

Briggs L. "The Pill" in Puerto Rico and the Mainland United States: Negotiating Discourses of Risk and Decolonization. In: Reed L, Sankko P, eds. Governing the Female Body. Gender, Health, and Networks of Power. Albany: State University of New York Press; 2010: 159-184.

Briggs L. Reproducing Empire: Race, Sex, Science, and U.S. Imperialism in Puerto Rico. Berkeley, CA. University of California Press, 2002.

Brodie JF, Contraception and Abortion in 19th Century America, Ithaca: Cornell University Press, 1994.

Bruner R. Neutral Stand Dropped. Doctors to Aid in Population Curbs. The Blade, Ohio, January 22, 1965: 5.

Burchfield RW, ed. A Supplement to the Oxford English Dictionary, Vol I·A-G. Oxford: At the Clarendon Press; 1972.

Cannon W. The Right and Wrong of Making Experiments on Human Beings. JAMA 1916; 67: 1372-1373. Reproduced in JAMA 2016; 316: 2680.

Cannon W. The Right and Wrong of Making Experiments on Human Beings. JAMA 1916; 67: 1372-1373.

Catholic Physicians Denounce Medical Assn. for Birth Control Recognition. The Guardian, June 19, 1937: 4.

Cavanagh J. The Popes, the Pill, and the People. A Documentary Study. Milwaukee: The Bruce Publishing Co; 1965.

Chesler E. Woman of Valor: Margaret Sanger and the Birth Control Movement in America. New York; Simon & Schuster.

Chung GS, Lawrence RE, Rasinski KA, et al. Obstetrician-gynecologists' beliefs about when pregnancy begins. Am J Obstet Gynecol 2012; 206: 132.e1-7.

Clarke A.E. Disciplining Reproduction. Modernity, American Life Sciences, and "the Problems of Sex". Berkeley: University of California Press; 1998.

Coleman HH. Obstetric-Gynecologic Terminology. J Obst Gynecol Neonat Nurs 1973; 2: 71.

Commission Pontificale pour l'étude des problèmes de la famille, de la population et de la natalité. Report of the Majority of the Papal Commission. Chap. IV. Objective criteria of morality; 1966.

Commission Pontificale pour l'étude des problèmes de la famille, de la population et de la natalité. Report of the Medical Session, 2nd May 1966.

Commission Pontificale pour l'étude des problèmes de la famille, de la population et de la natalité. Report of the 4th session of the Commission. p. 28. Documents disseminated by Grisez on the Internet. Accessible at: http://www.twotlj.org/BCCommission.html.

Committee on Human Reproduction. The Control of Fertility. JAMA 1965; 194: 462-470.

Committee on Terminology, American College of Obstetricians and Gynecologists. Terms Used in Reference to the Fetus. Terminol Bull, No. 1, Insert in Obstet Gynecol, 1965; 26.

Hughes EC, ed. Obstetric-Gynecologic Terminology with Section on Neonatology and Glossary of Congenital Anomalies. Philadelphia: FA. Davis Company 1972.

Cook HH, Gamble CJ, Satterthwaite AP. Oral Contraception by Norethynodrel. A 3-Years Field Study. Am J Obstet Gynecol 1961; 82: 437-442, 444-445. Reprinted in Katz, op. cit. 739-742.

Cook R, Dickens BM, Fathalla MF. Reproductive Health and Human Rights: Integrating Medicine, Ethics, and Law. Oxford University Press; 2003.

Curran CE. Contraception. In: Clarke PB, Linzey A, eds. Dictionary of Ethics, Theology and Society. Abingdon; Routledge; 1996.

Curran CE, Hunt RE, and the "Subject Professors" with Hunt JF and Connelly TR. Dissent In and For the Church. Theologians and Humanae Vitae. New York: Sheed & Ward; 1969.

Darwin, C. The Descent of Man and Selection in Relation to Sex, 1896 edition, D. Appleton and Company; New York, 1871.

de Riedmatten H. Relatio generalis, presented to the Commission of Cardinals and Bishops the 20th June 1966.

de Riedmatten H. Report Final des Travaux de la Commission Pontificale pour l'étude des problèmes de la famille, de la population et de la natalité, presented to the Pope Paul VI the 27th June 1966.

Dekker H. Prevenceptive and Abortion - Are They on the Same Ethical Plane. Med Critic & Guide 1920; 23: 213-214.

Derr MK, MacNair R, Naranjo-Huebl L. Reproductive Wrongs Unto Death: Eugenic Strictures (Late Nineteenth-Early Twentieth Centuries and Beyond). In: Derr MK, MacNair R, Naranjo-Huebl L, eds. ProLife Feminism. Yesterday and Today. 2nd ed. Bloomington, IN: Xlibris; 2005: 107-113.

Dickinson R.L. Conception Control. JAMA 1943; 123: 1043-1047.

Dickinson R.L. Control of Conception, Present and Future. Bull NY Acad Med 1929; 5: 413-434.

Dixon WE. The Action and Uses of Ovarian Extracts. Br Med J 1927; 2: 1070-1074.

Dvorak J. Natural Family Planning and the Christian Moral Code, which can be accessed at:

http://lapidesclamabunt.angelfire.com/nfpwinters.htm.

Editorial. The Prevention of Conception. JAMA 1924; 83: 2020-2021.

Editorial. Doctors Approve Birth Control. Violent Catholic Protest. Sunday Times, Perth, WA. Sunday August 1, 1937: 1.

Editorial. American Medicine Accepts Birth Control. Birth Contr Rev 1937; 4 (n.s.) (6): 1-2; Sanger M. Hail and Farewell. Nat Birth Contr News 1937 June: 3-5, available at:

http://sangerpapers.org/sanger/app/documents/show.php?sangerDoc=301422.xml.

Editorial. Birth Control Approved by Medical Assn. Altoona Tribune, June 8, 1937, p. 1.

Editorial. Birth Control Policy Change for Reaching. The Telegraph, Nashua, N.H., June 9, 1937, p. 7.

Editorial. American Letter: Contraception Approved, and Combated. South Afr Med J 1937, Aug. 14.

Editorial. The Business of Birth Control. JAMA 1938; 110: 513.

Editorial. Stopping the Pill. BMJ 1974; 2: 517-518.

Edwards RG, Steptoe PC. A Matter of Life, The Story of a Medical Breakthrough, London: Hutchinson, 1980.

Eig J. The Birth of the Pill. How Four Crusaders Reinvented Sex and Launched a Revolution. New York; WW Norton; 2014.

Engelman P. A History of the Birth Control Movement in America. Santa Barbara: Praeger, ABC-CLIO, LLC; 2011.

Engle ET, ed. Pregnancy Wastage, Proceedings of the Conference Sponsored by the Committee on Human Reproduction, National Research Council, on behalf of the National Committee on Maternal Health, Inc. Springfield, IL. CC Thomas; 1953.

Engs RC. The Progressive Era's Health Reform Movement: A Historical Dictionary. Wesport, CT: Greenwood Publ. Group; 2003.

Fishbein M. The History of the American Medical Association, 1847 to 1947. With the Biographies of the Presidents of the Association by Walter L. Bierring, and with Histories Pof the Publications, Councils, Bureaus and Other Official Bodies. Philadelphia; W.B. Saunders Co; 1947.

Fleming AS. Statement. In: Proposed Constitutional Amendments, cit. above, in note 11: 155.

Fletcher GP. Dogmas of the Model Penal Code. 2 Buff. Crim. L. Rev. 3 1998-1999.

Foote EB. A Summary of My Views on the Prevention of Conception. Med Pharm Crit Guide 1910; 12: 408.

Foote EB. Home Cyclopedia of Popular Medical, Social, and Sexual Science. New York: Murray Hill Publishing Company; 1902.

Foote EB. The Radical Remedy in Social Science or Borning Better Babies Through Regulating Reproduction by Controlling Conception. An Earnest Essay on Pressing Problems. New York: Murray Hill Publishing Company; 1886. To access the virtual version of the book, go to: https://archive.org/details/02531230R.nlm.nih.gov.

Frank JP. The American Law Institute 1923-1998. Hofstra Law Rev 1998; 26: 615-639.

Frank RT. Report on the Use of Roentgen Rays for Contraception. JAMA 1939; 112: 169-170.

Freidson E. Profession of Medicine. A Study of the Sociology of Applied Knowledge. Chicago: The University of Chicago Press; 1970.

Fried J, Ryan KJ, Tsuchitani PJ, eds. Oral Contraceptives and Steroid Chemistry in the People's Republic of China. A Trip Report of the American Steroid Chemistry and Biochemistry Delegation. CSCPRC Report No. 5. Washington, D.C.: National Academy of Sciences; 1977.

García CR, Pincus G, Rock J. Effects of three 19-nor steroids on human ovulation and menstruation. Am J Obstet Gynecol 1958; 75: 82-87.

García CR. Clinical Studies on Human Fertility Control. In: Greep RO, ed. Human Fertility and Population Problems. Cambridge, Mass: Schenkman Publ Co. 1963: 43-63.

Gibbons WJ, Burch TK. Physiologic Control of Fertility: Process and Morality. Am Eccl Rev 1958; 138: 246-277.

Goldman C. Voluntary Checks to Population. Med Critic Guide 1918; 21: 248-256.

Goldzieher JW et al. Study of Norethindrone in Contraception. JAMA 1962; 180: 359-361.

Goldzieher JW, Moses LE, Averkin E, Scheel C, Taber BZ. A Placebo-controlled Double-blind Crossover Investigation of the Side Effects Attributed to Oral Contraceptives. Fertil Steril 1971; 22: 609-623.

Goldzieher JW, Moses LE, Averkin E, Scheel C, Taber BZ.

Nervousness and depression attributed to oral contraceptive: A double-blind, placebo-controlled study. Am J Obstet Gynecol 1971; 11: 1013-1020.

Gordon L. The Moral Property of Women, A History of Birth Control Politics in America, Urban, Ill: University of Illinois Press, 2007.

Gordon L. Woman's Body, Woman's Right. Birth Control in America, 2nd ed. Penguin Books: 1990.

Gray M. Margaret Sanger: A Biography of the Champion of Birth Control. New York: R. Marek Publ.; 1979.

Greenblatt RB. Discussion. Fed Proc 1959; 18: 1055-1056.

Griffin PD. Pushing the Frontiers of Science. The WHO/Rockefeller Foundation Initiative on Implantation. Int J Gynecol Obstetr 1999; 67: S111-S116.

Grimes DA, Cook RJ. Mifepristone (RU486). An Abortifacient to Prevent Abortion? N Engl J Med 1992; 327: 1088-1089.

Grimes DA, Cook RJ. Mifepristone (RU486). An Abortifacient to Prevent Abortion? N Engl J Med 1993: 328: 254-355.

Grisez G. Abortion, The Myths, the Realities, and the Arguments. New York: Corpus Books; 1970.

Grodin ME. Historical Origins of the Nuremberg Code. In: Annas GJ, Grodin MA, ed. The Nazi Doctors and the Nuremberg Code. Human Rights in Human Experimentation. New York: Oxford University Press; 1992: 121-144.

Guttmacher AF. Oral Contraception Postgr Med 1962; 32: 552-558.

Hall DL. Biology, Sex Hormones and Sexism in the 1920s. Philosophical Forum 1974; 5: 81-96.

Harding J. Sex and Control: The Hormonal Body. Body & Society 1996; 2: 99-111.

Harman L., A Letter. In: Schroeder T, ed., Edward Bond Foote. Biographical Notes and Appreciatives. New York: Free Speech League: 1913: 62-65.

Harvey JC. André Hellegers and Carroll House: Architect and Blueprint for the Kennedy Institute of Ethics. KIEJ 2004; 14: 199-206.

Hayes TL. The Biology of the Reproductive Act. Insight 1967; 6: 12-19. This article was reprinted in a special issue dedicated to birth control, as indicated by Springer RH. Current Theology. Notes on Moral Theology: July-December, 1967. Theol Stud 1968; 29: 275-300.

Hayes TL. The Biology of the Reproductive Act. Its Application to Various Methods of Birth Control. Cross Currents 1965; 15: 393-406.

Heape W. Ovulation and Degeneration of Ova in the Rabbit. Proc Roy Soc Lond B 1905; 76: 260-268.

Hellegers A. Document CBCC 2/06 M-4. Survey of Contraceptive Methods [12] XI. The Pill.

Hellegers A. Report of the Medical Session. The significance of the stages in the development of life. May 4th 1966.

Hellegers A. Response of Doctors to Conclusions of Theologians, May 7, 1966, p. 12. (From the Marshall's archive).

Hellegers AE. A Scientist's Analisis. In: Curran CE, ed. Contraception: Authority and Dissent. New York: Herder and Herder; 1969.

Herranz G. The Ethics of Medical Research: A Christian View. Bull Med Ethics 2004; 200: 13-19 + bibliography and notes at: http://www.bullmedeth.info/).

Hertig AT. A Fifteen-Year Search for First-Stage Human Ova. JAMA 1989; 261: 434-435.

Hilgartner CA, Randolph JF. Psycho-logics: An axiomatic system describing human behavior, J Theoret Biol 1969; 23: 285-338.

Himes NE. Medical History of Contraception. The first edition of the book (1936), with a preface by RL Dickinson, was published by Williams & Wilkins Co, Baltimore. In 1970, the book, with a New Preface by Christopher Tietze, was reprinted by Schocken Books Inc., New York.

Himes NE. Note on the Origin of the Terms Contraception, Birth Control, Neo-Malthusianism, Etc. Med J & Rec 1932; 135: 495-496.

Hines DC, Goldzieher JW. Clinical Investigation: A Guide to its Evaluation. Am J Obstet Gynecol 1969; 105: 450-487.

Hodge HL. The Principles and Practice of Obstetrics. Philadelphia: Blanchard and Lea; 1864.

Hoolihan C. An Annotated Catalog of the Edward C. Atwater Collection of American Popular Medicine and Health Reform, Volume III. Rochester NY: University of Rochester Press; 2001.

Hughes EC, ed. Obstetric-gynecologic Terminology, with Section on Neonatology and Glossary of Congenital Anomalies. Philadelphia: F.A. Davis; 1972.

Hughes EC. Comparison of Intrauterine and Outer Space Life, New Physician 1963; 12: 57-59.

Hughes EC. Life in Inner Space, Oxygen and nourishment are primary survival factors for the fetus in utero in inner space and the astronaut in a capsule in outer space. Am J Nurs. 1963; 63: 92-94.

Hughes EC. Noblesse Oblige. Obstet Gynecol 1962; 20: 821-825.

Hughes EC. Terminología en Obstetricia y Ginecología. Revisada por J.M. Carrera. Barcelona; Salvat Editores; 1975.

Hughes EC. To Sow is to Reap. Inaugural Address. Obstet Gynecol 1963; 21: 639-645.

Hume M. Maybe Baby. Texas Monthly 1973; 1 (9): 43.

Hyde D.R, Wolff P, Gross A, Hoffman E.L. The American Medical Association: Power, Purpose, and Politics in Organized Medicine. Yale Law J 1954; 63: 937-1022.

Jacobi A. A Final Word to the Fellows and Members of the American Medical Association. JAMA 1913; 61: 633-635.

Jacobi A. The Best Means of Combating Infant Mortality. JAMA 1912; 58: 1735-1744.

Jensen JM. The Evolution of Margaret Sanger's "Family Limitation" Pamphlet, 1914-1921. Signs 1981; 6: 548-567.

Johnson MH. Robert Edwards: the path to IVF. Repr Biomed Online 2011; 23: 245-262.

Jütte R. Contraception: a history. Cambridge; Polity Press; 2008.

Jütte R. Lust ohne Last: Geschichte der Empfängsnisverhütung von der Antike bis zur Gegenwart. München: Verlag C.H. Beck; 2003.

Kaiser RB. The Politics of Sex and Religion: A Case History in the Development of Doctrine, 1962-1984, Kansas City, Mo, Leaven Press, 1985.

Kaiser RB. The Encyclical that Never Was. The Story of the Commission on Population, Family and Birth, 1964-66. Revised edition. London: Sheed & Ward; 1987.

Katz E, Hajo CM, Engelman PC, eds. The Selected Papers of Margaret Sanger. Vol. 1, The Woman Rebel, 1900-1928. Urbana: University of Illinois Press; 2003.

Kay LE. The Molecular Vision of Life: Caltech, the Rockefeller Foundation and the New Biology. New York: Oxford University Press; 1993.

Kennedy D.M. Birth Control in America. The Career of Margaret Sanger. New Haven: Yale University Press; 1970.

Kosmak GW. Contraceptive Practices. Am J Obstet Gynecol 1940; 40: 652-654.

Kosmak GW. The Broader Aspects of the Birth Control Propaganda as it Should Interest the Physician. Am J Obstet Gynecol 1923; 6: 276-285.

Kosmak GW. The Responsibility of the Medical Profession in the movement for 'Birth Control'. JAMA 1939; 113: 1553-1559.

Kutner L. Due Process of Abortion. Minn LR 1968; 53: 1-28.

Lader L. Margaret Sanger: Militant, Pragmatist, Visionary. http://www.ontheissuesmagazine.com/1990spring/Spr90_Lader.php. The full text of the journal, published between February 1917 and January 1940, is available at: https://lifedynamics.com/library/#birth-control-review.

Lader L. Three Men Who Made a Revolution. New York Times Magazine, April 10, 1966: 8-9, 55-56, 63-64.

Latkovic, MS. Is the Teaching of Humanae Vitae Physicalist? A Critique of the View of Joseph A. Selling, Linacre Quart 1995; 62: 39-58.

Lederer S. Subjected to Science. Human Experimentation in America Before the Second World War. Baltimore: The Johns Hopkins University Press; 1955.

Editorial. Legion of Decency Proposed Against Firms and Doctors Dealing In Contraceptives. The Guardian, June 19, 1937, p. 4.

Center for the History of Medicine, of the Francis A. Countway Library, Boston: 2013. Letter from Hertig to Streeter, dated October 22, 1938. Letter included in the presentation of a graphic story of the pill, entitled 'Conceiving the Pill' and produced by the Accessible at: https://collections.countway.harvard.edu/onview/exhibits/show/conceiving-the-pill.

Linton PB. Planned Parenthood v. Casey: The Flight from Reason in the Supreme Court. St. Louis U. Pub. L. Rev. 1993; 13: 15-137.

Mandelbaum J. Histoire de la fecundation in vitro. In: Poncelet C, Sifer C, eds. Physiologie, pathologie et thérapie de la reproduction chez l'humain, Springer Science, 2011.

Mark LV. Sexual Chemistry: A History of the Contraceptive Pill. London: Yale University Press; 2010.

Marks L. 'A Cage of Ovulating Females': The History of Early Oral Contraceptive Pill Clinical Trials, 1950-59. In Chadaverian S, Kamminga H, eds. Molecularizing Biology and Medicine: New Practices and Alliances, 1910s-1970s. Amsterdam: Harwood Academic Publishers; 1998.

Marks L. Human Guinea Pigs? The History of the Early Oral Contraceptive Clinical Trials. Hist & Technol 1999; 15: 263-268.

Marsh M, Ronner W. The Fertility Doctor: John Rock and the Reproductive Revolution. Baltimore: Johns Hopkins University Press; 2008.

Marshall R, Donovan C. Blessed are the Barren. The Social Policy of Planned Parenthood. San Francisco: Ignatius Press; 1991.

Maurovich F. Humanae Vitae at 45: A Personal Story. Nat Cath Reporter 2013 Jul. 25, 2013. Accessible at: https://www.ncronline.org/news/vatican/humanae-vitae-45-personal-story.

May ET. America and the Pill, A History of Promise, Peril, and Liberation, New York: Basic Books, 2010.

McCann CM, Birth Control Politics in the United Status, 1916-1945. Ithaca, NY: Cornell University Press; 1999.

McClory R. Turning Point. The Inside Story of the Papal Birth Control Commission. New York: Crossroad; 1995.

McGreevy JT. Catholicism and American Freedom: A History. New York: W.W. Norton; 2003.

McLaughlin L. The Pill, John Rock, and the Church. The Biography of a Revolution. Boston: Little, Brown and Co.; 1982.

Medical News. AMA's Population Control Program Keyed to Physician Role as Counselor. JAMA 1965; 191: 31-33.

Meigs CD. Obstetrics: The Science and the Art. Philadelphia: Lea and Blanchard, 1rst edition 1849.

Meigs CD. Obstetrics: The Science and the Art. Philadelphia: Henry C. Lea; 1867, fifth edition.

Meloy S. Pre-implantation Fertility Control and the Abortion Laws. 41 Chi.-Kent L. Rev. 183-206, 1964.

Mengert WF, Pearse WH. History of the American College of Obstetricians and Gynecologists. The First Quarter Century 1950-1976. Washington; ACOG; 2001.

Merz JF, Jackson CA, Klerman JA. A Review of Abortion Policy: Legality, Medicaid Funding and Parental Involvement, 1967-1994. Women's Rts. L. Rep.1995; 17: 1-61.

Mietus AC, Mietus NJ. Criminal Abortion: "A Failure of Law" or a Challenge to Society? Am Bar Ass J 1965; 51: 924-928.

Mintz M. Are Birth Control Pills Safe? In: Katz J, ed. Experimentation with Human Beings. The Authority of the Investigator, Subject, Professions and State in the Human Experimentation Process. New York: Russell Sage Foundation 1972: 751-754.

Mitchinson W. The Nature of Their Bodies. Women and Their Doctors in Victorian Canada. Toronto: University of Toronto Press; 1991.

Mohr JC. Abortion in America. The Origins and Evolution of National Policy, 1800-1900. New York: Oxford University Press; 1978.

Moll A. Aerztliche Ethik. Die Pflichten des Arztes in allen Beziehungen seiner Thätigkeit. Stuttgart: Verlag von Ferdinand Enke; 1902.

Morgan LM. Icons of Life: A Cultural History of Human Embryos. Berkeley: University of California Press; 2009. A section, entitled Egg Hunting (pp. 125-133).

Morris JM, van Wagenen G. Interception: The use of postovulatory estrogens to prevent implantation. Am J Obstet Gynecol 1973; 115: 101-106.

National Committee on Maternal Health. Program for Future Research on Birth Control. Memorandum on March 23, 1933, conference between Drs. Frank, Hartman, Dickinson, Bryant. Center for the History of Medicine, Countway Library, Harvard University http://collections.countway.harvard.edu/onview/file_upload/0002360_d ref.jpg.

Nelson WO. Survey of Studies Relating to Vulnerable Points in the Reproductive Processes. Papers on Biological Research Presented at the Fifth International Planned Parenthood Conference Held at Tokyo, Japan, from October 24th to 29th, 1955. Acta Endocrinologica 1956, Suppl. XXVIII: 7-17.

Noonan Jr JT. Contraception A History of Its Treatment by the Catholic Theologians and Canonists. Cambridge, Mass: The Belknap Press; 1965.

Noonan JT. Contraception: A History of Its Treatment by the Catholic Theologians and Canonists. Enlarged Edition. Cambridge, Mass: Belknap Press; 1986.

Oudshoorn N. Beyond the Natural Body: An Archeology of Sex Hormones. New York: Routledge; 1994.

Oudshoorn N. Drugs for healthy people: The culture of hormonal contraceptives testing for women and men. In: Gijswijt-Hofstra M, van

Heteren GM, Tanse EM, eds. Biographies of Remedies: Drugs, Medicines and Contraceptives in Dutch and Anglo-American Healing Cultures. Amsterdam; Rodopi; 2002: 123-140.

Pardo JM. Rationality of Openness to Life and Contraception. Scripta Theol 2009; 41: 113-141.

Parkes AS, Dodds EC, Noble RL. Interruption of Early Pregnancy by Means of Orally Active Oestrogens. Br Med J 1938; 2: 557-559, at 559.

Parkes AS. Biological Control of Conception. Nature 1961; 191: 1256-1257.

Parkes AS. Quest for an Ideal Contraceptive. Proc Soc Stud Fertil 1953; 5: 20-26.

Parkes AS. The Menace of Overpopulation. New Scientist 1961; 10: 566-570.

Parkes AS. Biological Control of Conception. The Fifth Oliver Bird Lecture. J Reprod Fertil 1962; 3: 159-172.

Parkes AS. The Biology of Fertility. Discussion. In: Greep RO, ed. Human Fertility and Population Problems. Proceedings of the Seminar Sponsored by the American Academy of Arts and Sciences with the support of the Ford Foundation. Cambridge, Mass: Schenken. Co.; 1963; 238.

Parkes AS. Biological Aspects of the Population Explosion. Nature 1964; 204: 320-322.

Parkes AS. Biological Aspects of the Control of Human Fertility. The Practitioner 1965; 194: 455-462.

Parkes AS. Biological Aspects of the Population Explosion. In: Parkes AS. Sex, Science and Society. Addresses, Lectures and Articles. Annotated by the author and illustrated by A.G. Wurmser. Newcastle upon Tyne: Oriel Press Ltd; 1966.

Parkes AS. The Future of Fertility Control. In: Meade JE, Parkes AS. Biological Aspects of Social problems. A Symposium held by the Eugenics Society in October 1964. Edinburgh: Oliver & Boyd; 1965: 205-212.

Patten BM. Early Embryology of the Chick, Philadelphia: Blakiston Co, 1920.

Patten BM. The Early Embryology of the Chick, 4th ed. New York: McGraw-Hill Book Co; 1951.

Patterson JT. On Gastrulation and the Origin of the Primitive Streak in the Pigeon's Egg: Preliminary Notice, Biol Bull 1907; 13: 251-271.

Paul VI, Encyclical Humanae Vitae, Vatican Press, 1968.

Paulus VI. Allocutio ad E.mos Patres Purpuratos, fausta et felicia ominatus Beatissimo Patri nominalem diem celebranti, anno ex quo ad Summum Pontificatum est evectus. Die 23 mensis Iunii a. 1964. Act Apost Sedis 1964; 56: 581-589.

Paul VI. Allocution à la Commission d'Étude sur les Probèmes de la Population, de la Famille, et la Natalité, Samedi 27 Mars 1965. Available at: http://w2.vatican.va/content/paul-vi/fr/speeches/1965/documents/hf_p-vi_spe_19650327_demographic-commission.html.

Pearson M. Millennial Dreams and Moral Dilemmas. Seventh-day Adventism and Contemporary Ethics. Cambridge: Cambridge University Press; 1990.

Pfeffer N. The Reproductive Body. In: Cooter R, Pickstone J. Companion to Medicine in the Twentieth Century. Abingdon, UK; Routledge; 2013: 277-290.

Pincus G, Chang MC, Hafez ESE, Zarrow MX, Merrill A. Effects of Certain 19-Nor Steroids on Reproductive Processes in Animals. Science 1956; 124: 890-891.

Pincus G. Some Effects of Progesterone and Related Compounds upon Reproduction and Early Development in Mammals. Papers on Biological Research Presented at the Fifth International Planned Parenthood Conference Held at Tokyo, Japan, from October 24th to 29th, 1955. Acta Endocrinologica 1956, Suppl. XXVIII: 18-36.

Pincus G, Rock J, Garcia CR. Effects of Certain 19-Nor Steroids upon Reproductive Processes. Ann N Y Acad Sci 1958; 71: 677-690.

Pincus G, Rock J, Chang MC, Garcia CR. Effects of Certain 19-Nor Steroids on Reproductive Processes and Fertility. Fed Proc 1959; 18: 1051-1055.

Pincus G. Reply to Discussion, Fed Proc 1959; 18: 1056.

Pirie NW. The Biochemistry of Conception Control. Eugen Rev 1952; 44: 129-140.

Pius XI, Litt Encycl Casti Connubii, 31 dec 1930. Acta Apost Sedis 1930; 22: 560.

Pius XII. Allocutio iis quae interfuerunt Conventui Unionis Catholicae Italicae inter Obstetrices Romae habito. Romae die 29 Octobri mensis a. 1951. Acta Apost Sed 1951; 43: 835-860.

Pius XII. Discorso alle Partecipanti al Congresso della Unione

Católica Italiana Ostetriche. In: Discorsi e Radiomessaggi di Sua Santità Pio XII. Vol. 13: 333-353.

Pius XII. Speech to the Congress of the Italian Catholic Union of Midwives, 29 Oct 1951.

Pius XII. Speech to the Participants in the First International Congress of Histopathology of the Nervous System. The Moral Limits of Medical Methods. September 14, 1952. Accessible at: http://w2.vatican.va/content/pius-xii/es/speeches/1952/documents/hf_p-xii_spe_19520914_istopatologia.html.

Polge C. Sir Alan Sterling Parkes: 10 September 1900 – 17 July 1990. Biogr Mem Fellows R Soc 2006; 52: 263-283.

Polityka T. From Poe to Roe: A Bickelian View of the Abortion Decision – Its Timing and Principle. Neb. L. Rev. 1974; 53: 31-57.

Population Crisis. Hearings Before the Subcommittee on Foreign Aid Expenditures of the Committee on Government Operations. United States Senate, Eighty-Ninth Congress, Second Session on S. 1676. Washington: U.S. Government Printing Office; 1966: 135-147.

Preciado B. Testo Junkie: Sex, Drugs, and Biopolitics in the Pharmacopornographic Era. New York: Feminist Press at the City University of New York; 2008.

Prelate Flays Medical Assn. in Statement. Blow Dealt at America Home, Prelate Says. The Guardian, 1937; June 19: 4.

Pusey W.A. Medicine's Responsibilities in the Birth Control Movement. Birth Contr Rev 1925; 9: 134-136, 156-158.

Pusey W.A. Some of the Social Problems of Medicine. JAMA 1924; 82: 1905-1908.

Ramírez de Arellano AB, Seipp C. Colonialism, Catholicism, and Contraception: a history of birth control in Puerto Rico. Chapel Hill, NC: University of North Carolina Press; 1983.

Ramsbotham FH. The Principles and Practice of Obstetric Medicine and Surgery, in Reference to the Process of Parturition: A new American Edition, revised by the Author, with Notes and Additions by W.V. Keating. Philadelphia: Blanchard and Lea; 1855.

Ramsey P. Reference Points in Deciding about Abortion. In: Noonan Jr JT, ed. The Morality of Abortion. Legal and Historical Perspectives. Cambridge, Mass. Harvard University Press; 1970: 60-100.

Reed J. Doctors, birth control, and social values, 1830-1970. In:

Vogel MJ, Rosenberg CE, eds. The Therapeutic Revolution: Essays in the Social History of American Medicine, University of Pennsylvania Press, 1979: 109-133.

Reed J. From Private Vice to Public Virtue. The Birth Control Movement and American Society Since 1830. New York: Basic Books; 1978.

Reed J. The Birth Control Movement and American Society. From Private Vice to Public Virtue. Princeton: Princeton University Press; 1984.

Reed J. The Birth Control Movement, Princeton, New Jersey: Princeton Legacy Library; 2014.

Rhonheimer M. Ethics of Procreation & The Defense of Human Life. Contraception, Artificial Fertilization, and Abortion. Ed. By WF. Murphy Jr. Washington, DC: Catholic University of America Press; 2010.

Rice-Wray E. Field Study with Enovid as a Contraceptive Agent. Proc Symp on 19-Nor Steroids. Chicago: GD Searle & Co; 1957: 78-82, 92-93. Reprinted in: Katz J. Experimentation with Human Beings. New York: Russell Sage Foundation; 1972: 742-745.

Robinson JW, Eugenics, Marriage and Birth Control [Practical Eugenics]. New York: The Critic and Guide Co., 1917.

Robinson JW, Fewer and Better Babies, or The Limitation of Offspring, 11th and 12th ed. New York: The Critic and Guide Co., 1917.

Robinson JW, Prevenception versus Abortion. [Editorial] Med Critic Guide 1918; 21: 206-207.

Robinson JW (editor). Do we Possess an Absolutely Reliable Prevenceptive? Med Critic Guide 1918; 21: 207.

Robinson JW, Reliability of Prevenceptives Tested on Animals. Med Critic Guide 1918; 21: 207-208.

Robinson V. Pioneers of Birth Control in England and America. New York: Voluntary Parenthood League; 1919: 72.

Robinson WJ. Sexual Problems of To-Day. New York: Critic and Guide 1912: 155.

Robinson WJ. The Ethics of Abortion. New York Medical Journal 1914; 100: 897.

Robinson, WJ. Woman. Her Sex and Love Life. New York: The Critic and Guide Co., 1917.

Robinson WJ. Prevenception versus Abortion. Med Critic Guide1918; 21: 206-207.

Robinson WJ. Editorials. A Doctor on Prevenception and Abortion. Critic & Guide 1918; 21: 410.

Robinson WJ. Practical Prevenception or The Technique of Birth Control. Giving the Latest Methods of Prevention of Conception, Discussing their Effect, Favorable or Robinson WJ. Comment by the Editor. Critic and Guide 1920; 23: 215.

Robinson W.J. Twenty-Five Years of Progress. Birth Contr Rev 1927; 11: 323.

Robinson WJ. Unfavorable, on the Sex Act; Their Indications and Contraindications, Pointing Out the Reasons for Failures and How to Avoid Them. Hoboken, NJ: American Biological Society; 1929.

Robinson WJ. Do Doctors Know About Prevenception? Birth Control Rev 1931; 15: 11.

Robinson WJ. Dr. Robinson and Saint Peter. How Dr. Robinson Entered the Heavenly Gates and Became St. Peter's Assistant. New York: Eugenics Publishing Co.; 1931.

Robinson WJ. The Law Against Abortion. Its Perniciousness Demonstrated and Its Repeal Demanded. New York: The Eugenics Publishing Company, Inc.; 1934.

Rock J, Loth DG. Voluntary Parenthood New York: Random House; 1949.

Rock J. Progress in Obstetrics. N Eng J Med 1932; 206: 77-87.

Rock J, Pincus G, Garcia CR. Effects of Certain 19 Nor Steroids on the Normal Human Menstrual Cycle. Science 1956; 124: 891-893.

Rock J, García CR, Pincus G. Synthetic progestins in the normal human menstrual cycle. Rec Progr Horm Res. 1957; 13: 323-339.

Rock J. The Time Has Come. A Catholic Doctor's Proposals to End the Battle over Birth Control. New York: Alfred A. Knopf, Inc; 1963.

Roelcke V. The use and abuse of medical research ethics. The German Richtlinien / guidelines for human subject research as an instrument for the protection of research subjects - and of medical science, ca. 1931-196. In Weindling P. ed. From Clinic to Concentration Camp. Reassessing Nazi Medical and Racial Research, 1933-1945. London: Routledge; 2017.

Rothman DJ. Strangers at the Bedside. A History of how Law and Bioethics Transformed Medical Decision Making. New York: Basic Books; 1991.

Rouche M. La Preparation de l'encyclique «Humanae Vitae». La Commission sur la Population, the Famille et la Natalité. Actes du Colloque de Rome (2-4 juin 1983). Rome: École Française de Rome; 1984. Accessible at: www.persee.fr/doc/efr_0000-0000_1984_act_72_1_2419.

Royle E. Radicals, Secularists, and Republicans: Popular Free Thought in Britain, 1866-1915. Manchester: Manchester University Press; 1980.

Saini A. Inferior. How Science Got Women Wrong, and the New Research That's Rewriting the Story. Boston: Beacon Press; 2017.

Sanger M. Family Limitation. Revised, Sixth ed.; 1917.

Sanger M. Birth Control or Abortion? Birth Contra Rev 1918; 2: 3-4.

Sanger M. Woman and the New Race (With a Preface by Havelock Ellis). New York: Brentano's; 1920.

Sanger M. The Pivot of Civilization. New York: Brentano's Publishers; 1922.

Sanger M. (Editor). Doctors and Birth Control. Birth Contr Rev 1923; 7: 144-145.

Sanger, M., My Fight for birth control. New York: Farrar & Rinehart Inc. on Murray Hill; 1931.

Sanger M. Comments on the Pope Encyclical, Birth Control Rev 1931; 15: 40-41.

Sanger M. An Autobiography. New York: W.W. Norton & Co; 1938.

Schwitalla AM. The American Medical Association and Contraception. Hosp Progr 1937; 18: 219-224.

Seaman B. The Pill and I: 40 Years On, the Relationship Remains Wary. New York Times, June 25, 2000: 15-19.

Sears HD. The Sex Radicals. Free Love in High Victorian America. Lawrence: The Regent Press of Kansas; 1977: 183-203.

Seipp C, Ramirez de Arellano AB. Colonialism, Catholicism, and Contraception: A History of Birth Control in Puerto Rico. Chapel Hill, NC: University of North Carolina Press; 1983.

Shannon WH. The Lively Debate. Response to Humanae Vitae. New York: Sheed & Ward; 1970.

Smith A.E. Council on Pharmacy and Chemistry. JAMA 1943; 123: 1043.

Smith J. Humanae Vitae. A Generation Later. Washington, DC: The

Catholic University of America Press; 1991.

Smith-Rosenberg C, Rosenberg C. The Female Animal: Medical and Biological Views of Woman and Her Role in Nineteenth-Century America. J Am Hist 1973; 60: 332-356.

Speroff L. A Good Man: Gregory Goodwin Pincus. The Man, his Story, the Birth Control Pill. Portland, Or: Arnica Publ.; 2009.

Stein I. Contraceptive Methods. JAMA 1939; 112: 1311-1314.

Stillman JB. Birth Control Movement. In: Ross JA, ed. Encyclopedia of Population, Vol. I. New York: The Free Press; 1982, 58-64.

Stone A. The Control of Fertility. Sci Am 1954; 190 (4): 31-33.

Sullivan P. Raymond T. Holden, 102; Longtime District Obstetrician. Washington Post, March 22, 2007.

Thomas TG. Abortion and Its Treatment, from the Standpoint of Practical Experience: A Special Course of Lectures Delivered at the College of Physicians and Surgeons, New York, Session of 1889-1890. New York: D. Appleton and Co.; 1890.

Tietze C. Voluntary Parenthood. Quart Rev Biol 1950; 25: 12.

Tone A. Contraceptive Consumers: Gender and the Political Economy of Birth Control in the 1930s. J Soc Hist 1996; 29: 485-506.

Tyler ET, Olson HJ. Fertility Promoting and Inhibiting Effects of New Steroid Hormonal Substances. JAMA 1959; 169: 1843-1854.

United States Adjutant General's Department. Trials of War Criminals Before Nuremberg Military Tribunals Under Control Council Law No. 10 (October, 1946 - April, 1949), The Medical Case. Vol. 2. Washington, U.S. Government Printing Office; 1947: 181-183.

Veatch RM. 'Experimental' Pregnancy. The ethical complexities of experimentation with oral contraceptives. Hastings Cent Rep 1971; 1 (Jun): 2-3.

Veatch RM: Disrupted Dialogue. Medical Ethics and the Collapse of Physician-Humanist Communication (1770-1980). New York: Oxford University Press; 2005.

Velpeau AALM. Traité Élémentaire de l'Art des Accouchements, ou Principes de Tokologie et d'Embryologie. Tome Premier. Paris: J.B. Baillière; 1829.

Velpeau AALM. Traité Complet. Tome I, 2ème éd. Paris: J.B. Baillière; 1835.

Velpeau A. An Elementary Treatise on Midwifery: or Principles of

Tokology and Embryology. Transl. by Ch. D. Meigs. Philadelphia; John Grigg; 1931.

VV.AA. Working Party of the British Council of Churches. Human Reproduction. A Study of Some Emergent Problems and Questions in the Light of the Christian Faith. London: British Council of Churches; 1962.

Wechsler H. The Challenge of a Model Penal Code, Harvard Law Rev 1952; 65: 1097-1133).

White ME. Oogenesis and Early Embryogenesis. In: Aldridge RD, Sever DM, eds. Reproductive Biology and Phylogeny of Snakes. Boca Raton, FL: A.K. Peters / CRC Press; 2011: 101-102.

Wood JR. The Struggle for Free Speech in the United States; Edward Bliss Foote, Edward Bond Foote, and Anti-Comstock Operations. New York: Routledge; 2008.

Woodward W.C. Contraceptive Advice, Devices and Preparations. JAMA 1937; 108: 1820.

World Health Organization. Report of a WHO Scientific Group. Technical Report Series 753. Geneva: WHO; 1987.

World Medical Association. Declaration of Helsinki. World Medical Association. Principles for Those in Research and Experimentation. World Med J 1955; 2: 14-15.

The authors

Gonzalo Herranz. He is a recognized expert and a reference in Medical Ethics, Medical Deontology, Research Ethics and Bioethics. He studied Medicine and Surgery at the Universities of Santiago de Compostela and Barcelona. He has been president and member of numerous national and international organizations dedicated to medical ethics and deontology. Dr. Herranz is currently Professor Emeritus of the Faculty of Medicine of the University of Navarra. https://bit.ly/2KNOANw

Pilar León-Sanz. Tenured professor of History of Science in the School of Medicine of the University of Navarra. https://bit.ly/2YjtOIZ

José María Pardo. Professor of Moral Theology at the School of Theology of the University of Navarra. https://bit.ly/2SpYxoE

Jokin de Irala. Tenured professor of Preventive Medicine and Public Health. School of Medicine. University of Navarra.

https://bit.ly/2YmJFv7

amazon.com/author/jokindeirala